Jayne Wilkinson, an identical twin, from a council estate in Birmingham, born to a factory worker father and a housewife mother. Travel for her was the local park or a coach trip to the seaside, not driving around the world in a Land Rover.

As an identical twin, she came out of the womb, firstly, pissed at having to share an egg, and secondly with half a personality. Jayne is competitive and artistic, while Jenny is studious and always on time, but neither had confidence or self-belief. By the age of twenty-five, married, with two children, Jayne realized alcohol and debt were not what she wanted and found her feet.

To my mother, lost to me through the fog of Alzheimer's; my son, Ricky; daughter, Adele; and twin sister, Jenny.

We lose people not just in death, but in their life choices. Whenever I was lost, lonely, and afraid, they would write:

'Mom, you said you were driving around the world, now shut up and get on with it!' So I did.

Jayne Wilkinson

WHEN 'WILL' IS MORE THAN 'WON'T' - YOUR JOURNEY BEGINS

AUSTIN MACAULEY PUBLISHERS™

LONDON * CAMBRIDGE * NEW YORK * SHARJAH

Copyright © Jayne Wilkinson 2023

The right of Jayne Wilkinson to be identified as author of this work has been asserted by the author in accordance with sections 77 and 78 of the Copyright, Designs and Patents Act 1988.

All rights reserved. No part of this publication may be reproduced, stored in a retrieval system, or transmitted in any form or by any means, electronic, mechanical, photocopying, recording, or otherwise, without the prior permission of the publishers.

Any person who commits any unauthorised act in relation to this publication may be liable to criminal prosecution and civil claims for damages.

A CIP catalogue record for this title is available from the British Library.

ISBN 9781035807260 (Paperback)
ISBN 9781035807284 (ePub e-book)
ISBN 9781035807277 (Audiobook)

www.austinmacauley.com

First Published 2023
Austin Macauley Publishers Ltd®
1 Canada Square
Canary Wharf
London
E14 5AA

Table of Contents

Preface	9
Introduction	10
Chapter 1: The Idea	11
Chapter 2: And So, It Began	22
Chapter 3: The Importance of Being Lizzybus	36
Chapter 4: The Curse of the Visas	48
Chapter 5: The Pull of Home	58
Chapter 6: Life Then and Now	65
Chapter 7: What Were We thinking?	79
Chapter 8: The Respite	90
Chapter 9: Falling at the Last Fence	101
Chapter 10: Where Is Home?	115
Chapter 11: Readjusting to Life Now	123
Chapter 12: Capital Cities and Embassies	134
Chapter 13: Milestones: Vous Franchissez L'équateur	151
Chapter 14: The Real Beauty of Africa	162
Chapter 15: The Goal Is in Sight	181
Chapter 16: Becoming Part of Something	191
Chapter 17: Our 'Mission' Is Accomplished	199
Epilogue	205

Preface

This book came about when David, my partner of ten years, and I decided to 'buy one of those Land Rover things and drive it around the world', starting in Africa. From the very first moment I stepped foot on African soil, I wrote a revealing personal account of the impossible being made possible. I've been asked many times to publish my missives about this journey, from those on their all-inclusive holiday, to those hitch-hiking, cycling, driving, or simply living vicariously, so here it is. For the women shuddering at the thought of digging their own toilet or changing a tire, or the man looking for just that sort of woman, for those sat in the garden to a setting sun sipping wine, soaking in the bath, tucked up in bed, or out chasing their own horizons.

It's not a travel book as such, but it does take you on an epic journey, through countries and continents, but mostly through life. It's the reality of living that dream of the relationship, sex, hygiene, illness, corruption, pollution, poverty, despair, loneliness, wonder, laughter and total utter joy of it.

This is Book 1, from England to South Africa, written with complete candid honesty, in the moment, as it happened, by me, Jayne. I am not a writer, I've screamed, cried and questioned my abilities daily, but somehow, like the journey, I did it.

Book 1: West Coast Africa
Book 2: East Coast Africa, Middle East, Far East, and Australia
Book 3: South America

Introduction

This is not a travel book as such but it does take you on an epic journey, through countries and continents but mostly through life. It starts on a rainy day in Birmingham, the reality of a dream, of a relationship, sex, hygiene, illness, corruption, pollution, poverty and total utter joy.

On 16 August 2009, we, sold, donated and trashed all our possession, gave up our jobs, rented out our house, bought 'one of those Land Rover things,' and set off to drive it around the world. Having never done anything like this before, no one thought we would even make it to France, and quite honestly, nor did we.

This is the beginning of the odyssey, raw and of the moment but above all else honest, written on the journey, as it happened, by me, Jayne. I was told I was living the dream; I question how living two feet from your other half, twenty-four hours a day, is living a dream?

There are moments in all our lives when something changes forever when we wander down a path, that becomes 'our' path, this is my path and where it took me.

Chapter 1
The Idea

In that fuzzy, hazy moment of the morning when sleep is replaced with consciousness, when reality blurs with make-believe, I imagine peering through a mosquito net into a tree canopy from a roof tent in Africa, to realise I am! How did I get here? How did this happen?

It all started on a Jeep Safari, whilst backpacking in Chile three years earlier. David, my partner of ten years and I were in the back of a vehicle, sandwiched between two huge guys, who stunk and three girls, who didn't, sitting up front. My view was blocked sideways by the guys and limited to the front by the girls. Whilst everyone else was commenting on the wonderful landscape, all I could see was the vehicle ahead, which just so happened to be a Land Rover. I was transfixed with how effortlessly it maneuvered over the huge rocks, up this near-vertical track. Realising I had actually said out loud "We should get one of those Land Rover things," not just thought it in my head, when David replied "Yes and we should drive it around the world" for some reason making it a 'fact.'

There are moments in all our lives when something changes it forever, when we wander down a path that becomes 'our' path. We both loved to travel but no more than the next person; the desire to drive around the world had never been a goal, a dream, or part of any conversation we had ever had, in any of our time together. The fact we had never owned or driven a Land Rover or a four-by-four (which I've learned is what these vehicles are) was insignificant. These words, words I thought were silent but had actually been spoken, sealed our fate and became our destiny, as if set in stone.

Just like that fateful evening, ten years earlier, when destiny, or fate, took over and David and I met.

But first, a bit about me and how I got to be with David in this Land Rover in Chile in the first place.

I was born to a factory worker father and a housewife mother of three girls and a boy, living in a three-bed council house on a huge council estate. On discovering my mother was pregnant again, not with one but two, you could say we were not exactly planned. Being identical twins with a mass of blond curls (that later coarsened to become afro frizz), we were just adorable and full of mischief and won the hearts of everyone, or so I'm told.

By the time we were aware of others in our universe, in the form of siblings, my eldest sister Jan was in the air force, the middle two Chris and Annabel were working as live-in Nannies in Canada and my brother Ivan was far more interested in girls than to be bothered with us. It was just Jayne and Jenny, the twins. At age five, thanks to my mother, we could both read, write and tie shoelaces but this made not the slightest difference when stood in front of the head of the Infant school, quivering behind my parents. The full glare of the head and his deputy upon us, a finger was pointed first at Jenny, with words of "You in the upper," then at me and "You in the lower." We later realised this meant upper and lower 'class,' as government policy at the time was to separate twins to give them the independence of character.

Jenny thrived, with reading, writing and arithmetic, even having homework (which my mother insisted, much to my dismay, I did with her, as I was not given any). For me, it was very different, when in my first reading lesson, the girl who was asked to read did not. I was scared for her, for not doing what she was told, shocked and confused, until realising she couldn't read! As was the case, for most of the children in the class. My reward for being able to read was to spend the lesson washing greenfly off Mrs Jackson's treasured geraniums (I cannot stand the smell of these plants to this day) or washing the staff tea and coffee cups, whilst eating any remaining stale biscuits.

This lack of learning followed me to senior school. Not surprisingly, as not a single question related to washing greenfly off geraniums, I failed the eleven plus. Jenny, whilst not quite passing, scored enough to be put in the top class to do French, English and Business Studies. Once in the bottom class, my subjects were limited to Domestic Science (cookery), Needlework—which I hated and will now throw a shirt away, rather than sow a button on it—and Art, which I loved and excelled at but no one cared. I did have the obligatory, very basic, English, Maths, History and Geography but I became a rebel, bored and embarrassed at what I felt was my ignorance and started bunking off and acting the fool. My only respite and challenge was sport, winning the Martlet for the best hockey player for four years but neither my parents nor my school were impressed with this: I was constantly in trouble.

Like the time me and my best mate Gayle launched a power ball off the desk in our Geography lessons. It bounced in slow motion, onto one wall and then the other, until landing on the bald head of our teacher Mr Smoulden. The whole class dissolved into hysterics but Mr Smoulden was less impressed, locking us in the stock room for the duration of the lesson.

Gayle had nicked one of her dad's fags and we thought it would be so clever to smoke it here, in the stock room. Neither of us smokers, we coughed, spluttered and turned green, as the smoke filled this little room, finding its way under the door.

Panicked, on hearing the door unlocking, we flung the offending fag behind us, setting fire to some crumpled paper.

For reasons never fully explained, Gayle was expelled and I spent most of my foreseeable lunch hours sat with teachers, ecstatic it didn't involve any teaching of Geography, oblivious to the importance of this in my future. Not surprisingly, academically I failed and at sixteen left school to work in a factory. Jenny, having been given no other guidance, came with me.

David's experience was worlds apart from mine, with a younger sister, Sue, his parents met whilst both in the Royal Airforce, Mr T Senior as an aircraft engineer and Mrs T Senior, would you believe, ferried pilots to their aircraft in Land Rovers. Mr T became a fire fighter and then a local bobby, Mrs T a mother and civil servant. David went to the prestigious King Edward Grammar School for Boys, getting a bunch of O and A levels to go to Polytechnic, before qualifying as a quantity surveyor. After a downturn in the property market, he changed career and went into criminal law.

David admits having been given every opportunity in life to underachieve but I will always be in awe of his academic achievements, even a little jealous. My lack of, for want of a better word, 'qualifications' has always made me feel less than I really am, an embarrassment to me. Even though I know it was as a direct result of 'adults' decisions,' it still stings. Knowing, despite their decision, I made the best of what I had been dealt with, I do wonder many times if I was to have been given the opportunities, the education I needed and craved, how different my life could have been.

Jenny and I had ten very difficult, what I call, wilderness years. Still only children, at sixteen Jenny was pregnant and in an abusive relationship. Neither realising you could want anything more in life, or achieve it, other than having children and getting married. That's what we both did: got married at a local registry office to the first person who asked us and went on to have four children between us. We did eventually figure it all out, find our inner strength; Jenny getting out of her abusive relationship and me dealing with the aftermath of an alcoholic husband that led to his death and my destitution.

Jenny and I leaned on each other during this time, sharing a small flat, getting jobs in a pop canning factory on nights, scrimped, saved and lied on the mortgage applications to buy our own houses. My little two-bed terraced house for me, my son and daughter was the first time in my life I began to feel proud, to believe in myself. One thing that had been instilled on us growing up was, 'it's your bed, you lie in it!'

My parents at this point had gone their separate ways, trying to make sense of their own lives, unable to help us in ours. It was a very difficult time, living mostly on beans on toast, saving coins to put in the electric and gas meters, whilst pay the mortgage. I look back on these years with hurt, laughter and pride. I know that what we couldn't give our children materialistically, we tried our very best to give in all other ways.

Without a shadow of a doubt, we both loved them all as our own and they will always be one of our greatest achievements.

Having put myself through a typing course, whilst working in a supermarket, I secured a job working twelve-hour nightshifts, coordinating callouts for on-call duty solicitors, vets, electrical industrial breakdowns etc. This, before smartphones, apps and Wi-Fi were a thing, I would take the call from the police, or person needing an engineer, page the 'on call' who would call the help desk, me and I passed the information on.

Going out was never an option but one night my workmate Lynn insisted I join them for a drink after work. Lynn was quitting work to go travelling. I never thought people actually did this? That it was just a dream, a fantasy but they didn't do it. Never, for one single solitary moment, in my wildest dreams, did I ever envisage one day I would not only do this but drive around the whole world, never ever. I roped my sister into coming with me, the thought of going into a pub on my own was not one I wanted to entertain. As the barman handed us our drinks, I regretted this immediately when paying and of how much shopping I could have bought instead. Behind me I heard a familiar voice, on turning I didn't recognise the face and intrigued, I went over and said, "I don't know your face but I know your voice." It was David, David Turner from Michael Purcel Parker Solicitors, who I had been speaking to on the phone for the last two years, whilst passing calls to him.

I imagined, in my lonely existence in the early hours of the morning, David to be a tall, handsome James Bond look-alike, who one day would sweep me off my feet but what I got was a Homer Simpson look-alike. Unable, or unwilling, to believe it was him, David showed me his chequebook, (which was a thing then), with his name printed on it but it was when he produced his gold American Express card, as further proof, I became interested. We laugh about this today, as I'm the least impressed person possible, to materialistic shite, cars, houses, watches, or your chosen method of payment.

But something about David intrigued me and much to my sister's alarm, half an hour later, Jenny, bored and wanting to go home, I told her to, "Get the bus, I am getting a lift with David." We had a stand-up row in the pub, Jenny pointing out I had only just met this guy and my insistence I had known him for two years, which in reality I had but had just never met him. It was the first introduction David had to the complicated world of twins, one where you will never win, one you never interfere in, one you will never figure out and one where your opinions, or side, will always be wrong. Two minutes later we hugged, cheek-kissed, before Jen went off to get the bus home, as my life and David's became one.

David, as I knew he would, dropped me home safely; it was no passionate affair, a confirmed bachelor, more interested in motor bikes, fast cars and music. My focus was on paying the mortgage, buying school uniforms and keeping my Ford Escort, bought for two hundred quid from the auction, on the road. What we both shared was a work ethic. I knew David's job came first and would always be prioritised over me. I didn't care, in fact, I wanted it. Also, fiercely independent, there was no way I was going out on a date without being able to buy my own drink, meaning it was only every few weeks I could afford to go on one.

Somehow our lives slotted together; Adele became, not exactly fond of David but tolerated him, until a year later he moved in. Neither of us changed, we didn't have to, we just accepted who and how we were. David was a lot more of a traveller than ever I was, this he got from the Seniors, putting him and his sister in the back of a Mini and driving them to France at ten and twelve years old. This progressed to an old Ambulance, taking 'Gran Griff' with them all over Europe.

Our first holiday together was to America. On arriving, we picked up the hire car to go in search of a cheap motel. I was totally freaked out, on the six-lane highway, driving on the opposite side of the road, humiliated, stood, negotiating a room at a local motel and homesick. But, on my return, I knew I wanted more. Working shifts, we were able to tie days off to working days and get three weeks off together so could venture further afield.

That's how we ended up in Chile, in a Land Rover, with what we thought was a 'good idea' to get one of those Land Rover things and drive it around the world.

Now, all we had to do was get one and get it ready for such an adventure, one thing we both knew for definite was, we were going to do it! Family and friends humoured us, thinking it to be nothing more than a fanciful holiday romance, something that would never happen. We knew differently, it was no dream, it was fact, a fact we were going to make happen.

To us, driving around the world in a Land Rover seemed pretty simple: get a Land Rover and piss off. Surely the hardest part was getting the money together to do it? This, we realised, was going to be a huge task but simple in that, the more you worked, the more you earned. It just so happened on our return, I was made redundant from my present job, which enabled me to pay off my small mortgage. I immediately took a job working with a team of six, on twelve-hour shifts, a mix of days and nights on an IT Help Desk for a government outsource company. I hated every second of it, it was pressurised and confusing, even having a piss was timed, or how long you spoke. It was technical, I'm not and rigid, in what you could and had to say. With team leaders who liked nothing better than to dissect each call, to report back to their boss on how long you breathed, or a word you might have misspelt, or not asked and how helpful you were.

This only cemented my determination, all thoughts focused around escape: escape from this mental torture, to stick two fingers up, to live the dream. To not have to sit at a desk, with a headset wrapped around my head, for twelve endless hours, day and night, solving things I knew jack shit about. The Jayne in me would never not do her best, it was this that was pushing me to a meltdown. In these sorts of 'environments' it's nothing to do with your best, it's all to do with fobbing people off.

As David had been living with me for the last six years, his house had been rented out, all the rental income having been used to pay the mortgage and it was now mortgage free. The house next door was up for sale: I got it into my head we needed it, with three houses rented out, this would give us our income. As I had worked since sixteen, paying a full contribution to my pension, it would be at least another ten years before I would receive it. Speaking to the agent, they said the house was under offer!

Undeterred, I went to see the owner, a South African, offering him what I thought was two thousand over the asking price but was actually four thousand. David, knowing nothing about my little deal, when returning from work, was congratulated by the neighbour and thanked for the generous offer by his 'missus.' This was financed by a small loan against David's house and the selling of all David's premium bonds.

We now had three houses, two paid for and rented out, the other we lived in, which would also be rented out when we left. These three rental incomes would give us sixty pounds a day between us to live on, for as long as it would take for our little drive around the world.

Now that that was set in place, it was time to get a pot. We settled on a target of one hundred thousand pounds. The thinking was, if for any reason Lizzybus was totalled, we could at least replace her and carry on. It would also be a safety net for big items, like tyres, shipping and mechanical needs, or emergency flights home if needed. In savings, we had around forty-five thousand, only another sixty-five to go. I made a chart on the wall and every time we squirreled away some more, I moved the red line closer to our goal.

During all this David had been looking for 'the one,' a Land Rover, to do it in. It was late afternoon, I was getting ready for my night shift when I heard what would become very familiar to me, the rattle of a diesel engine. Looking out of the window, pulling up was a twelve seat Station Wagon Land Rover Defender with David driving. David handed me the keys and left me to it. I sat in it, didn't even try to start it up, went back inside, gave David the keys back and said, "Forget it, I can't drive that thing, it's too big," got showered and went to work. David was crestfallen.

I think it made it all feel too real for me; I panicked—up to this point, it was just a thing. Returning from my nightshift, 'it' was still there, David having already left for work, I took the keys, started 'it' up and drove to my sister's. With Jen still in her pyjamas, I told her to get in, I'm taking you for a ride.

Trundling around our local park, the rising sun dissolved the morning mist, revealing a glorious day.

It brought with it a moment of time, one that just is, that hangs, as I was smitten, the smell, the noise but most of all I was ready, ready to have this adventure. It was in this moment, that Jen also realised I really was doing this. She saw it as that of a traitor, all our life, there was an almost unwritten law that we would always be there for each other, seeing it only as an abandonment, left to make a life without me in it, was too painful.

'It' finally got a name, Elizabeth, which came about when fitting the Brown-Church Roof rack, which to me looked like a crown. As a nod to being English, Queen Elizabeth herself, driving a defender and of Jen's street name being Elizabeth, David suggested Elizabeth. I was not that sure, until the day, with twelve of us in her, off to the circus, James my son-in-law, said "Are we going in the Lizzy-bus?" and that was it, 'it' became The Lizzybus.

When my fiftieth birthday came, with it went the loose plan to set off, knowing the one thing we could never ever get back was time, which was slipping through our fingers, to become the enemy. Working every minute of every day, time for David to work on Lizzybus, or for us to take any courses, like mechanical or off road, which we realised might be useful, was impossible, changed tact and started paying others to prepare Lizzybus.

At this point, David had already stripped out the bench seats at the back, not exactly fitting, more filling, it with plastic boxes for kit, had taken out the middle seat between the two back seats and fitted a fridge. David's dad's garage was full to the brim with eBay bargains, like long range fuel tanks, rock sliders, high lift jacks and a complete roll cage, which needed welding to the chassis. Both totally overwhelmed, as the simplicity of it all just got complicated, it was time to take action.

Lizzybus was booked in with a company specializing in such preparation and several weeks later when picking her up, we found a shoddy cover up job. Stuff they had fitted was not bolted down or secured, things were just covered in grease not replaced. A little broken by this, David vowed to never let anyone work on Lizzybus without him being there.

We did find good honest people and slowly Lizzybus came together, with a new chassis, full external roll cage and updated electrics. Not being part of any club or group or even Facebook, it was all down to good old fashion research by David. But time was still passing by, our one hundred-thousand-pound target was twenty thousand pound short. Having paid back the loan on the third house, we were spending so much money on Lizzybus and getting the house ready for rental, with a new kitchen and double-glazing, it seemed an impossible dream.

Going into the third year since our decision, the end was further away than ever, we were running out of steam. It was at this point, I insisted David go to the doctors, he was having pains in his shoulder and shaking. The doctors said, "Change whatever you're doing, or you won't be doing it anymore!" Overweight, with high blood pressure, irregular sleep pattern and drinking a bottle of red a night, David was not good.

The Seniors stepped in, giving us twenty thousand pounds, taking us to our one hundred-thousand-pound target, telling us, "It's time to go." With Lizzybus and the house almost ready, I took the plunge and handed my notice in to focus on the final push. This I knew would force our hand, as David continued to work, I made a to-do-list, shocked at the amount of things 'to-do' on it.

One of the biggest was filling in my twelve-by-six-foot pond, with over twenty beautiful Koi Carp. I'd built this with my most treasured possession, a tangier orange electric cement mixer, a Valentine's Day present. I was sad at having to sell this; watching sand and cement come together into a smooth dough, ready for my creations, was therapy after a long day at work. Not as much though as David was when his adored Aprilia Mille R Motor bike also had to go. I was shocked when reading the description posted on the sale of this bike, the gushing fanciful description of this Italian beauty, words I thought beyond him. It took me all my time to get a "You look pretty" comment, used only after asking how I looked.

Both adamant to make coming back the hard option, not one we could fit easily back into, everything had to go. I do wonder how two normal, everyday people, who enjoyed a bit of sight-seeing, became so focused, so determined, so tunnel-visioned, never once really questioning why, or if, or how. Yes, we were both having moments of being totally, utterly, overwhelmed by the logistics of it all but never did we question, why?

With the Koi Carp swimming in a new pond, the cement mixer and Aprilia sold, I donated, sold and trashed all our clothes and household paraphernalia. But the days flew by and David, still, had not given in his notice and the to-do list just got longer. I arranged some house viewings and agreed to a letting at the end of next month. This forced David to give a month's notice and us to get our act together.

After a load of us manhandled the 'Hannibal roof tent' bought off eBay onto the roof, Jenny and I got it into our heads to piss off for the weekend to Wales with our horse-riding buddies and test it out. Ten minutes in, on the first night, I realised there was 'no way' I could sleep with David in this for a night—let alone the foreseeable future; we could barely turn over. Jen and I, not wanting to 'touch' each other, slept one in the awning and one in the roof tent. Unable to prime the Coleman cooker, having paid no attention to David's instructions, we couldn't even have a hot drink, with the typical Welsh mountain downpour all night, I decided it was absolutely not for me. I was going to forget all about any stupid idea to live in a roof tent and drive around the world.

I made it clear to David, I could not sleep in 'that thing' like a sardine, with him (now, there are lots of alternatives to a roof tent but then it was more of less a roof tent or nothing). At the last minute, David ordered a German-made, brand new roof tent, based purely on it being a foot wider and assuring me, that in Africa it will not rain!

We had one of those rare moments: a day off together. I had not seen or been part of the 'eBay must-have, needed bargain purchases' that filled Mr T Senior's garage. I had assumed they had all been fitted, today we were going over to take one last look. On opening the garage, I was shocked. How much stuff? This was the first, real indicator as to David's, I can't say hoarding, as such, more of needing and wanting every washer nut, bolt, tool and spare part you would, or could ever need to rebuild a Land Rover.

I looked at it in horror. Knowing somehow we had to find space for it, I laid it all out on a huge tarpaulin, trying to categorise stuff. I could feel myself getting more and more infuriated as Mr T Senior kept adding to the pile, "Son, this will be useful, take this and this," handing David half-full tins of some gunk or other and old biscuit tins with rusted nuts and bolts. I just exploded. Unlike Mr T Senior, with two garages, a spare room and a home to live in, we had a box and, in that box, had to go all this stuff and US!

With Lizzybus full to the brim and us barely speaking, once home, I emptied the lot onto the living room floor, to realise what I already knew: no way would it fit into the six plastic boxes, the boxes that would contain my life, for the foreseeable future. We bought a huge soft roof bag, for 'our stuff,' so all the Lizzybus 'stuff' could be stored inside, along with one of the two spare wheels, the other fitted to the swing away back door carrier. On the two back passenger seats were stuff bags, which effectively became our wardrobes.

David rigged up a pump, to pump fuel from the long-range fuel tank to the main tank and water through a ceramic water filter system, fed from two twenty-litre Jerry Cans. Our third Jerry Can was filled with petrol for the Coleman cooker. I worked on a food, shelter, water basis—and to me we had all three.

The final week was focused on paperwork, Lizzybus had her Carnet De Passage, a sort of passport, secured by an eight-thousand-pound bond, which required stamping in and out of each country. We had an extensive medical kit, with enough equipment to do a blood transfusion and a year's supply of malaria tablets, for when we reached Malaria countries. Our arms throbbed, from all the vaccinations against the tropical diseases waiting to infect us and die an agonising death from. One EpiPen as, despite being anaphylactic, one was all the Doctor would prescribe and a six pack of one hundred percent body rotting DEET.

You would imagine the enormity of what we had done, of the comfortable life we had just trashed, would be freaking us out but we just didn't have the time to think about it. It had become like a runaway train, all focus was on running, to catch it. The constant "When are you leaving?" was on loop in my head.

I wanted to scream, "I have no idea!"

Chapter 2
And So, It Began

In the early hours of a typical wet miserable grey day, we slipped away. I just had to see my sister one last time, so instead of heading for the motorway we headed to hers. Jen was doing such a normal thing, putting on her boots ready for work, amongst the plants in a garden centre. Neither really having any words for a moment like this, we just hugged. It helped that it was Jen driving away from me, even if only to work, rather than me from her. To have watched me drive off into the unknown, an unknown that didn't include her, would have been too unbearable for us both.

The realisation that we had no jobs, no possessions, no wage, our home rented out and of there being 'no going back' was not allowed into our heads. I know in this moment, had we had a choice, we both would have said, "No! We're not ready" and, the reality was, we never would be. It seems crazy, to not have discussed how we felt but any doubts either of us had were far better left unspoken. The biggest emotion was of relief, to not have to face the constant question of, "When are you leaving?"

Our rough plan was to head to Morocco and follow the West Coast of Africa to South Africa. David had mentioned heading North first, to the Arctic but since my weekend in Wales with Jenny, I wanted to go somewhere hot—be careful what you wish for.

The simplicity of our decision-making beggar's belief; I had no understanding of the implications of getting us and a Lizzybus through these countries but I sure as hell was about to find out.

Arriving at Dover for the ferry to France felt so normal, like a little jolly, like children playing house, only in a Land Rover. The biggest, scariest thing for us both, having worked since leaving school, was of having no salary. With the journey funded solely by rental income and savings, we determined the costs that could not be avoided were visas, diesel and for now camping fees, as no way was I ready to Bush Camp, alone in the wild. Meals out, or even coffees, were to be a luxury, to enjoy only with others. I'd filled the fridge with cooked chicken, homemade bags of pasta sauce and the plastic box, my 'pantry,' with tinned tuna pasta and rice.

It took one night before realising what a shit set-up we actually had; even when making a morning coffee, most of the boxes had to come out. This started an ongoing, kit shuffling and prioritising routine, the cause of many heated arguments, as my priorities, like clean knickers, were a lot different to David's, of grease guns. It was decided that the second of the two spare wheels inside Lizzybus just had to be stored elsewhere. It got 'ratcheted' to the bonnet, with words of "I told you that bag of ratchet straps would come in useful!" A phrase applied to every other needed bag of something from here on in.

The lesson of constant kit shuffling was also one of compromise. Yes, there was more space for personal kit but you had to bench press the bonnet for the nightly ritual of checking oil and staring at the engine and it partially blocking the driving view. Even taking off and putting on the ex-army Directors chairs, now ratchet strapped to the external roll cage, was an effort but we decided it looked super cool and at this stage looking cool pleased us no end.

David and I were taking it in turns to drive but as my map reading, or ability to programme, or follow a GPS was non-existent, I tended to drive through cities whilst David navigated. That was, until driving towards the Eiffel Tower, through six lanes of gridlock traffic, approaching an island, on the wrong side of the road, I stopped, got out and refused to drive. David looked at me with disbelief at my stupidity. As traffic swerved to avoid me, he ordered me back in but my mind was made up, no way was I driving with these idiotic crazy Frenchmen, one single inch more.

Somehow, we made it through France and into Spain, heading now for Algeciras, the bottom of it, for the ferry that would take us across the Straits of Gibraltar and into Morocco and Africa, the unknown and the real start of this ordeal, I mean, epic journey.

We were staying a few days en-route with my best friend, sealed with a piss, Gayle, having moved to Spain three years earlier to open Lobo de Mar restaurant, with husband Bob and son Gary. Gayle got her name when, for some unfathomable reason at junior school, when going for a pee we each had to put a foot under the door of the next cubicle to prove we weren't looking over the top at each other. With my foot diligently under Gayle's cubicle, I felt something wet and warm run over it. Gayle, so focused on getting her foot under, had missed the pan and peed all over my foot.

Disgusted, I shot out of the toilet, knickers around my knees to put my whole foot under the tap in the sink. Everyone was in hysterics; it took a very long time before I saw the funny side.

I remember the night of Gayle's leaving party in England, on seeing her crying, I wondered what all the fuss was about, it was only Spain, a skip and a hop away. Gayle and Bob, both divorcées, had sold their houses to start this new life, effectively burning all their bridges. The pressure was on to make it work, as a couple and as a business. I see the enormity of this, now, of leaving friends and family, the life she loved. It was their fourth year here, the Lobo de Mar was a huge success, they had a beautiful villa with pool and convertible car.

(Five years after this, Gayle and Bob got itchy feet, sold up and moved back to England. Sadly, Gary, Gayles only son died in an accident and Bob a year later to cancer.)

We rented an apartment close to Gayle's, decorated the Lobo for free meals and joy of joy, Jenny and her husband Richard came out for a two-week holiday. Life was wonderful but the reality was, we were only putting off the inevitable, of getting on with this journey. David continued to work on Lizzybus, fitting a re-enforced bonnet with wheel carrier to secure the spare wheel, getting rid of the ratchet straps.

A month passed before finally heading off to the port of Algeciras. In the distance, we can see the silhouette of Africa, just a short ferry journey away, scaring us shitless. Camping on the beach, we keep telling ourselves we will go tomorrow, until committing by booking and paying for the ferry tickets, sail in two days' time: it just got real.

Waiting at the docks, like a mirage, are ten Land Rovers on a three-week organised trip into Morocco. With no shame whatsoever, we tag on behind them, with every intention of sticking to them like glue. This day, this journey, this life just got real, we're on the ferry crossing the Straits of Gibraltar taking us to Africa, our destiny, a destiny that is about to change us and our lives forever.

Arriving at Ceuta docks, utterly overwhelmed by the heat, the dust, the people all wanting to help us, we follow our group into a cordoned off area where immigration and customs is completed. With Lizzybus' insurance typed out on a manual typewriter, at eighty dollars for the month, we're not entirely sure it's valid, placated slightly by the official-looking stamp on it. It's fair to say, we're both pretty traumatised at this point but with the group being in awe of what we're doing, like ducks, we act cool and calm above the water, whilst paddling like hell underneath.

Following the group, David, driving, notices the indicators won't switch off; although indication is not necessary here, we don't want ours flashing, just in case someone thinks we might be turning. This is the first 'indication' of how overwhelmed David is—he just won't listen to me when asking him if the hazards are on. I lean across and switch them off. A rookie mistake, one of the many times I will say something that David will pay no attention to but actually is something useful. It's not that he doesn't want to hear, or value my input, it's just in these situations he can't. It helps that I'm a far simpler person, with only a basic understanding of what could go wrong, unlike David, who knows all the worst-case scenarios and that's his starting point.

Arriving at the pre-booked campsite as dusk settles, the realisation we have no beer or obvious place of buying any is a big concern. Our group generously donate beers to the cause and over a plate of pasta, it dawns on us we're here, we made it, we're in Africa—this is our life now and will be for the foreseeable future.

Making it to our first morning, on peering out of the roof tent, my first thought is to the heat, followed by the mosquitoes, which, despite the liberal coating of one hundred percent body rotting DEET, I'm covered in pulsating bites specifically on my arse. Getting down the roof ladder and to the toilets with a full bladder becomes a sprint; squatting over the open hole of toilet with my trousers around my knees, trying to avoid piss-soaked trouser bottoms is an art, an art I'm yet to master. As is protecting my bare arse from the mosquitoes lying in wait.

I'm a lot freaked out, waving farewell to the group on their three-week 'raid' into Morocco, as we are now totally on our own heading for Chefchaouen. The group are heading directly to Meknes (where we will go tomorrow), as they are here for only three weeks, unlike us who have the rest of our foreseeable life.

As the days, months and years pass on this journey, we will become semi experts at packing, driving and surviving in this heat, dust and general mayhem, become experts at negotiating and bargaining, understand who is and who is not, official. But, for now we're just getting through each day, facing each task as it comes along, like buying food at the French speaking market, without getting ripped off. I'm still far too nervous to ever consider 'Bush Camping' out in the open alone, insisting on a campsite, which is putting a huge dent in our daily budget, as is paying for a traditional Terineen (Stew) served in a ceramic conical pot baked in the oven, even though it is delicious.

We're in the Mountainous fertile area of the Rif Valley, Northern Morocco heading for Meknes, one long slog of vertical and horizontal gravel roads with hairpin bends and sheer drop offs. David, perched on a vertical junction, the clutch starts slipping, yet to become at one with Lizzybus, to understand her rhythm, her noise, her strength, this shatters our already fragile confidence and begins my ongoing education of what a knackered clutch, or anything knackered, could mean.

I wish someone could have put their arm around me, assured me: time will give me the experience and confidence I need. Not fully understanding the mechanical side, or its implications, or realising that voicing worst case scenarios, does not mean they will happen, it's just David's way, whilst to me, it feels like the end before the beginning has even begun. All this is doing very little to change my mind about driving—since the incident in France, I'm still refusing. I'm ashamed but so terrified of the total chaos on the roads, the longer it goes on the more I'm filled with self-doubt. It's just so alien to what was my Monday morning commute on the M6 in my suit, phone in my bag, with the AA on speed dial speaking English.

I wonder what's happened to me, where the daring, go-for-it Jayne has gone, I feel totally out of my depth, intimidated by it all. One thing I'm good at is talking to myself, so that's what I do. I wake feeling a lot more positive, on realising I had no expectations of this journey, I can see it now for the adventure and challenge it is. I am ready, today I will drive. It's also helped by having reached the valley and flat. An arid dry landscape as far as the eye can see of over ploughed fields, it's dusty and grey but I don't care as for now it's wonderfully flat. This sets a routine, where I drive for two hours in the morning and through hard to navigate city areas, David drives the rest of the day.

Arriving in Meknes I'm still wanting, needing the security of a campsite, the evening search for one from the guidebook begins. Despite having the latest edition, this is no guarantee it's open or even exists. The Garmin used mainly for compass points (later we will get 'Tracks for Africa' with detailed maps) loses satellite, making it impossible for David to even head south. We're in the heart of the city in a rabbit warren of narrow streets, destroying my new-found confidence, as buildings, businesses and people live, eat and sleep here in the street, it becomes so narrow we're stuck. I'm sweating, David is shouting and the locals are holding tight to their tomatoes making sure we don't squish them. We ask a policeman where the campsite is, to be told the campsite does not exist: it's a crushing blow.

Heading back out of town to a sign we noticed on the way in, taking us into the grounds of a 'Riad' set around a courtyard with swimming pool, water feature and walkway of ornate decoratively tiled arches. The pool is half-full of garbage with broken gold and blue ceramic tiles, the fruit of the once carefully tended orange and lemon trees make a carpet of autumn colours leading to a Pagoda, which lists drunkenly.

We thought all life had been abandoned years ago until two mangy dogs bark, waking the unshaven tee-shirt clad guy asleep on a raised platform. It's cheap and despite a generator off the Richter scale for noise belching out black acrid smoke, we even get a hot shower.

Back in Meknes we find a supermarket selling beer, what we thought would be the luxury of a cold beer from our Engle fridge at the end of a day par boiled in Lizzybus, we have now realised is a necessity, to wash away the dust and mayhem of it, the day that is. Not even looking at the price, we buy two cases, along with a bag of chicken pieces and vegetables.

Back to our 'handsome' camp site, after a hot shower, my dry split filthy feet soaking in a bucket of hot water, a chicken stew bubbling away in the pressure cooker, we crack open a beer. Both agree, right now, in this moment in time, there is nowhere else we would rather be. Inwardly I smile, realising we're still very much in our honeymoon period.

Today we visit Volubilis, a UNESCO registered ancient Roman city. A few coaches litter the car park, its occupants disgorged, dissolved amongst the ruins: and best of all, it's free. Later we find an internet café, as Wi-Fi is yet to become a 'thing' this arduous task becomes a weekly trial of poor connections, broken keyboards, and worn blank keypads, desperately trying to download and send precious emails to and from home. My only connection to a life that was. On reading the emails from Jen (who will write every day for the rest of this journey), I realise that losing someone comes not just through death but through life and the choices we make.

I've seen or spoken to my sister every day of my life since we shared our embryo, it's a huge missing, an actual physical pain.

Being English we're still noticing a sunny day, where commenting on this is as asking how you are, so it's another sunny day! This vast city encompasses life as it was and the life it is becoming, as high-rise buildings provide shelter for lean-to wooden shacks the roads are clogged with as many motor cars as donkeys and carts—and now a Lizzybus.

Each area of the city is specific, metal work, woodwork, fleece harvesting, etc. in the market area, on wooded stalls are whole cows' heads with glazed eyes that follow you, all shaved to look their best. The futile swatting to remove the crust of flies is automatic, along with assurances they have the best cows' head. It's kind of repulsive, a little nauseating, with the smell of blood and rotting, at the same time as intoxicating and alluring, with the ever present calling to prayer.

Treating ourselves to a coffee in the town square, an overly made-up middle-aged woman sucked into a silver glittering tee shirt and jeans pushes her two-year-old towards us, dwarfed in a tatty pageant dress hand out begging, as is the man playing his cymbals. A wizened old man struggles to push his cart full of fresh fish and flies in the gridlock traffic, in what is becoming a familiar scene to us in our new life. A part of our new life, which we will always find incredibly difficult, is being faced with so much poverty, broken bodies and begging. Along with the nightly serenade of wild dogs and camp site skinny cats, all with bulging bellies, or trailed by the latest litter of kittens.

We know that giving money to beggars, especially children usually forced into this by adults, will be something to try and avoid. To buy wherever possible from locals, avoid tourist places and always give of our time. It's time to move on.

We met a wonderful couple last night, Marianne and John in a yellow zebra stripped Land Rover. John English, Marianne Spanish, living in Malaga, visit Morocco twice a year to buy rugs and artefacts. We sit open-mouthed listening to all their past adventures, with the conclusion we're not so sure this travel thing is actually for us, getting the feeling we're just lambs to the slaughter. What is becoming obvious to us is any traveller, experienced or not, suffers from an amount of clutter at the start of any journey. The first days, weeks, months, are of prioritising the everyday needs and access to them. On this journey, we had visions of picking up hitchhikers, even of people joining us and paying. It soon becomes apparent this could never happen; we can't even sit inside Lizzybus, let alone other people with their kit.

We know we have to dump kit but being so far from home and unable to replace or source parts or equipment, for us or Lizzybus, ditching it becomes a necessary, agonising choice. We know people who buy mementos along the way, either shipping them home or just cramming them into their vehicles. With little intention of returning home anytime soon and hating mementos, we determine not to fall into this trap. Much to our irritation, we have a new addition to the Lizzybus camp, not bought but donated, by Marian and John, a black Mamba four-foot plastic snake called Sid.

Feeling almost obliged to accept him, we're not convinced he will be the security feature we're assured he is, as apparently Africans are terrified of snakes.

A sort of routine develops and with it we become a little less critical of each other's efforts. The hardest task when packing up is the roof tent ratchet straps, which totally baffle me, no matter how many times David shows me. During our ten years together, the domestic chores were mine, apart from cooking which we both did depending on my shifts or David's call outs. It might also have been that David could never see the point in ironing shirts for the week or having things in drawers. The confirmed bachelor, David would even put boxer shorts in the microwave, directly from the washing machine, to dry.

It's struck me that I have to spend every minute of every day, a few feet away from David, this after not really spending more than a few hours together. I remember Christmas days, or my rare birthday meals out, David would most likely leave halfway through, being called out to a police station. This never bothered either of us, I know the last thing David wanted was to sit half the night in smoke-filled interview rooms, floating just above the underbelly of society, any more than I wanted to celebrate without him. It's what we did, we worked, it was who we were, an inbuilt need in us both, not having this now and being in such close proximity to each other is taking some adjusting to.

Driving on through what feels like a fog, we realise it's a haze of pollution and I end each day with a nose full of snot and soot. We were told that being obvious over-Landers specifically in a Land Rover, you will always need a garage sooner or later and that you don't need to find local garages, they find you. That is exactly what happened, when sat having coffee a guy covered in grease and rags is trying to get David to go to a local garage. One of David's prioritised close-at-hand items is his grease gun. This is to be used constantly during the end of day ritual of crawling under Lizzybus to grease. The wisdom and necessity of this, along with the most important thing to grease being nipples, I'm still to recognise. The prospect that all Lizzybus nipples would be greased for two dollars, less than the cost of the grease, fills David with need and he agrees to go to his garage tomorrow.

First, we're off to visit the Old Cedar Tree, an apparent scenic walk through the Cedar Forest. A few ramshackle huts selling fossils adjacent to a tarmac road led you to a dead tree under which sit two people begging. I decided it's not the destination but the journey. On returning to Lizzybus, the same guy is waiting and no number of refusals will put him off us agreeing to take Lizzybus to his garage, now. What we find there are other over-Landers mainly in Toyotas returning from, or on their way to, Africa. It occurred to me that most were doing their trip in aid of charitable causes or had the backing of sponsors.

Feeling slightly alarmed that we are actually doing this for us, just us. Un-sponsored un-supported and, beginning to realise, un-hinged. I remind myself of my precious days off spent donating blood, doing the Three Peaks Mountain challenge, when I nearly fell off the cliff edge, the years of volunteer twin research, eating raw pigs' eyes for children in need. All raising money for charitable causes and progressing medical science, think sod it whilst commending their noble deeds.

Along with greased nipples, David has agreed to upgrading the Lizzybus springs, as now fully loaded, she is sitting low, my mechanical education continues. Sat in the shade daydreaming, I think back to my money challenged, basically poor, childhood, when every Christmas our hand scribbled notes of much wished for Bicycles were sent up the chimney of smoke and hope. Trying desperately not to be disappointed, with the pogo sticks Santa left instead a metal pole with internal spring and foot pegs.

Our school allowed us to bring in a present from Santa; Jenny and I pogoed the three miles to school, arriving knackered but triumphant, alongside the pupils whose wish didn't go up in smoke but materialised into bicycles. Eventually the spring gave up, giving us a jarring thud every hop and the worn-out rubber left a trail of metal sparks in our wake. I think how amazing it would have been to have one of these bright red, upgraded springs for our pogo sticks, Lizzybus now has.

The desert dust gridlock cities and smoke spewing chimneys change, here in the town of Azrou, it's like an Alpine ski resort. The king has a private airfield next to the huge, brand-new sprawling university. It's so at odds with life now, walking around collecting conkers from autumnal aged oaks I'm transported back to the forests of England, minus the bluebells. The valley and surrounding forest bring a cooling breeze into the immaculate campsite, with sit down toilets and hot showers, almost as shiny as my conkers.

We're in the rugged spectacular heart of the Middle Atlas Mountains, the remote villagers here live a subsistence life, we seem to be the only vehicle on the road, to be seen way before we arrive. Children appear from the remotest of places, blocking our way, hands out, shouting, "Cadeau" meaning gift or present; it's unsettling but we know if we stop, we will be overwhelmed. Endless days of driving become just that: endless. It's so difficult when a life has been spent dedicated to an alarm clock, to allow it to have a natural rhythm.

Now I'm driving, it has become apparent our driving styles are very different. This is becoming a real issue, as we begin to bicker constantly over it, to the point of aggression, it needs addressing. I'm one for talking things over, David is not, seeing everything as a criticism, I have a one-sided conversation, which will become the norm. Settling on an unwritten understanding, that neither will be judgemental of the other's driving, this works some of the time, as we sit in silent irritation of each other and perhaps not so silent at others but it's progress. Being a right-hand drive vehicle, it's the passenger who faces the oncoming traffic; with no control of the vehicle, you are putting all your trust in each other. One thing I am beginning to realise is, he who falters is lost, causes confusion, or gets you run off the road.

My map reading, or any form of navigational skills, have not improved, by the time I've finished reciting N-ever E-at S-hredded W-heat, we have passed where we need to turn, or to be, or to go, I'm now, not just the dedicated but the set in stone, official driver in towns and cities, David the navigator. Applying my newly acquired point and shoot skills, only giving way to vehicles bigger than me, never showing facial expressions like terror and never stopping, is working well.

Both wanting and needing, this journey to be more than just a calculation of countries driven through, or a ticking off of bucket list places, neither of which have, we know we need a target, a rough plan. For now, it will be South Africa, the very bottom of West Coast Africa, at over seven thousand five hundred kilometres and another twenty countries away. It's supposedly the toughest leg, due to civil war, border crossings, police and military corruption and poorly maintained, if maintained at all, roads. I don't for a single solitary second let any of this information into my head, just focus on the issue at hand, of how I can turn dry bread and a cheese triangle into breakfast.

The opinion held by most is that of David and I being workaholics and only spending a few hours of each day together, we would never survive each other, let alone the journey. It has become quite apparent their misgivings are misguided and a great relief, on realising conversation is futile above the rattle and noise of an old Land Rover Defender engine, we can sit in harmonious silence. The deciding factor to pushing on will be the dreaded visas, still, we determine, each day, or as many days as possible, to visit or see something of interest along our way.

Today it's the source of the river Oum Er-Rbia and waterfall, amongst the collection of ramshackle huts selling tourist trinkets is a Peugeot on English plates, the driver asks if we're here to join the hippy commune Rainbow Gathering. Hike with him, to the plunge pool of the waterfall, where groups of people have set up camp, enjoying life at one with mother earth. I can't ignore the discarded piles of tin cans and dirty Nappies, I'm a bit, no, a lot pissed off by it. David and I have a policy: burn, bury, or take it with you. We leave in disgust.

Arrive to a setting sun at Aguelmame Aziza, one of the milky azure hanging limestone lakes in this area and our first night of 'Bush Camping.' I'm overwhelmed with its magnitude and remoteness, totally humbled by its pure beauty. Under the vastness of sky, a full moon illuminates David, stripped naked showering stood on the wooden Ikea shower tray. This item of equipment was nearly ditched but has become invaluable, placed at the bottom of the roof ladder with a bucket of water, allowing for the offensive aroma of David's feet and sand to be washed off before getting into the roof tent. It's bitterly cold, David's shrivelled testicles join his kidneys as the campfire is another skill we have yet to master. It flickers and fizzles giving only the illusion of warmth. I'm in hysterics wrapped up in my sleeping bag. Little things please and believe me little things doth come of cold water.

We have found wild dogs to be very selective, white people are non-threatening and to be trusted, unlike black who are to be barked at and feared. Knowing we have to be cautious as wild dogs carry rabies, we find leaving a scrap of food on the perimeter of camp, for now stale bread soaked in a stock cube, that they stay all night on guard. It's comforting and feels protective; they don't enter camp, just watch silently from afar.

Tucked up in the roof tent, somewhere in Africa, protected by wild dogs under an inky vastness of sky, I begin to feel a belonging I've never felt before.

Waking this morning to a knocking, in that moment between sleep and reality, I think it's someone knocking the door, to realise, there is no door. Peering through the moggie screen into the tree canopy is a woodpecker preparing his home, unlike most birds who build a structure to form a nest in branches, Woody Woodpecker carves his out of the bark itself. Thank you for sharing this with me, Mr Woodpecker.

Pressing on towards Kasba Tadla, the bread we would have had for breakfast being the reward to our wild dog protectors, at Za-ech-Cheikh we treat ourselves to lunch. David tries out his schoolboy French compulsory at Boys Grammar. Admitting to getting unclassified in the exam, revert to the universal language of pointing at the steaming bowl of something on the next table. What we think is chicken is some sort of offal with white beans and carrots, it's chewy, slimy and smelly but with all eyes on us we smile and give a thumbs up whilst tucking in.

I'm becoming homesick and isolated, days upon days of not speaking to a single person are tough. Being in a Muslim country, David is the one spoken to, or addressed, I find myself looking away, lowering my gaze, standing behind. This is most agreeable to David and something to be greatly encouraged.

Our route over the middle Atlas Mountains is a steady climb, I save all my fear and terror, not for the hairpin bends, sheer drops or disintegrated road but as to whether Lizzybus will make it to the top with her slipping clutch. This colours the mood, plunging David into worst-case scenarios. This area inhabited by The Berbers or Berber, ancient nomadic herders of sheep and goat, they silently appear from everywhere and just as silently, disappear to nowhere. Forced to stop by a setting sun, we find a campsite nestled in the trees overlooking a vast reservoir, it's a mirror image reflection of the magnificent mountains taunting us, a reminder we have to get our sickly Lizzybus over them tomorrow. For now, we're just grateful at having water to wash the day away, a beer and roast chicken bought from the roadside, in the 'now' ready for the 'whatever' tomorrow.

We're heading for Marrakech, apart from "Quite frankly my dear" Casablanca, it's the only other city I've heard of in Morocco, working only on the fact I'd heard of it, assumed it to be the capital but that's Rabat. It's important to remember you are in the presence of someone who thought Jamaica was in Africa, since my geography lessons were cut short.

Thinking only of the day ahead and not the journey, which I now realise is a 'thing' and involves many 'things,' most of which I'm totally unprepared and unskilled for. I give up trying to figure David out, other than right now he is taking Lizzybus and her failing clutch as a personal betrayal. I'm as worried as David but I can't bare regurgitating things over and over. I let him waffle on for a while then tell him to "Shut the f…up."

In the beautiful red brick town square of Azilal stop for a coffee to lighten the mood. It's in the Beni Melal-Jenifra region with Las Cascade Ouzoud Falls flowing into the El-Abid River (Arabic for 'Slaves River'). 'Ouzoud' is the act of grinding grain and reflected in all the mills dotting the area, a reminder of its past and its present. It's out of season, the few tourists (us) are bestowed with all the best-selling techniques (harassed), once free of this, huff and puff our way through shaded paths of olive trees to plunge pools fed by spectacular cascades of tumbling water. David and I will from now on be dusty and dirty but never unclean, swim fully clothed in the plunge pools washing off the sweat and grime of travel.

We're still at the point of washing food, I had bought boxes of baby sterilizing tablets; once re-hydrated, I would soak the vegetables in, before soaking our clothes, this gives them a most agreeable fresh aroma, even to David's humming ones. It's still early, not completely at one with this life yet, there's a 'what to do now?' end of the day boredom. With no internet or Wi-Fi, David's either tinkering with Lizzybus or bent over maps, reading his bible, *The Haynes Manual*, or watching *Fawlty Towers and The Simpsons* videos. Never one for small talk, it's all about engines, gearboxes, routes and visas. Of course, I am interested, I know how important all this stuff is to us both, it's just occasionally, I just want a chat. I'm almost drowning in an enormous wave of loneliness, of missing, I feel it as a physical pain.

Last night feeling a long way from anywhere, not just home, three months having passed since we left England and life as it was. As David chuckled away to a *Fawlty Towers* video in the roof tent, I laid a blanket on the ground and set up the Yoga video my friend recorded for me. To hear her words, the soft music carried on the breeze, to a setting sun sent shivers down my spine. My body complained bitterly on being bent into positions it could only do immediately after birth but it felt good, because it was a familiar pain. Sat in the lotus position eyes closed, I could hear the tinkering of bells and bleating; on opening my eyes

I found myself surrounded by the most beautiful auburn longhaired herd of goats. I knew in that moment; I might be alone but I won't ever be lonely.

Chapter 3
The Importance of Being Lizzybus

It's exciting today, as we should actually make it to Marrakech in the foothills of the Atlas Mountains—to me, this means mercifully flat. The first half of the drive was beautiful, the vegetation changing over each set of mountains according to its allotted sun or shade; the silhouette of Marrakech and the Kingdom of Morocco appears in the distance.

I had taken over the driving, on what might have been a dual carriageway once but now broken-down vehicles, donkey drawn carts, cows, bicycles and life have reduced it to a single lane of mayhem, where oil, grease and traffic had polished it to a mirrored sheen slippery as an ice rink. The heat inside Lizzybus made open windows essential, bringing in a thick choking acrid smoke, turning day into night. My eyes and nose streamed, only short gulps of breath were possible, until I felt nauseous and light-headed.

Several hours of gridlock traffic later, our nerves in tatters somehow, we find the campsite in the heart of Marrakech, well not us exactly but from the directions of a very nice policeman. Not yet accepting or understanding the importance and difficulties of each other's role, as driver or navigator, on arriving we have a blazing row. We attract attention anyway, just by being in a Lizzybus, even more so when hurling abuse at each other. Not being able to slam a door, or go into another room, or just go out to calm down, we use the next best thing, words. "How the hell do you expect me to navigate when you don't listen to directions?"

"How the hell do you expect me to turn when I'm on the opposite side of the road?" This is quite new to us, never being the argumentative type. Oblivious to the onlookers, it carries on for the next hour or so, until camp is set up and we're cracking open beers.

Waking to a sunny clear blue sky, last night's argument forgotten, we're told the blackout happens all the time dependent on the wind direction, from the constantly burning municipal dump. Slowly we're beginning to feel at home, not at home in a place but at home in a Lizzybus, as things are finding their own place and places have things that belong in them. This camp not only has a pool but the pool has water in it, there are washing machines and hot showers. It feels incredible shoving offensive smelling washing into a machine, pressing a button and heading off to buy beer.

Once back, with the washing blowing on the line, a stew bubbling away in the pressure cooker, we head for the pool, totally ignoring the gathering black clouds. It's only minutes before steroids of the watery stuff fall upon us; I think it's nature trying to put out the combusting rubbish tip. Our pitch becomes our very own swimming pool, we sit it out in the bar area, sodden, rejected but worse, the Wi-Fi promising precious emails from home is down, it's a bitter blow.

Last night Malcolm, an English guy on his BMW 650, arrived in the middle of the thunderstorm. Malcolm, the owner of Street Bikes, a shop used by David back in England, having survived a major heart attack, took stock of his life and went travelling. This "Oh what a small world" is what we will find throughout the whole of it (this was to be Malcolm's last journey—on returning to the UK Malcolm did not survive the next heart attack).

Tonight, with Malcolm, we visit the Jemaa el-Fnaa (assembly of the dead) in the centre of the old city. A vibrant mass of people flowed between row after row of stalls piled high with spices, dates etc. Food cooked over charcoal before you are served on, or in, paper, we squish together on a single plank bench feeling a belonging in our little group of three.

The rest of the area gives way to storytellers, musicians, bakkachat (henna tattooists), hook the ring over the coke bottle and miniature monkeys dressed in dolls' clothes, silhouetted by sandstone buildings and the imposing Mosque. Taxis can be horse-drawn carriages adorned with tassels and tinkering bells, or the knackered suspension-less, seatbelt-less, mad Moroccan rent a wreck Taxi that David and Malcolm booked.

Malcolm's gone and we visit The Menara Gardens, a twelfth century UNESCO heritage site basin reservoir and green tiled Pavilion. I've seen the image on postcards, it's a tourist recommended place to visit. Its seven-hundred-year-old innovative hydraulic system of getting water from the Atlas Mountains is a feat but it's a lot underwhelming.

Overcast and cold today, the Lizzybus clutch colours the mood, it has to be sorted but where to start? The Wi-Fi is still down, it makes me feel desolate and alone knowing I have emails from home but cannot get them. I keep going over to the bar area in hope, only to relive this bitter disappointment. Sitting at the bar sheltering from the rain, I go outside to see if it's still raining, okay to have a fag, that David, as a non-smoker, assures me will stop as soon as the contraband purchased in Spain evaporates in the smoke they leave behind. This infuriates me, as I smoked when I met David, it's not something he said would be a deal breaker, I didn't hear him saying, when zipping his flies up, thanks Jayne but I can't date a smoker.

Outside smoking, I meet Justus, a Dutch guy with his friends returning to his campsite in Atar, Mauritania, our next country. Justus tells us we can get Mauritanian visas on the border, giving us a beautiful hand-drawn map of how to get to his campsite. David spent the evening drinking red wine with them, until finding the tent and getting up the roof ladder was a blur.

This morning Justus and his friends leave David with his hangover and us with information for our onward journey, which is how we will forever more find out information, not from books or websites but from word of mouth and local knowledge. This local knowledge is why we're heading for the garage beside the 'Old Tyre Factory' to get the Lizzybus clutch sorted. Calling in at the Central Train Station, locally known as Gare de Marrakech, which despite only having been rebuilt in 2008 has a colonial grandeur to it but what is most impressive is the working, free Wi-Fi, this day is already looking great.

Despite David's instructions and our Tourist To-Do street guide, it's several hours before eventually finding the 'Old Tyre Factory' as piles of old tyres are everywhere. In our old life everything was researched, prices compared, feedback considered, now just finding a place, any place is good. Lizzybus is booked in next Monday at eight in the morning.

Jenny, Mick and their children Mimi, three and Tao, six, arrive in an old Citroen pulling a trailer: English living in France. Having rented out their farm in France they are heading to the Gambia to set up a beekeeping charity. This is the magic of this journey, the crazy, focused-driven, no excuses people you meet along the way.

What a tonic, all speaking fluent French including the children—I am in awe they could travel with what seems to me so little. Lizzybus looks military spec next to their set up; her steering wheel is bigger than their tyres. We spend the afternoon in the shade around the pool chatting, such a simple thing of being able to speak my sister's name 'Jenny' is very special. One precious day is all we had,

Jenny, Mick and their children leave and on their travels I donate a bag of lollipops and pack of sterilising tablets. Jenny was using a mild bleach solution to sterilise their drinking water! Hard core.

Areane & John (the couple we met in Meknes) said we should black out all the back windows to stop prying eyes and to keep the sun out. With a couple of silver bubble wrap sunscreens, I empty Lizzybus out and cable tie them to the internal grills, it's a real success, as prying eyes can no longer see into Lizzybus and it's quite amazing how much cooler it is. Whilst I'm doing this, David permanently fixes the solar panel stored inside Lizzybus to the roof, to give a permanent charge and it occurs to me how well we're working together today.

Today is the day Lizzybus is getting a new clutch and I've decided to wait it out here on the empty sun beds. As the early morning sun kisses my skin, I munch my breakfast apple. The vacant sunbeds begin to fill with the migrated French, who come in convoy fully equipped in massive camper vans, complete with vacuums, irons—even washing machines. The sun is no longer kissing but biting me as six hours have passed, with only one phone between us, unable to phone David, I begin to feel a rising sense of panic.

How will I report a David lost at a garage, next to the 'Old Tyre Factory' with my passport, my home, my everything. Ten hours turn into twelve, it's pitch black, I couldn't care less about Lizzybus or her clutch, just about David and driving alone in the dark. There is a desolate helplessness about my situation, I'm furious with myself for not going with David, determine if he comes back alive, this will never happen again, we will always go together.

I hear that wonderful rattle of a Lizzybus engine well before seeing the familiar box square shape silhouetted by the moon. Relief washes over me, so traumatised I barley register the successful fitting of the new clutch and seals. Today's lesson, 'Inshallah,' a huge part of life on the road, will apply forever more.

As I write this, I am lying on a mattress on a mud floor in the house of a Berber family in the heart of the High Atlas Mountains. Having left Marrakech in great spirits now that Lizzybus has a new clutch, the adventure ahead filling us with excited anticipation on our way to Ouarzazate. As Marrakech became a dot in the rear-view mirror, David navigated a route once taken by merchants and caravans (not white caravans but donkey and camel caravans). How intoxicatingly romantic, so full of mystique and quite stunning ascending ever higher, the lush green of valley getting farther away, a contrast against the imposing mountains. Clinging to the sheer edge of a rubble track, apart from occasional clusters of mud-built red earth houses, we're totally alone.

David's nickname for me is 'Miss Daisy,' as apparently you could walk faster than I'm prepared to drive. What I am learning and it's a revelation, is just how strong Lizzybus is, giving me a newfound respect, cementing my love for her. But even Lizzybus cannot walk on water, or in this case climb the mountain of fallen rock completely blocking the next bend. Incredibly a tractor appears manoeuvring the larger boulders to form a rough path, I can see and try to ignore the driver signalling for me to pass. The road cut into the mountain has an overhang of rock, I'm convinced we will never fit under it. I sit momentarily frozen in time and terror, before inching forward, saying a silent prayer we're right-hand drive, as I'm spared the full view of the edge and sheer drop.

Somehow, I found myself further along the track and not dead in the valley below it, flattened to a Frisbee. Out of sight of our road builder tractor I got out and refused to get back in. It's hard to imagine how intimidated and scared I felt; nothing in life had ever prepared me for what I am facing. It's not just me, this is not exactly within David's experience either, his anxiety does jack shit to alleviate any of mine. David takes over the driving whilst I walked behind, registering the fact mountains are not just one up and one down but a constant series of ups and downs and their roads are not straight but snake to follow the mountain contours and always on the very, very edge.

Above us I can see two men watching, they scramble to the head of each bend on the switchback faster than we're driving. David is getting agitated (bloody cross) with me walking behind, as it's getting late and dark. I'm just appreciating the sheer joy of being on two legs, enjoying the panorama around me, whilst breathing. On the next bend, the guys are sitting with a thumb out wanting a lift—in this vastness of nothingness we can't leave them. They're now both squeezed onto the front seat, with me having finally agreed to get back in, wedged in amongst the kit in the back. With no common language, communication reverts to the universal hand signals, for sleep and where we can get it.

We're surrounded by endless mountain, quite literally as far as the eye can see, in all directions. Each time we reach another bend it's another mountain. The road widens slightly, revealing built into the mountain a house, with stone outbuildings and the family cow. What a magical evening, drinking fresh milk still warm from the cow, a delicious meat Tajine, followed by pancakes lathered in homemade honey. Sitting with the children, on the laptop show them pictures of our journey, our family and the homes we left behind in England. Looking up at the night sky, the full moon has a complete halo around it. David sees this, for us both the trauma of the day disappears into that halo.

I hear a timid knock on the door to find more pancakes drizzled with delicious honey and a bucket of hot water. Freeing ourselves from the three-inch thick warm as toast hand woven traditional Berber blanket, incarcerating our bodies all night, we tuck in. We are not asked for any money but know how precious food is here and how hard life is, we leave some anyway. Back on the road the tractor that rebuilt the road behind us is now ahead of us and for what we can see, dismantling it. Out of everywhere children appear carrying books en-route to school. It's a wonder as to where the school is and how these little, tiny dots of cloth draped children skip and play like mountain goats on their way to it.

We now understand the importance of not just storing kit but securing kit, as yesterday a litre bottle of gear box oil broke free, leaving a thick oil slick coating everything. It's the stick in your throat nauseating aroma reminiscent of your local tyre garage.

In the distance, we see the sprawling Ait Ben Haddou 'Ighrem' 'Ksar' meaning Fortified Village. One of the largest complexes of traditional packed earth buildings in Morocco. As a UNESCO registered (United Nations Educational Scientific and Cultural Organisation) site, which recognises buildings, places and things for their historical importance, it is protected and funded. Famously the film location for the likes of Lawrence of Arabia, Jewel of the Nile, Jesus of Nazareth and the Gladiator, some of my favourite films. I can hardly believe I'm here, to see, feel and be part of it all.

Traditionally constructed of rammed earth, it's most impressive seen from a distance, close up its extensively rebuilt and dare I say, feels a tad clinical and quite touristy. But of course, I have just spent the night drinking warm milk from a cow, incarcerated in a hand-woven Berber blanket, under a full moon halo, in the High Atlas Mountains.

Back on tarmac heading to Ouarzazate, 'The door to the desert,' we reach the plateau at one thousand one hundred and sixty meters above sea level. A once isolated French military post now has an international airport, luxury hotels and a municipal campsite, where we're heading to empty Lizzybus out, with the intention of filling her back up, minus her stinking aroma! Despite all our efforts,

Lizzybus still stinks of EP90 gear box oil and will continue to stink of it for many months to come.

We're crossing the planes of Ouarzazate heading for Zagora through the Jbel Anaouar Mountain range into the Draa Valley. It's totally beyond anything in my wildest imagination, both in its remoteness and utter wonder. I still and always will, marvel how the hell I, we, even got here, in Lizzybus, alone, with little more than a dream but am beginning to have a strange feeling it was always meant to be. Dropping into the Draa Valley, the intense cultivation forms a carpet of green waving us through the dessert. At a campsite nestled between palms, shedding their heavily laden crop of sun ripened dates, a man brings us a pot of rot-your-teeth, incredibly sweet green Tea. It's a traditional drink here, the more sugar, the wealthier you're thought of. It's quite delicious. David is not convinced, he is a black coffee, no sugar guy.

Confidence in us and Lizzybus begins to grow; today, just like real adventurers we're going to follow coordinates given to us by the Italians we met in Spain. The coordinates David has programmed into the GPS (Global Positioning System), now a very familiar piece of kit available to the masses but like all of this journey, something we need to familiarise ourselves with and most importantly, know when to ignore it. The biggest issue for us is to not cross into Algeria now we're running along its border.

It's a long, long and tough day, descending this single track of road with hairpin bends, humongous potholes and giant rocks, we can keep the windows closed and par boil, thus avoiding the thick blanket of bull dust sucked in, or open them to enjoy the furnace-like wind. Finally, knackered, covered in dust, we reach level ground to set up camp between two lone trees giving a pretence of shade and belonging. The full moon, taking the place of the setting sun, highlights the surrounding mountains into exquisite folds, like a gigantic hug. The complete silence ringing in our ears is broken only by the frying of couscous and hiss of beer pulls. Any conversation would spoil this moment, we just share it in comfortable silence, lost in our own thoughts.

Woken by the rising ball of sun changing the dark, brooding mountains to folds of glittering golds, with a cup of water each, clean teeth and wash bits, meat paste on stale bread is breakfast, the remains saved for lunch, we're off. David drives, I climb onto the roof, gripping tight, hollering and whooping on an exhilarating ride through this emptiness of rock and sand desert. It's getting rockier and sandier, my knuckles are white from gripping on, my internal organs fight for position. The relentless ball of sun begins to sting, I get back into Lizzybus, to find my organs are not the only victims of the violent shaking: the eggs we planned for tea have been scrambled before they were even cooked.

With no real track, David relying on the sun and his co-ordinates, we're both incredulous and relieved to see, on the horizon, what looks like a town, with its promise of a shower and food, then it all falls apart. Nature has a way of making impassable any co-ordinates you might have, destroying them with wind and rain. Crossing what looked like a dry riverbed, find it little more than a thin crust, Lizzybus sunk door-deep into the thick black silt and mud. Momentarily overwhelmed, sit under a tree pondering our situation; despite being amateurs, we still came prepared. It's time to get out the 'equipment' David brought along to get us out of just this sort of predicament. I dismiss the 'all the gear, with no idea' thoughts, knowing it's us and we're not about to give up without a fight. First, the electric winch, without a suitable tree or rock to secure to, is of no use, it's down to sand ladders and a shovel.

Having sat on our backsides for the last few months, with this physical activity in such heat, we're puffing and panting just getting the metal sand ladders off. Taking it in turns to dig, the other holds the umbrella for shade, only to realise a group of men swathed in vibrant blue djellaba have surrounded us. Ignoring them, continue digging hoping they are local villagers and not the Algerian border control.

Sinking ever deeper into this quicksand of clay, the flies sticking in our throats get swallowed, the sweat instantly dries on our parched skin. Our onlookers start gathering tree stumps and rocks, laying them out before us to make a solid path. Lizzybus has her own secret weapons to help free herself from this bog, low ratio and locking diffs (giving power to the wheel with the least grip), something I have no idea about but will become very familiar with soon enough. With lots of pushing, pulling, rocks, fallen trees, diffs and ratios, to a resounding cheer we make it to solid ground.

We might be free of the riverbed but not free of our party of rescuers, who are joined by two men on motor bikes. On their insistence, we reluctantly follow them, with no accurate maps and the co-ordinates wanting us to go back into our swamp, figure it the best, okay, the only option. Still learning about this life we voluntarily stepped into, I wonder if we should be more concerned, as our escape route closes, not just follow two men on motor bikes. That thought is fleeting, it's all such an adventure, thoughts David found and will continue to find, far harder to dismiss, understandably as he feels the weight of total responsibility for both me and Lizzybus.

In the middle of this vastness appears an Auberge; we're shown a room with shower and squat toilet and, as haggling is part of life here, feel compelled to do it but are crap at it. We settle on twenty dollars to include an evening meal and breakfast, with a guide to take us back to the main road tomorrow, we think.

The new day arrives bringing with it a newfound confidence, having survived and conquered our first real challenge, evident in a Lizzybus, sand-ladders and shovel that no longer glint in the sun but are baked in a rather fetching mix of okra and black mud. Full of cheese spread and delicious pancakes drizzled in honey, two of which are wrapped in serviettes for lunch, showered and in good spirits, we follow our motorbike escort, with its Turban-wrapped pillion inside Lizzybus, giving us directions on how to follow a motor bike! An hour later, there it is, glorious, wonderful tarmac, grateful for their local knowledge and of no further money being demanded, our passenger hops on the back of the bike and disappears, our love of these people and Africa moves up a notch.

There is actually a reason for taking this route and not just because it's a challenge, it's taking us to the magnificent limestone Gorges de Todgha. Accustomed but still uncomfortable, to the begging children, who now throw clods of earth and stones into the potholed road before us, wanting payment for their efforts. It makes not the slightest scrap of difference to an almost non-existent road, we just give them a smile and continue on.

With the bag of vegetables bought in town simmering away in the pressure cooker, I remind David it's not the vegetarian option, as I am using two chicken stock cubes! We love being in the roof tent under the inky vastness of sky, woken not by an alarm clock but the ball of red appearing on the horizon, stirring us to another day.

Now we're intrepid explores, take the 'four-wheel drive' only route to Gorges de Todgha, checking tyre pressures are firm for rock crawling, fuel tanks are full, making a mental note of the warning to watch out for the tyre-splitting road edge. I heed this warning, by not looking through both eyes, only one and keeping that one half shut. They forgot a word, sheer, oh and another hairpin, if I add bends, does that count as three? What a day—we shared the driving along with road building and spotting.

Spotting, I have learnt, is when the co-pilot outside of the vehicle guides and signals the driver, who can see jack shit with a bloody big spare wheel on the bonnet, through the safest rout. It hinges on trust and good signalling, of which, by the end of the day, we've grasped the fundamentals of, well the fundamentals of spotting, as for trust, that needs a lot more work.

With the progress terminally slow and our learning curve in its infancy, it being bitterly cold, we book into a small Auberge, settling on the cheaper option of a communal room. It's a huge room with mattresses laid out around the edges; as no-one else is here to share, I choose the mattress the farthest away from David, to work on my trust issues and have some much-needed personal space. Agreeing to pay extra, get a steaming hot, goat terrine, delicious, hearty and a perfect end to a tough day, spoilt slightly by the hard selling of fossils, carpets and constant requests as to what we can give them whilst sat eating it.

Up early after a good night's sleep, we even manage to laugh over yesterday's antics, refuse the ten dollar each breakfast, brave a cold shower and head off. Surprised at the progress we made yesterday, find we're only ten minutes from the mouth of the Todra Gorge; I know it was all down to my incredible spotting! Lizzybus is dwarfed by the mouth of the gorge, arching to one hundred and fifty meters above us, with the river winding through it like a slippery eel. Exiting into a thick blanket of fog, it's eerily romantic, of course that would be if David was the romantic type, so it's romantic in my head only.

Would you believe, after all that has happened in the last two weeks, we're right back where we started in our old campsite, in the heart of Marrakesh. Fortunately, the wind being in the opposite direction, it takes with it the acrid smoke from the communal tip. We are very different people from the two who arrived here a few weeks earlier, most noticeably in that we are not arguing. From our baptism of fire, we found skills we never knew we had, gained a mutual respect for each other and Lizzybus; manage to laugh about it, even have a night of passion, when all you have is a cup of water to wash pits and bits, getting down and dirty in a sleeping bag is never going to happen.

This newfound harmony lasted the weekend, as I am now a 'non-smoker'—much to non-smoker David's total delight, finally my stash of duty-free fags have run out. Everything is making me pissed off, agitated and conspired against, hating this life where I can't just go into a shop and get a packet of fags when I want.

Governed not so much by our time but the time allowed on the visa of the country we're in, on our first leg of this around the world ordeal (I told you I'm grumpy) of West coast Africa, with over thirty countries, each needing a visa. You can't pre-order visas, as most are valid from the date of issue, or require your physical presence at the embassy of the country you want it for, in the country you are in. Lizzybus, with her Carnet De Passage, will become a major cause for concern the further we travel, as corrupt boarder officials want money to stamp it and somehow it needs renewing in twelve months' time.

Our next country, Mauritania, despite assurances from Justes that a visas can be issued on the border, a couple here, having just crossed, are saying people are being refused entry without visas. The last thing we want is to be stuck on the border, in Lizzybus with an expired visa. I realise why David is so good at this, he never takes a chance and is adamant we have to get the visas from the Mauritania Embassy in Casablanca. Pitching up at a campsite on the outskirts of Casablanca, accustomed to squat toilets and cold showers, what we find most disturbing is the amount of garbage in towns, cities and highways. Clinging to and from, every bush, tree, corrugated shack, anything protruding above ground level, is an anchor point for plastic bags and a dump for rotting garbage.

What's a morning without a fag and a coffee? Miserable, even in paradise or a campsite on the outskirts of Casablanca. Climbing down the ladder that hurt my feet more in the morning than at night, I decide to surprise David and prepare the morning coffee.

Having decided against gas, as getting gas bottles in the African bush might be a problem, settled on a Coleman two ring petrol cooker. It's taken some time for me to learn the knack of pumping and coaxing it to a rewarding blue flame, rather than a sooty black-yellow one but it's a most pleasing morning ritual, one David enjoys.

Watching my every move, I'm told I need more water in the bottom of the coffee pot. It's hard to justify how infuriating I find this criticism. When spending every minute of every day together, you cling to each other's compliments and criticisms, pondering and regurgitating them, unable or unwilling to let them go. It's caustic and destructive but part of adjusting to each other and life now. I leave David to it and go take a bloody freezing cold shower.

Chapter 4
The Curse of the Visas

Casablanca grew from a small trading port into one of Africa's biggest cities, its vast smoggy and sprawling with gridlocked traffic, skyscrapers that dwarf shantytowns as progress marches on. Several hours later, in what seems the Casablanca rush hour traffic but is an all-day thing, we find the Mauritanian Embassy has become a mobile phone shop. The security guy tells us the Embassy has moved to Rabat, writing the address on the back of his fag packet, I just wish he had left a fag in it.

It's these moments that are the most testing, with the days counting down on our Mauritania visa and Rabat being sixty kilometres back to where we came from, it's not a challenge but an ordeal. I drive, David navigates, a few hours later, triumphant at actually finding it but crestfallen as it's closed. I never thought stress would be part of this journey but we're both beginning to feel it, knowing it takes a few days to apply and issue a visa and still having to get to the border. There is nothing more for it than to return to last night's campsite and come back tomorrow, Friday thirteenth.

Tucked away off a boulevard amongst opulent houses will be where most embassies are to be found, as is this one. Noticing a few people gathered around an imposing door with an armed security guard, join the not quite a queue gathering. Armed with a folder full of photographs, photocopies and copies of copies of all our documents, the Carnet De Passage, the logbook for Lizzybus and a few pens to give out to officials. This is our first real experience of an embassy; they will always be significant moments in this journey where it could all end. Our English need to form an orderly queue is not working; we start elbowing our way in and hold firm our position. Once inside we're faced with blanked out screens and post-box sized cutouts to pass documents through to the faceless voice. Thirty minutes later a receipt for the documents and seventy

American dollars is posted back through the slit, with instructions to return at thirteen hundred hours.

Leaving Lizzybus at the Embassy, wait out some of the hours in the café, the cafe where all the men sit with a coffee 'smoking.' Everything in life has changed, none more so than our diet, finding a set of scales in a chemist weigh ourselves, feeling a little chuffed whilst surprised, to have lost thirty-five pound between us. I see our reflection in the full-length mirror, our skin is no longer sun kissed but rugged, my Afro frizz hair is becoming dreadlocks, our embassy outfits hang on us. David has started shaving less, hairs curl out of his ears and nose, a wiry pubic hair-like grey beard meets his white chest hair. I hate this.

Back outside the consulate we wait, wait, wait and wait some more, wondering where everyone else is, until the security guard in French David did understand but wished he didn't, said being Friday the Embassy shuts early and will not reopen until Monday. We obviously got the thirteen hundred hours right but not the Monday bit. I've had it. I don't even want to go to stupid Mauritania, despite David's explanation of it being the gateway to Black Africa and if we don't go then we have to go back to Spain. This will not be the first time on this journey that thought is most appealing, Spain, France, England, home, where I can smoke, drink and talk all day long to anyone and everyone.

For our enforced weekend break, book into the Sieed family-run hotel, our spirits lifted by the luxury of a room with en-suite and hot showers. On the laptop watch a nineteen sixty British comedy classic 'Carry on Regardless.' All thoughts of passports, visas, or if we will make it to the Nouadhibou boarder two thousand kilometre away before our Moroccan visa runs out, banished.

Back at the Mauritanian Embassy people are collecting visas and submitting applications, along with another group who had been refused entry at the Nouadhibou border. Unable to cross, they had to make the four-thousand-kilometre round trip back to Rabat, some even leaving their vehicles and taking internal flights to avoid heavy fines for overstaying, we feel justified in David's insistence to get one here.

Once inside the reception area, which accommodates five comfortably but has twenty uncomfortably, adopt the elbows in the ribs and holding firm our position technique. It's a physical thrill, to once more be in possession of our passports, one full page of which has a beautiful Mauritanian visa on it. I just can't get the words "One small step for man, one giant leap for mankind," out of my head, as to its significance to us and our journey. David and I dance around

Lizzybus, like kids getting that wished-for bike on Christmas morning, things are starting to get real.

Last night David, cutting a piece of tube (on his leg) with a Stanley knife, cut into his leg just above the knee. With our extensive first aid kit I lovingly attend to David, whilst quietly muttering on "What a stupid thing to do!" Perhaps not that quietly, as he now refuses to drive with his 'injury.' It feels fantastic to be heading in a direction that progresses the journey, through a rugged, harsh environment where trees grow bent against the prevailing winds. Quite incredibly, in the gnarled twisted thorny branches of the argon tree are climbing goats. Eating its fruit, that look just like tiny, shrivelled apples, which pass through their digestive system and undigested the seed is pooped out, to be collected and used to produce argon oil.

The oil is eaten over couscous or as a dip for bread, or spread over your skin—who ever thought goat poop could be so beneficial? It's commercially produced nowadays but goats still climb trees in search of the shrivelled apple argon fruit. Camping that night, sat writing my journal, I feel something rather than see it running over my feet and, shining my torch under the table, see lots of little mice, I feel the warmth of their fluffy bodies comforting. It's moments like this I wonder where Jayne has gone, I remember a mouse in the house once, it fell into the swing bin, I was terrified it might jump out. I put a sheet over it and carried it out into the garden, to wait for my son to come home and take it into the fields. Why I never thought to let it run over my feet to warm them up, I don't know?

The border seems to be getting farther and farther away, there is an urgency now our days are counting down on the visa. With the cold of evening meeting the heat of day, heavy condensation makes everything wet—well, wetter than it was before we packed it away. A sweaty body aroma and damp permeates everything but we cannot afford a day to give the ball of sun chance to dry it all out. David has always refused to use any form of deodorant, insisting his body needs to sweat naturally. With his arm propped on the open window and the wind in my direction, I find myself covering my nose with my sarong to stop retching, the smell is that bad.

Tonight, we need to find a campsite with water, on the horizon silhouetted in the setting sun see the skeletal remains of the old fish factory, bringing with it a rotting fish aroma, to me a refreshing change to David's. This once bustling port town of Sidi Afi has become a ghost town, there is no traffic, I don't just mean cars but nothing: not even a moped, a mule, or donkey, just the odd person sitting, their djellaba blowing in the dusty wind. At the deserted local campsite on the shores of the mighty Atlantic, with David still nursing his self-inflicted wound, I decide to swim. On hitting the waves, I was swept up as if in a washing machine, tumbled and tossed, disorientated and semi drowned, somehow got back to shore. Looking up I could see David casually chatting to a huddle of fishermen pointing at his knee, whilst I drown. I determine from now on he can sort his own stupid knee out.

As I've been doing all the driving due to David's knee, with my understanding nature, today I've told him to 'get over himself and drive.' In fairness, David would, could and sometime does, drive all day every day, he loves being behind the wheel. But he is being a right primadonna over this 'man injury,' did I mention it being a self-inflicted, man injury? Incredibly, this two-thousand-kilometre drive to the border is more or less one road, it stretches before us onto the distant horizon, a horizon you just never reach. Today is different, we have to turn off the V1 onto the N1 at an island in the middle of this vastness. With no other traffic anywhere, David slows but does not quite stop, to be pulled over by the police parked behind bushes. Not having come to a complete stop as indicated on the rusted, illegible, lollipop signpost cost four hundred dirham (forty dollars). As negotiating is not yet part of our skill set, or calling their bluff, just pay up.

David takes it personally, along with his morning telling off for filling up a bowl with hot water from the shower to do the washing up. I on the other hand, find it hysterical knowing full well it would have also happened to me but it happened on his shift!

Today the border is in sight but progress is terminal due to the deteriorating road and building traffic, admitting defeat camp for the night close to the cliff edge overlooking the mighty Atlantic. I always imagined camping in a roof tent overlooking the sea to be spectacular but it's not. Waves crashing to shore sound like gunfire and although well off the main road, the wind that carries the thundering noise of lorries, is the same wind that pushes us closer to the cliff edge. The roof tent acts like a huge sail, I'm almost seasick, terrified we will be blown over the cliff.

Both knackered mentally and physically, carry out the morning ritual of brushing teeth and washing pits with our mug of water in silence. We're facing constant police and military roadblocks now, where all our details are laboriously handwritten in ancient, dog-eared ledgers. Following the advice of a German guy, wrote out all the relevant information and printed fifty copies off, they can then write our details into the ledger at their leisure. It's better but it still takes forever for them to cross-reference the printed sheet against our original documents.

Just as we were about to leave the last checkpoint, a Police Officer asked for our insurance. David had renewed the insurance bought when arriving in the country but with the five-day hold up for visas it had run out. A fact I was blissfully unaware of as I handed over the invalid document. It's important to understand how honest I am as a person, this is a very bad trait in me in this environment, when a poker face and calling people's bluff is needed.

Having this pointed out to me, I immediately turn to David to ask if he knew this had run out? Of course, poor David said "No," which starts an argument as to how the hell he would not have known this? This is the old Jayne, that has so much to learn, the officer is a little taken aback with this altercation and not sure what to do.

Looking through the rest of our documents he sees the leather-bound wallet, one half containing a laminated identity card of David in full police uniform, the other a gold enamelled five-inch crest (very similar to the West Midlands Police crest issued to Policeman Mr T Senior). For some reason, he got the impression David was a Police Officer in England. At this point, David's hand is shook as a fellow comrade in law, email addresses are exchanged and assurances made, our home is his home, when or if we ever make it back to England. We're free to continue our journey; I vow from now on to become the most dishonest person my honesty allows.

Ahead rocky desert becomes a vast 'sand sea,' wind-driven sand forms huge horseshoe curves and delicate folds. Before the rising sun brings its surface temperature to a burning feet point, I climb barefoot to one of its peaks. On its lee side is a sheer drop, taking giant strides down it, the sand gives way and folds around my feet, to ever so gently lower me to its base, a moment in time I will forever treasure. The tarmac road is being swallowed by sand, we keep losing it, I imagine being lost here amongst it forever, until just like that, appears a gateway across it. This is not unusual, as each village has these elaborately adorned gateways, to what is little more than a few huts but this one has armed guards.

We're at the border, our intentions were to get as close as possible today, camp overnight and cross first thing tomorrow. It's thirteen hundred hours, the border into Mauritania closes at sixteen hundred, not wanting to get trapped in no-man's land, or hang around, decide to risk it and cross now. Nothing has prepared us for what we are about to face.

On leaving Morocco, you have to clear immigration and customs but most importantly, is to get the Lizzybus' Carnet De Passage stamped. This document is passed between officers, with no one really wanting, or willing, to stamp it. The clock is ticking, each person wants us to acknowledge their importance and how honoured we are to be given their time, realise donating our pen, (of which we have spares) speeds up the farcical process.

Now it's time to cross 'No-Man's Land' a five-kilometre, non-existent road, where the blown up remains of a Land Rover remind us it's mined. I'm almost numb with fear, seeing the skeletal abandoned cars and trucks which provide shelter for the blackest people I have ever seen, it feels like a film of the living dead. Without a clear path to follow, it's not long before we're lost in this forgotten in time place, in the rear-view mirror see a battered windowless car driving towards us. With no intention of stopping, keep going until it pulls alongside, the four men inside are waving and shouting in words we don't fully understand but get the idea we are heading for exploding mines. Lizzybus struggles crossing the deep sand, the car chasing us gets stuck, in the distance we see a truck that was at the border, as we head for it, it disappears, at least we can follow its tracks.

Somehow find ourselves at a rope with plastic bags tied to it strung across what has now become an actual track; behind it are a few buildings, one of which is flying the Mauritanian flag. The vehicle we saw earlier is also parked here, they tell us it is the border and it's closed. What! We have to spend the night in no-man's land, amongst the living dead? A few minutes later a French couple in a Land Cruiser and a truck packed full of locals, their djellaba billowing from the windows, goats tied to the roof, pull up behind us. This makes us feel united in our plight, we get out the table and chairs to do what we English do, make a cup of tea. I'm just finishing my tea when the rope is taken down, it seems I was not the only one having a tea break: the border has re-opened.

This ordeal is never ending, Lizzybus is searched over and over, working as a team, one doing documents, one guarding kit is best. By the time it's all over, dusk is settling around us, we feel abused, whilst euphoric at having survived our first proper border crossing, heading into the 'real Africa' fills us with both terror and joy.

Mauritania, almost three quarters desert, or semi desert, occupied by Berbers, Arabs, colonised by the French, gaining independence in nineteen sixty. What will always be the case when crossing borders is how stark the difference that strip of no-man's land makes. Borders are desolate places anyway, with the dispossessed and vagrants, this doesn't change, what changes instantly are the houses, the people, the vehicles. I'm still looking at countries through my western eyes, one day I will see much more than a country's wealth but for now it looks and feels a lot poorer than Morocco.

Facing constant roadblocks, checking the same documents checked at the border, with no pens, no Mauritanian Ouguiya, sit with our fixed smile whilst handing out the photocopied sheet, relieved to have bought insurance at the border, as it's the first document asked for. Heading for the secure camp listed in the guidebook, along a single-track dirt road, find it behind a high wall with barbed wire, it's secure and has a very welcoming owner. Both shaken by the day's events, feel privileged to have this experience, perhaps not one I might have chosen but now it's over we're filled with a sense of accomplishment and a little chunk of pride.

Of course, that was just the start of what is to come, a tiny weenie part of a massive journey, far too enormous to contemplate, focus purely on the task ahead. We're in Nouadhibou, heading for Nouakchott, once a small village, now Mauritania's capital city. Where not to expect majestic monuments or cultural landmarks but slums, rubbish-strewn streets, no street signs, in fact no signs at all. This is a relief for David, as he can't be accused of not stopping at them. Adjacent to a deep-water port built by the Chinese, plans to clear the slums to build social housing started in two thousand and nine, the year we are in.

Navigating is not that difficult as there is only one road if it didn't keep getting swallowed by the sand sea. In the distance, we see the incredible 'iron-ore railway,' a three-kilometre slithering snaking chain of over two hundred and fifty carriages transporting twenty-two thousand tonnes of crushed rock across the Sahara. You can hitch a ride in one of the iron-ore open top carts, die in the forty-degree daytime heat, or bitter cold desert nights, or by simply falling off it. Nouakchott, it's true, is a sprawling maze of garbage-strewn streets, houses sit behind high barbed wire topped walls but it feels welcoming. Looking for but unable to find, the campsite recommended to us, with the details scribbled on a piece of paper, a motor bike pulled up. Showing him the piece of paper, he motions for David to get on the back of his bike and off they go, I'm left here, with Lizzybus, totally alone.

The minutes turn into an hour in the scorching midday sun; I think, like the hitchhikers on the iron-ore railway, I will meet my death. Visions of David mugged and left for dead play out in my head, a rising panic chokes me. On the dust-strewn streets, not another soul passes, at the point of desperation, hear the missing beat of a motor bike with a smiling David upon it. I'm overcome with emotion, if I was able, I might even have shed a tear but all bodily fluid stopped in the intense heat. What felt like a lifetime to me is nothing in the 'Inshalla' of my life now. Without local knowledge, we would never have found this French-run auberge, decide to try and trust locals a little more. Lizzybus is squeezed into this vibrant bougainvillea laced courtyard, shaded by feather leaf trees dripping in small fruits, the colours are incredible to our eyes after so much blond sand.

With the roof tent erect, showered, rank clothes in the washing machine, dinner bubbling away in the pressure cooker, I read my emails, as joy of joy we have Wi-Fi. After the challenges of the last few weeks, tonight, clean, full and totally at peace, sleep.

Dragged from our comatose state, thinking we are under attack, realise it's hundreds of mega fruit bats raining discarded fruit stones upon us.

Nouakchott does not have a lot to do or see, the market selling mostly things we throw away lie directly in the sand. Mauritania is a dry country (not dry arid, although it's that but dry as in no alcohol) you can buy it, at great expense, in some restaurants and hotels, or at our auberge, so each evening we share a cold beer. What a difference a few days make, totally refreshed, washing done, emails to and from home updated, we're ready to get going. Mauritania has suffered over the years and still does, from terrorism, muggings, scams, kidnappings, armed bandits etc. Specifically, Nouakchott where we are leaving and Atar, where we are heading.

This land's beauty is in its isolation, occasional caravans of camels with child herders, clusters of wattle and daub homes, family goat and sand. We're heading for Bab Sahara campsite, to meet up with Justus, the owner, who we met in Marrakesh. In the middle of this nothingness is Terjit, a promised 'lush oasis fed by warm springs,' as it's getting dark and the entrance has a makeshift fence, set up camp in the desert dreaming of our cool oasis awaiting us in the morning.

Okay, a slight exaggeration but there are palm trees, the water seeping from the gorge collected in a concrete plunge pool is cool and refreshing. In this desolate isolated place where life itself is a constant struggle, homes little more than bamboo huts, we're trailed by locals wanting payment for the guided tour. Paying for a perceived service, rather than direct begging, just feels the right thing to do. Finally, we arrive at Bab Sahara, Justus is as amazed to see us as we are at making it, greeting us like lost puppies finding their way home. I'm beginning to realise people, with a lot more experience and knowledge than us, are incredulous at what we're doing. Even more so, on knowing we are totally alone, having never done anything like it before.

In camp are a group of ex-army guys, Germans and Canadian Richard, in Toyotas, on their annual desert raid, this apparently is driving their vehicles as hard as possible for three weeks, leaving them here in Atar and returning back home. What a fantastic evening sitting around the campfire chatting, I can't believe all the adventures we have to tell already, how much has happened to us since setting off. They are so interested in how we got this far, I almost feel admired but realise they, like many, are just incredulous we got here. I've not mentioned for a while the smoking, have I? I have to admit as they all smoke, it felt rude not to accept a fag along with the beer. Or, from the hut on the corner, buy a pack of Marlboro, just so I could give them one back and as easy as that I'm smoking again much to David's disdain.

Today, leaving our kit in camp, go exploring to Chinguetti, a two-hour drive across the Adrar Plateau, a desert pavement or 'regs' formed from packed rock fragments to a former medieval trading post once famous for its Islamic Scholars. Ascending up over the Ebnou Pass we're transported to a lunar landscape of blue-green dome shaped rocks rippled with tiny fossils, stromatolites dating back millions of years, earth's earliest life forms. The trick to driving these roads, apparently, is to take them at speed so you 'float' across them, at over fifty kilometres, it's fast for us. Lizzybus is not exactly floating, just not juddering quite as much, a trail of bull dust swirls two storeys high behind us.

I'm driving when the steering becomes incredibly heavy, David is shouting but I can't hear him, to realise, he is shouting for me to stop. We have our first puncture, with the sharp volcanic rock, the tyre is shredded. Changing tyres is something we have both done in the past, changing a Lizzybus tyre is a whole lot of other. Getting the spare off the bonnet, accessing the tools, jacking her up, is totally exhausting in this heat. We gave up on Chinguetti, back at Bab Sahara in the evening breeze, sway in a hammock under a bamboo roof, I could be on a *Raiders of the Lost Ark* film set. African thin, hair in dreads, feet like leather, bleached planks of wood fashioned into chairs and tables, a cobweb draped pottery lampshade with single light bulb, the bookshelf full of old maps and dog-eared over-read books, next to animal skulls and a rusted rifle.

David is chatting about our onward journey with Richard; we should retrace our route back to Nouakchott and follow the coast road to Senegal, our next country. But he is being seduced by the idea of forming a convoy through the desert, back to Nouadhibou (the border from Morocco) alongside the iron-ore railway. This would mean doing the Three hundred-and thirty-kilometre Nouadhibou to Nouakchott road again, the road where yesterday three Spanish aid workers (two men and a woman) were kidnapped at gunpoint, whilst refuelling, the last vehicle in the convoy of thirteen. It took nine months for their release, after an undisclosed ransom payment by the Spanish government, something we know the British government would rightly never consider.

Chapter 5
The Pull of Home

It's the first of December, nearly four months since we set off and for reasons I don't fully understand, other than we're both committed in this journey, to push ourselves, to do more than just follow a tarmac road, we are heading out of Bab Sahara in a four car convoy, on a non-existent sand road, into bandit territory back to Nouadhibou with Richard and the Germans. As ex-military guys, they're equipped with the latest satellite tracking and navigational systems. I wonder and sort of hope, if this also includes a gun, to increase our chances of avoiding the same fate as the Spanish. I feel an expectation of us, on knowing we're 'driving around the world,' like as if we're being tested. In our backpacking days, when staying in hostels, almost the first question asked of you was, 'where have you been?' and 'where are you going?' Interest in you, or of you, afforded, as to how much, or how long you have, or will travel. On that basis, I realise we are most interesting.

Of course, it's not about this, we all do what we can and its life that gets in the way, not least earning the money to do it. It makes no difference a day, a week, a month, your local seaside resort, or deepest darkest Africa, it's all an adventure and something we can all enjoy and be proud of. Setting off, in the middle of the convoy, bandits are the very last thing on our mind, facing an almost whiteout from their dust, our fully laden Lizzybus and us, are no match for their vehicles and experience. Driving through sand, you're pushed and pulled to wherever it has a fancy: hit at speed, it's hard as concrete, hit it too slow it swallows you up. We're just about keeping up and as of yet, have not had to be rescued, a testament to us both. Abusing Lizzybus like this, pushing her to her limits, hurts—we question, why?

Having made it through the first day, pitch camp at the base of Ben Amera, the world's second largest monolith, to Ayres Rock. Unlike Ayres Rock, there is no tarmac road to it, no cafes or visitors centre, just armed guards at the railway crossing, warning you to stay on the track as there are mines. I'm freaking out, I want to go back and forget all about this bloody convoy. Not least as the Germans have the biggest dog ever, which is running everywhere. David tries to calm me, saying they are only anti-tank mines, not anti-personnel, so the dog won't set them off. Having never faced mines, of any description, in my day-to-day life, I have not the slightest interest whatsoever in finding out about them now. I do, however, get the gist in the 'personnel,' and 'tank' mine prefix, in regard to the dog but question how very similar Lizzybus is to a tank!

Shit, its morning, peering out of the roof tent, cross my fingers our convoy have abandoned us, and we can try to find our own way back out alone, at my Miss Daisy driving speed, bandits or not. But no, they are still here talking, scheming and planning the most terrifying route for the day ahead. Setting off, fully loaded Lizzybus struggles to keep up, in the deep sand and gale-force winds, which have produced huge horseshoe dunes. Our convoy, under full power, drives up the back of the dunes, teeters on its rim, before the sand crust breaks, to very gently lower them to its base.

It's quite incredible to watch but watching is all we want to do, refuse the offer of revving the nuts of Lizzybus to do the same. We smell the familiar whiff of clutch and as Lizzybus keeps losing power, we can't get the speed needed to get through the deep sand. Bogged down, we're winched out, for our convoy this is great fun, adding to their adventure but makes us physically sick at the abuse we're giving Lizzybus. Eventually hit tarmac, I'm more than a little relieved as our convoy head off; their vehicles will get a full service before being stored for another year, they fly home. Instead of being euphoric at having driven one of the toughest sand roads, through the heart of the Sahara, we're just broken to have done this to Lizzybus, when we have the rest of the world to get her through. It was an amazing adventure, if your vehicle was not your life, your home, your everything.

Determine we will always seek out the most adventurous off-road routes but at our own pace avoiding convoys.

After a night at the campsite, we started out at when arriving in Mauritania, head off for the second time to Nouakchott. Due to the kidnapping, there is a high military presence, which is both a comfort and a frustration. The chances of being kidnapped are lessened but, with all the security checks, progress is terminal, we're relieved to still have a pile of photocopied sheets with our information on, to hand out. Back in Nouakchott, there's a scabby toothless spitting white camel in camp, I'm already loving it. It belongs to a Japanese man who is trekking across the Sahara to Egypt, a country we will drive through eventually but for now we're heading south, to South Africa. I find this eccentricity most comforting; it puts our little 'idea' into perspective. I wonder who, or if, either of us will ever make it.

The responsibility of Lizzybus and to an extent me, for David is taking its toll, especially after the last few days and the consequences of the choices he makes. This pressure never goes away, it comes with us, follows us, is part of us, filling him with doubt about this journey. I'm not exactly sure what it was David was expecting and have no intention of making up his thoughts but with only each other, his mood brings us both down.

David in his legal profession was good, very good, respected and in control, everything that life, now, is not. I can't offer any words of comfort, as I'm in the same boat but my storm is different.

I take it personally, to me he is allowing himself to feel like this, an indulgence we can't afford: you owe it to each other to be strong. We can't just pack up and leave, having given up our jobs, rented out our house; sold, donated and trashed all our possessions. I imagine answering the question, as to why we gave up? Lizzybus was blown up, we were robbed at gunpoint, she fell off the cliff. No, just that we didn't like it, it was not what we expected! Sod the expense, let's have a beer each tonight.

And just like that the cloud of doubt has lifted, heading now for Senegal, our third country on West Coast Africa. The arid desert sand sea flattens out to be replaced by dark red mud and low-lying marshlands. We see lakes full of flamingo, warthog, a huge lizard and trees with squabbling monkeys in, the change is spectacular. Camping now is just a case of making sure we're far enough off the road not to be seen, although I'm not sure by whom, as we're the only vehicle on it, whilst close enough to navigate back to it in the morning. As dusk settles, sat on the roof of Lizzybus, I see flocks of roosting birds, their mass casts a shadow onto the ball of setting sun.

Marshlands bring mosquitoes, lots and lots of mosquitoes, despite the heat, sweat it out in long trousers and shirts. But nothing can take away the magic of this moment, knowing we have made it through that imagined gateway, into proper 'Black Africa.' It's the middle of the night, we're woken by loud squealing and grunting; once my eyes adjust, find we're surrounded by a group of warthogs. Under a full moon, they look prehistoric, with long shovel-faced heads, four intimidating tusks, warts and an almost hairless square powerful body. I'm glad I'm in a roof tent.

Filled with apprehension, knowing we will reach the border today, pass herds of Kudo, traditional African cattle, perched on their backs are linen white Cattle Egret. Symbolic in their relationship, the cattle ignore them, as they peck away at the tics and parasites. We're here, we're at the border, first we have to get stamped out of Mauritania and cross no-man's land, the main objective is to get the Carnet De Passage stamped when leaving. Once this is done, despite being harassed by moneychangers, the transients, beggars and dispossessed, just not having to face a mined no-man's land is a relief.

At the Senegalese boarder, know it's just a process, a nerve-wracking process it's true and one that takes several hours, includes several searches of us and Lizzybus but a process. There is an unspoken question as to what we can give them, other than our documents but we hold firm, smile, never show any irritation, just our respect and understanding of how important their job is and how humbled we are they are doing it, for us.

Welcome to Senegal; on the tip of the peninsular, it's an odd country as it has another country inside it: the Gambia. Senegal does suffer from petty crime, pick pocketing, etc. but to us, having faced the threat of kidnapping and terrorism, it's nothing. We can now get back to worrying about getting a Lizzybus around the world and the more immediate issue of contracting malaria. It's time to start taking the Mefloquine Larium anti-malaria bought with us, despite its side effects including hallucinations and depression, the consequences of not taking it would almost certainly be death. Mosquitoes here carry the Falciparum parasite responsible for almost all malaria deaths in Africa.

Saint-Louis, Senegal's once capital and the first French settlement in Africa, from afar has a grandeur from its Colonial Architecture. UNESCO registered since two thousand, it's undergoing 'gentrification,' turning its magnificent houses into hotels and restaurants. Close up it is a crumbling, rotting bygone era, dead animals lie next to fly-encrusted fish for sale along garbage-strewn streets forgotten by time. Parking Lizzybus amongst all this, we go off in search of an internet café. On our return, a small group have gathered around Lizzybus, which is not unusual. It's a while before we realise, the stick chewing man and woman in brown tunics with a sown on Yellow Patch, are apparently Traffic Wardens. With a piece of fashioned metal and padlock they had clamped us!

David was hysterical, letting down the tyre to release the clamp, in broken Fran-glish we're told we would be arrested if we did. Realising, if we did end up in prison, we'd still have a flat tyre and a clamp to sort out, relented. I loved that a little bit of him still fought for justice, on these litter-strewn streets with no road markings or signs, we both saw the funny side and burst out laughing. Negotiations began, the six-dollar fine was reduced to four, the clamp was removed, we were given a receipt and with our on-board compressor, re-inflate the tyre before heading off to Zebrabar campsite, laughing our heads off.

On the way start seeing the mighty Baobab, The Tree Of Life, an upside-down looking tree, as its branches are like stunted roots, stuck into an oversized vase. Velvet covered rugby ball-sized fruit hang from its branches like a pearl necklace. These can be blended into a drink and its young leaves eaten like spinach. They survive great droughts and fires, living for many hundreds of years. Like Elephants among animals, Baobabs among trees have no equal, it's an incredible sight to see. Finally, we are finding the rhythm and the joy in this journey and more importantly in each other, we feel its spirit. At Zebrabar, nestled on the shores of the salty Senegal river and Langue de Barbarie National Park, African music is piped through camp, accompanied by a lone accordion player: it's incredibly soothing. It's time to address the issue of my African Dreads hair, for five dollars, five French speaking women, with bamboo skewers rip it apart, pausing only to squat over a lunch of fish stew eaten with their hands. Plaited back into neat rows, I wonder if my hair now has the aroma of fish.

In the early hours of the morning, I get a text message, my mother is in intensive care having had a massive stroke, paralysing her left side. I'm consumed by a desolate ache for home; I imagine how terrified Mom would be, locked in her world, where dementia took any comfort, she could have from the familiar, unable to recognise family or friends years ago.

When I left to start this journey, my mother was lost to me in all but her physical being, my father had passed away years before. It hurts, neither will know what I'm up to but I like to think that, despite despairing of me, they would be proud. For us all it's never quite the perfect time in life to fulfil that dream, to take that step, education, work, children, grandchildren, money, etc. all good reasons to stay. Until the day the voices to go shout louder than the voices to stay, with the realisation that life, like time, is running out. For now, I need to be with my family, if only to support them and be supported, so it is decided that somehow, I will return to England.

Having set off five long months ago, this journey has been so removed from what was my life, or my experience of it. Dealing with the enormity of what lies ahead was dealt with by focusing only on the day ahead. Which is what we do now, on getting to the Gambia, to its capital Banjul and its international airport to be with my mother, one day at a time. It's with heavy hearts we leave Senegal; we're at the beginning of this journey and still full of adventure and curiosity for it but for now that has been overshadowed, it's all about mileage now. The constant police checks, broken tarmac roads, heat and incessant flies, become a chore not a challenge.

Pulling over as darkness falls, we check into a dimly lit hotel, at least it has a barbed wire fenced in the courtyard for Lizzybus, running water and a single hanging light bulb. With the steady stream of men going in and out of the adjacent rooms, the grunting, groaning and screaming we hear through thin concrete walls, we realise we are in a brothel. I feel nausea at the prospect of lying on the animal hair stuffed stained mattress, so put our cotton cocoons over them. Despite being fully dressed, wrapped in cocoons, lathered in DEET, the bastard moggies are eating me alive. I'm miles from home, my mother is desperately ill in hospital, in a brothel, on a semen-soaked mattress, living the dream.

Breakfast is bread and chocolate spread, served directly onto a plastic tablecloth, watched over by a group of yellow eyed, very black men who look at us like you would an alien species. The Gambia is a slice of country through the middle of Senegal, at its widest only fifty kilometres, running through it is the 'River Gambia.' Leaving Senegal and getting into the Gambia, is greatly eased by the assumption David is a Police Officer, a comrade, a keeper of the law. With all our documents stamped and insurance for Lizzybus bought, join the queue for the ferry over the River Gambia. This would have been spectacular but I'm still lost and hurting, the dust, the heat, the fumes, are overwhelming me.

Stationary, we're surrounded by people wanting to sell us stuff, begging, or just curious. I leave David to face it and hide in the back amongst the kit, covering my head with my sarong.

Three hours later, getting to the front of the queue made no difference, as vehicles are directed around us and onto the ferry. These vehicles had paid, not just for the ticket but to the crew loading us. We're pissed we forgot, as in Africa, corruption is a way of life, even if you don't agree with it, it's how life works. We will always refuse to pay corrupt officials, making life harder for fellow travellers but giving the guys who board you a 'tip,' avoiding sitting several hours in the blistering heat, will be something from now on we have full intention of doing.

Finally, we are loaded to join the locals, their cattle, goats and worldly possessions, inside or tied on the top, the vehicles packed so tightly we share breath. Get out of Lizzybus, before the next vehicle is parked, if this ferry goes down, she is on her own. By the time we cross and unload, it's pitch black, driving at night is dangerous anywhere but here it's suicidal, with little or no lighting. We're so consumed with getting to Banjul and sorting out a flight for me, decide to push on, head for Secuta Camping, a German-run campsite recommended to us.

I've always felt a helping hand, something looking over me, I don't know who, or what, it's just there, for now, it's in the full moon lighting the road ahead. Making it to Secuta Camping, we find the sanctuary so desperately needed. They have a telephone, internet and flight details but, best of all, a secure compound to store Lizzybus, so David can fly back with me.

At seven o'clock tomorrow morning, seven hundred dollars and seven hours later, we will be back, in Birmingham, the place we set off from five long months ago. We're different people now, not just in our physical appearance but in us, David and Jayne. I didn't think through what this journey entailed and certainly would never have undertaken it if I had. I'm Jayne, from a family of six, brought up in a council house, to a factory worker father and a housewife mother. Never did I ever imagine being on a journey like this, why, or how would I?

As for David, I think wanderlust was always in his genes, passed down from the seniors. It has taken a few months, but the journey is becoming a part of him, it's all he ever thought it would be and more saying if he had to travel with anyone, it would be 'me.' Is that a compliment? I'm not sure, or just that I will live in a box, I am not bothered about having to wash in streams, dig my own toilet, and to not have cupboards full of shoes, handbags, or make up. That's it for now, until my return, I am relieved and sad all in one but know it is the right thing to do, I only have one family.

Chapter 6
Life Then and Now

Only a few hours ago in Birmingham, England, I was scraping inch-thick ice off my sister's windscreen. Now, back here in Ghana, reunited with Lizzybus, I perspire in forty-degree heat. It was tough seeing my mother, a very different mother to the one I left, as even though her mind was a thick fog, she could wash herself, walk and talk. The mother I now have is a broken shell, mentally and physically, totally reliant on others, paralysed, unable to even smile.

I found no comfort in this, just a sense of injustice, that my mother, a free spirit all her life, was reduced to this. As Mom to six of us, living on a council estate, she would appear in the morning, hair bouffant, with bright red lipstick on, legs stained with coffee and a line drawn with eyebrow pencil down the back of them, as if wearing the latest French silk stockings. Even her familiar smell was gone, replaced by a metal disinfectant one, it was when I gave her hand three little squeezes, a sign used when growing up to say, 'I love you,' and got no response, I knew, for all intents and purposes, she had gone. I questioned why they would not have left her to slip away peacefully, rather than waste away, there in that hospital bed.

I thought, being back in England, David and I would question this path in life we had put ourselves on, or at the very least, had some doubts about returning to it. But being in England felt wrong, even flushing toilets and doors with locks didn't seem as important. In fact, I was beginning to feel alarmed by it, taps left running, unwanted food scraped into bins, my brain rattled with the noise of televisions, the harshness of electric lights, the pace and speed of life. I quite like the effort involved now in getting water, food, to only have what you need, not what you want. The thing we have most of, 'time,' seemed the most elusive there, I decided for now, we have the most valuable thing, that of 'time.'

Being reunited with Lizzybus we both realise how much we missed her, like you would an old friend, or comfy pair of slippers. How can this inanimate piece of metal take on such huge importance to us both? Lizzybus has become our past, our present and our future and most importantly, we know there are three beers in her fridge.

Last night with Lizzybus, on her palm, bamboo and bougainvillea edge concrete pitch, decided, not to sleep in the roof tent but under a mosquito net, on roll mats under the stars. I needed this, to feel alive, to find a quiet place to prepare myself for what lies ahead. We are five months and fourteen countries, into what is becoming an epic journey, the focus for now is West Coast Africa, the target South Africa, twelve countries and many thousands of kilometres away. Then, the rest of the world!

Today, find the wired and padlocked canvas roof bag has been cut open and most of the contents stolen. It's our winter gear, sleeping bags, hiking boots, pup tent etc.

Having paid for secure storage it's a blow, it's not like you can claim on your insurance, or replace it here in Africa. The campsite owners offer to pay but when they realise the value of the kit stolen, change their mind, giving us a quarter of its value. What is incredibly frustrating is, apparently, they knew who it was! What? Well get our bloody kit back then! It leaves a bitter taste but I'm still hurting from the last few weeks and can't be bothered.

After emailing Jenny, Mick, Tao and Mimi, who we met in Marrakesh as they were heading for the Gambia to set up a beekeeping charity, get an immediate response. Amazingly they are living in a village only an hour's drive from here; we're off to meet up. Concrete wattle and daub houses make up the village, at its centre a little bakery, tucked behind it the house Jenny and Mick are renting. Inside the once whitewashed walls, now charcoal black, light entering only from the holes in the disintegrating curtains and mosquito mesh, it takes a while for my eyes to adjust. A main room with concrete floor, two pallets make a futon, off of which are two bedrooms.

To the rear is a makeshift kitchen, with separate toilet and hanging pipe for showers, leading to a small yard. It strikes me how stark my life is now, from what it was, how we both have changed in ways we don't realise. Visiting friends in the past, almost the first thing they would say is, "excuse the mess." The reality being there was no mess but it's what they said. All that protocol and bollocks is so refreshingly irrelevant, here in this place, in this time.

It's such a simple pleasure, chatting over a beer, when Tao and Mimi arrive home from school, at four and seven they walk the two kilometres with the other children, if Jen and Mick are out when they get back, they play in the compound. I have visions of parents in England doing the school run by car and ponder being in dangerous Africa, where children can walk home alone. It has a sense of community and pride, the bakery its heart, earth packed floors are expected to be swept of dust and leaves daily—and they are.

In our family group of six, we navigate the open sewers to the eight stalls making up the market, with a bag of spongy green potatoes, overripe tomatoes and a carton of wine head off to the Jetty to buy fish. The Jetty has long since rotted, no match for the mighty Atlantic, its crashing waves make landing these highly decorated, heavy wooden boats impossible. Fishermen bob like corks offshore, a chain gang of people balance crates on their heads out to the boats to bring in the day's catch.

Many have lost their lives doing this, thrown against the wooden hulls for little more than a few fish to feed their family. It's one of the many humbling moments in this journey, when the life of its people become our life. There is a joy and camaraderie to this, watching the distribution of fish, no one is left out. Although the best of the catch is taken to be sold at market, the smaller, less desirable ones feed the locals and us.

Digging out a fire pit in the sand, leaf-wrapped potatoes sit directly on the coals, the fish grilled on an old piece of wire mesh above it. We ignore the blackened, rock-hard potatoes, fish like leather stuck solid to the wire rack, soaking wet and shivering in the ocean spray. The magic of this moment is in the company, a much-needed time for me, to laugh with and at, each other's charcoal toothless grins (Jenny lost a battle with cancer a few years later).

Here in Africa, it is a fact that being white, we are immediately perceived as being rich, this of course is true by comparison but we're only able to do what we do from money earned from our working life, putting us on a tight budget. I question, how we can give, as much as we take, see the reasoning of others, whose journeys are in aid of different charities, or causes. We never took sponsorship, or tied ourselves to a charity, knowing this would compromise us, I know over time we will find the right balance, the right thing for us.

Jenny and Mick's focus is on their beekeeping charity and teaching locals how to build a beehive. This will be a skill, once learned, they could get paid for, but they cannot understand whilst being taught how to build them, they won't and are refusing.

Mick decided to build a couple himself, so at least he can move onto the next stage of honey production. In his tiny back yard, with reclaimed wood, Mick is making the most exquisite beehives. I can't help thinking, the African bees are going to have better homes than the African people. Just being with Mick and Jenny has been the tonic we both needed, easing us back into our life now, like the tortoise inside its shell, slowly our heads are poking back out.

Today as the temperature soars to above forty, I collapse in the shade reading whilst David works on Lizzybus. Fitting new rubbers to the air filter stops it hitting the bonnet and sounding like a rattling machine gun but he needs help to take off the bonnet and spare wheel, to fit new rubbers to the hinges. The exertion leaves me lightheaded, weak and dizzy, dripping in sweat I head for the open-air shower amongst the trees, the shafts of sun and cooling water so refreshing. Access to and having, clean water, has been an issue for us, we can only carry forty litres, which we filter for drinking, or use directly for cooking and washing. This focuses the mind to the value of water and although I want to stay under the shower forever, I just can't.

A restlessness engulfs us to get moving but we have agreed to stay at Jenny and Mick's for a week to look after the three kittens Tao and Mimi sort of adopted, whilst they go back to Senegal to renew their three-month visas. When we set off on this journey, we were constantly asked how long it would take us? It was easier to make up a time, so we settled on ten years. What we both knew is that we would 'not' do it at all costs, family will always come first. Both agree the journey will only ever be over, if, or when, we took Lizzybus back to England, having driven her around the world or not.

We're in early February twenty ten; on the twenty sixth of April Adele, my daughter, will get married, it's important to us both to try and be there. Despite this, David is still wanting, needing, to see and do everything we can in each country, to max out the time allowed according to our visa, to not 'miss' anything. It's also, as we're relying on rental income, slowing the journey down, allows the money time to catch up. Scouring over maps and routes, David thinks Ghana, with its international airport, should be a good place to find secure parking for Lizzybus and get a flight back for the wedding.

At over two thousand four hundred kilometres, the six countries of The Republic of Guinea Bissau, Guinea, Sierra Leone, Liberia, Cote d'Ivoire and finally, if we're still alive, Ghana. It's a massive journey but hey, you're talking about two people who are driving around the world.

Having never heard of most of these countries, or unable even to pronounce them, David shows me on the map. It's like an out of body experience, as if I'm looking over the shoulder of someone who has a clue, who knows what they are looking at. But it's me, Jayne, sat looking at it, not just looking but with an expectation, that somehow, with David, I'm going to be driving in Lizzybus to it. I'm overwhelmed, aware of what we are about to face, my coping mechanism kicks in, I shut it all out of my mind, focus only on what I need to do right now.

What it did momentarily do, is give me an insight into David's world, his reality, of knowing what lies ahead, of what we face. The punishing, gruelling roads, the securing of visas, you can't just arrive to a border and cross it. It's a process, filled with obstacles, like closed embassies, no embassies, wrong documentation etc. I'm in awe of how, with what little internet access he has, none of the social media groups and websites available to us all now, he even comes up with a plan, let alone actions it.

Of all these countries it's the visas for Sierra Leone that we need to secure here in Banjul, the capital of Gambia, before we leave. It's in Banjul, on the third floor of a crumbling building at the Sierra Leone consulate, that we hand over our completed applications, passports and seventy-five dollars each with instructions to return tomorrow at eleven a.m. On our return, interviewed separately by three consulate officials, is like a full-on interrogation and very intimidating. Having found no one ever understood my profession, I just put 'infirmiere' Nurse, now they want documentation and non-existent nursing certificates, along with bank accounts. I'm asked where I have been and where I am going, I try desperately to remember the countries David showed me on the map but my mind goes blank, I can't even remember the ones we have driven through.

I wanted my lip balm; my mouth is so dry my lips are not moving in unison but sticking together as one. Peeling them apart, I manage a smile but avoid giving them any of the information they ask for. David faces the same interrogation and like me gives none of the details requested. We're sent home again, for them to process and consider our applications. Not used to being faced with such interrogation, we're both a little shell-shocked.

Still living at Jenny and Mick's looking after the kittens, the electricity is off, not unusual in Africa, it's more unusual to have it on. In the tiny kitchen, on the wooden plank with a hole cut for the metal bowl sink, it does have a tap and drain. Using the two-ring gas camping cooker, in candlelight I make dinner. The village children squeeze in and those who can't fit in watch from the open door. In the darkness, it's like a sea of disconnected white teeth and eyes, I feel the kittens scratching at my feet. Slicing into six, my tin of corned beef bought back from England, dip each slice in egg and couscous to fry. I cut two, into tiny squares for the children and with the bread still warm from the bakery make corned beef fritter sandwiches for us. All thoughts of getting visas gone in that first delicious mouthful.

We're back at the Sierra Leone Consulate for the third day, the security guard in his perfectly ironed white shirt recognises us, unlocks the door, to lock it behind us. We're left sitting, until an hour later, called to the frosted glass window, our passports are slid under the post box slit. Barely able to speak, scanning the pages, find a very impressive visa covering another whole page of our quickly filling up passports. Jenny and Mick are back tonight, we buy a whole chicken and crate of beer. It's a tonic of an evening celebrating their safe return and our Sierra Leone visas, marking the restart of our journey around the world, or at least Ghana and Adele's wedding.

It's tough leaving, Jenny, Mick and the children have become our family, no airs or graces, just people like us wanting more from life, we will miss them. Firing Lizzybus up, the familiar puff of smoke from her exhaust feels like a deep breath taken before entering the now familiar, whilst uncharted, territory. We're going back into the other half of Senegal, the country we were in when I got the news about my precious mother. I imagine the Gambia as the filling in a sandwich, it's the only way I can make sense of it in my head.

Hitting the border after only a couple of hours, join the queue of cars, vans and lorries in the midday scorching, blistering, heat. Becoming familiar with the process of crossing borders, Customs, Police and Immigration, arriving, or leaving, with a no-man's land in-between, it's still nerve-wracking. A day-long process, where getting all the documents stamped, specifically the Carnet De Passage, takes teamwork, nerve and determination.

Jenny and Mick gave us the name of Solos Beach Bar, where you can camp for free, our instructions are to, 'follow the main road from the border, turn where you see signs for a hotel and keep going.' When you hit the beach, park behind the last hut and tell the owner you are camping there, all seems pretty simple— not! The main road disintegrates from tarmac, to dirt, to sand, we give up guessing if we're on it or not, just head in the direction of the sea. Our newly acquired sand driving skills come in, as were literally driving along the beach, tempers and the temperature sore at the futility of our mission, in finding this hut, as all we pass are 'huts.' Just on the point of murder, see a wooden hand-painted sign nailed to a palm tree, Solos Beach Bar.

This part of Senegal is dominated by Rastafarians, a religious group originating in Jamaica, brought to the masses by Bob Marley through his reggae music. A religion that forbids the cutting of hair, sees colourful knitted woollen hats struggling to contain matted dreads. I'm right at home with my dreaded locks, I just need to get me one of them knitted colourful hats to contain it and of course keep my head toasty warm.

Although their religion frowns on drinking alcohol, or smoking, it would seem this does not include Marijuana; we are constantly, to the point of being harassed, asked if were looking for it. It's so colourful, from the painted shed homes to the brightly dyed cotton adorning the voluptuous bottomed and busted women. Everything is carried on the head in pots or baskets—up to seventy percent of their bodyweight can be carried this way. Everything that is apart from children, who are strapped to their backs in colourful cotton sheeting.

Sitting on the beach having coffee, the morning bringing with it the rising of what will be a fierce sun, a woman and her Rasta friend appear. It seems it is her beach we are now camped upon, as is the little wicker hut we are propped against. I am asked for a cigarette and feel unable to refuse. She sits in silence to smoke it, before disappearing, to what we later find out is a little hotel complex (six circular mud huts thatched with palm) nestled in the pines. Returning almost immediately, to give us a bagful of fruit, papaya oranges and lemons, we never see them again.

I am finding the lack of any toilet facilities a real nightmare, I have not yet had to resort to the she-pee my sister bought me, with its little vagina shaped cup. There are trees but as soon as I go into them people appear. Peeing is not that much of a problem; I don't need to dig a hole for a pee but anything else is. I'm just grateful that age has spared me the curse of a monthly period. I think, not about the luxury of a flushing toilet but just of being back in the desert, where I could be on my own with my spade. We have not showered for several days, washing in the sea is okay but it leaves a crust of salt on you. Collecting water from the local village two kilometres away, we find a padlock on the only well, it's not just us but the locals who have to pay. Solo said there is an internet café in the village, walking to it for the last few days, the familiar chant of 'cuduo' is replaced by 'My Friend you are from England, I have family there' is draining. We're still being polite but realise it just prolongs the agony, begin to walk on in silence but worse, the internet is always down when we get there.

Our water pump has given up, this is a disaster, by pumping through the carbon ceramic filter it provides our drinking water. It's too early to face, turn ground coffee into a morning that can and sit in the sand watching the sun appear from the ocean. We see lots of fish, flapping and jumping along the shore, apparently a boat capsized, releasing its bounty of fish. From everywhere an army of women collect them, expertly slinging them into wicker baskets on their heads, above us the mighty white-headed African Sea Eagle swoops. It's an incredible sight, all thoughts of our water pump are forgotten.

Back in camp, David stripped down the pump, its inners exploding are now scattered like seeds upon the sand. David if nothing else is methodical, on hands and knees collects the renegade pieces to re-assemble them. Bravo! We once more have a working water filter system, what more could a girl want of her man?

We forgot this morning to collect fish for our own tea, just up the beach are a few fishing boats, their flags shredded like fish fins, hauled onto the beach by the ancient art of rolling over wooden poles. Women, bent double, expertly crack fish over the head before gutting them, throwing the guts to scavenging gulls and stray dogs. I'm in hysterics as David bargains with a weathered, toothless old crone, then like my very own Robinson Crusoe, two fish tethered through their gills swinging from his hand, head back to camp. Building a fire pit in the sand, once the wood burns to charcoal, place a flat stone over it, putting banana-leaf wrapped fish, sliced potatoes and onions, more banana leaves, then sealing it with sand. With our bare hands, dig, like getting a gift at Christmas, peel back banana leaves: it's quite delicious.

It's Valentine's Day, David doesn't know it, but I have six pieces of Belgian chocolate hidden in the fridge I brought back from England. I crave a bit of romance, my hand to be held, words of love whispered in my ear, to gaze into a starlit sky. For David it's expected that I know he loves me, he is more likely to say, "Do you love me?" than "I love you," which immediately irritates me. I hate feeling this need, I never felt it before but being so far from home, with only each other, I'm beginning to feel lonely.

At the back of Lizzybus cutting mango, a little boy drowned in a faded man's T-shirt sits quietly watching. I plop pieces of mango into his open mouth, like a mother bird to its chick, I'm comforted by his presence where an agitation stood before. It's been a nearly a week, if we are ever going to make it to Ghana for April we have to push on, also, having lent our solar panel to Solo for his 'Beach Bar' need to run the engine each day to top the batteries up but it's not enough, Lizzybus needs a good run. It's decided we will make a move tomorrow. As dusk falls, we hear the enchanting sound of Djembe drums, a skin-covered, goblet-shaped drum with great spiritual meaning across West Coast Africa.

If I could have picked a date for Valentine's, then here on the beach, with three Rastas, a lifetime of dreads contained in their huge knitted red and yellow hats, playing their drums to a full moon would be up there. Ash dropping from their cigar-sized spliffs turns their fingers a sooty grey, the pungent smell of marijuana heavy on the cooling sea breeze. Getting going is always a wrench, being so transient I cling to these pockets of domesticity, the sheer luxury of language but there is a restlessness in us both, it pushes us, to explore, to see what's out there.

What I'm only just getting used to is, although on the map a distance can look tiny, the reality is, it can take days, even weeks, specifically if it involves sand, mud, or both, which it usually does. Oh and the constant stop checks, by police, military and anyone who has a fancy to put string across a road tied with plastic bags, wanting payment to take it down.

Leaving Ghana, cross no-man's land to the border of 'The Republic Guinea Bissau,' which apparently is different from our next, next, country of 'Guinea.' Like many African countries their past dogged by slavery, corruption and civil unrest, which to an extent still continues. Colonised by the Portuguese, it gained independence in nineteen seventy-four, significant to us, in that neither know a single word of Portuguese. Women are at risk here, forced into marriage as little more than children, face domestic abuse, violence, even female genital mutilation.

I tell David not to leave my side; although I realise I am well past my sell by date, there is a definite hostility here towards me, I'm never addressed directly, only spoken to through David. Despite the heat, I wear long trousers and a long-sleeved shirt buttoned to the neck, with my cap on and stand behind David.

The border crossing is long and drawn out, with repeated searches of Lizzybus, it's difficult to stay together. We're asked but refuse to pay, the Police for not having photocopies of the Carnet De Passage (which we don't need, as once stamped, they have a tear-off section to keep with all the details). It's relentless and draining, reluctantly David plays his trump card and the assumption he is a 'Police Officer' changes everything. Apparently, police don't need to pay, or provide photocopies, which is why, finally after several hours we are free to go due to the confusion David is one.

Following the coast road, take a forty-kilometre detour to remote Varela and its beaches, accessible only by four-wheel drive vehicles. The advice at the border is not to go, as recent rains have made it almost impassable; if we do, be sure to take plenty of food and water, as its charm lies in its remoteness. I'm still at a loss to know what has happened to David and I, what insanity has poisoned us, pushing us to do this stuff? I knew when they said it was impassable, it was something we would do. From a distance are miles of soaring golden grasslands, once in it, find it little more than swamp.

I am instantly devoured by mosquitos, we have wires attached from the bull bar to the roof rack, 'Bush Wires.' What a triumph these are at holding back the bush, despite the insect life, with no air con, we have to drive with open windows, they prevent the bush from taking our eyes out. It's tough, we're having to constantly build the washed-out road or clear it of fallen debris. We're way past the point of being able to justify why we're doing this, or retreat, the adventure becomes an ordeal, ask, "Whose stupid idea was this anyway?"

Passing what look like a load of derelict buildings, find a decent track, and an hour later hit the blond sandy beach. Nothing but beach, as far as the eye can see. I don't think we really thought this through, as David and I are not and never have been, beach people, with no water, little shade, remote and desolate, it's certainly not our idea of paradise. But, as it took so much effort to get here, we need a few days to get over it so set up camp under three palm trees, hammock strung between them. Fully clothed, head for the sea, to wash away the crust of dried sweat and cool throbbing mosquito bites.

Looking back, Lizzybus looks like she is on a film set, nestled between the palms, hammock swaying in the breeze, roof tent erect, I see this image as clear today, as I saw it then. Darkness has settled, sat writing by head torch, I hear a rustling from behind me, which I initially ignore. When I do look up, I see, like leaves on an autumn breeze, children draped in all manner of cast-off rags, from a swimming costume to dungarees and the obligatory oversized torn, faded football shirt. They settle around me in silence watching, until finally disappearing back into the mangroves.

The morning brings with it my 'autumn leaves,' accompanied by twenty-eight-year-old Solomon. Solomon, born in Guinea Bissau, had been adopted, by whom he said, was a 'white man' putting him through school and two years university in Canada, speaking perfect English. For the next few days, Solomon appears every morning, afternoon and evening, all day, every day. We're taken to his African Round House, a traditional mud built round circular building with corrugated metal and reed covered roof. Inside it's cool and huge, with six rooms, one the toilet, basically a hole covered in palm leaves but, for some reason, there is no smell or flies from it.

Solomon is in the processes of putting in a well, dug manually by himself, its sides reinforced with concrete, mixed with cockleshell. Trekking through what feels like virgin jungle, we find other houses, full of people and children, one of which is his brother's. On our way here a few days ago, passed what we thought were derelict buildings, we are now inside the compound of these 'derelict buildings' to find it's actually an army barracks and full of soldiers, one of whom is Solomon's brother—well it would be. A group of soldiers in khaki trousers and white vests tend a fire under two huge cauldrons, one of rice, one of fish stew, another group huddle around a tiny screen, watching a film.

Amongst piles of rubbish, are pots and pans, stacked anywhere and everywhere, chickens roam freely, whilst ducks are tethered with fishing line. On the verandas of the buildings drape disintegrating blackened mosquito nets, the soldiers' sleeping quarters, each complete with wooden bed and line to hang clothes. It's like an out of body experience, sitting on upturned oil drums eating delicious rice and fish stew, apparently being in the army is not quite a career choice but one step up from poverty.

We now realise Solomon just wants to parade his 'white friends' to anyone and everyone, as a sign of his importance in the world. It has an advantage in that we're able to get water from Solomon's and him showing us the hut selling bread, eggs and onions but this constant attention is draining. Tonight, David is going over to Solomon's to put some films onto his laptop, it's just so incredible to be alone. It lasted five minutes, before my 'autumn leaves' settled around me. I open the tin of apricots, (a present from my daughter) to share but before I know it, I have put every last piece into their open mouths. I didn't have a single slice or save any for David. Licking the juice off my fingers, I'm transported to

Sunday afternoon tea with my family, eating jelly and peaches, swimming in evaporated milk. Did I ever imagine, as that ten-year-old, I would be on a beach in 'The Republic Guinea Bissau,' with the blackest of children dressed in rags, living in a Land Rover, eating from a tin? Never, ever!

It's early morning, walking along the beach we hear the familiar 'David my friend,'—it's Solomon. He instructs us to follow him, taking us along the same dusty tracks away from the cooling sea breeze, to stand around whilst he parades us to more of his friends. This is so tiresome, I am hot, irritable and getting more and more agitated, even watching the wild pigs foraging in the undergrowth can't distract me. Solomon takes us to a group of palm trees where two guys are propped up sleeping. Shaking them from their stupor, we watch fascinated as the guy, tying his feet together with bamboo, like a monkey climbs the tree to where a 'tapper' had been inserted into the cut flower stump. A plastic bottle tied just below it collects the milky white sap, to be fermented into alcoholic palm wine.

They offer us a child's yellow plastic bucket and a large jam jar full of the stuff. Solomon took the bucket; we share the jam jar. It's semi sweet, semi sour, with an earthy yeasty flavour, having seen this on documentaries, to be sat here drinking it with the natives is quite incredible.

Back at camp I have an ache in my bones and a thumping head, Solomon sits in silence with David. Feeling faint and nauseas I crawl away into the roof tent oblivious. Waking to a setting sun, my temperature soars but I'm clammy and cold, throughout the night, my body evacuates all it contains from every orifice. I'm so weak, climbing up and down the ladder is impossible, I sit in the sand below it. David follows me, digging hole after hole, until, unable to squat, I just stand letting the vile stinking liquid trickle down my legs at the same time as dry retching. On all fours, crawl to the sea, leaving more of my evacuated body as a slug's trail behind me. Cleansed by the salt water, soothed by its coolness, my weight supported, I feel the gentle breeze under a vastness of sky, stars and full moon.

With the absence of any doctor, being so remote, David diagnosed me with possible malaria, despite having been religious in taking our Larium. In the three medical books, the advice is, 'If you think it is malaria, treat it as if it is, or it will have dire consequences, leading to death!' When you only have each other, like your kit, it's up to you to protect and look after it. I'm forced to swallow five (calculated by weight) foul-tasting Larium horse tablets, I am now a piece of needed kit. Finally, forty-eight hours later, I can stand un-aided, shaken by the seriousness of the last few days were subdued. I'm feeling sorry for myself, when I remember the little pot of Marmite from home, with a teaspoonful in a mug of hot water, I find the familiar taste such a comfort, nourishing me and lifting my spirits.

Chapter 7
What Were We thinking?

It's been almost six months since we set off on this adventure. I want to scream "F...k it I never expected this!" But that would mean I actually expected something. I know I should never have agreed so easily, let alone to actually have been an active participant in it.

I've never been a shoes, handbags, hair or make-up kinda girl. Each year for the annual works Christmas Party, I would raid my daughter's drawers for one of her many clutch bags, that didn't even fit my packet of fags and my sister's shoe cupboard for an acceptable pair of heels I couldn't wait to take off. I felt completely liberated, selling, donating and trashing all my worldly possessions, left with one bag of clothes, a pair of flip-flops and boots. No iron, no vacuum, no duster, suits me just fine. But I am missing the smell of England, of cut grass, of rain, the colour of it, in the bright yellow spring daffodils and summer meadows.

I am becoming familiar to and in a way comforted by the mechanical vehicle smell of Lizzybus, of baked earth, of salty ocean. To be having this experience is incredibly humbling, it fills us with wonder and magic; we feel nothing can take away its magic but we're about to be pushed to breaking point, putting in jeopardy if we're physically strong enough, let alone mentally, to carry on.

Leaving Varela beach, a little daunted by the road we know lies ahead, relieved to find in the dry weather the swamp has receded slightly. Heading for the capital of Guinea-Bissau, to get visas for Guinea (Guinea-Conakry, bloody confusing), know once we're out of this jungle, we'll be back on the main road we came in on. I'm not looking forward to this one bit, having faced constant roadblocks on the way in. I am still so weak and nauseated, I don't feel up to it but not only do they remember us (not many white people in a green Land

Rover), they still assume David is a Police Officer; we're pulled over but the checks are cursory.

Bissau, described as having narrow nineteenth century houses with wrought iron balustrades, of some architectural interest. Crippled by civil war, almost destroying it, special attention must be made to lock your room, as theft is rife and women should always be accompanied. We're both about broken, David worries for me having to drive whilst he navigates with a basic map, through a city without a single signpost. I'm incredulous as David announces we have arrived at Pensao Creola Hotel. For us an oasis, run by a Swiss man and his African wife, a whitewashed room, with bed, clean sheets, a pillow you can put your head on, a flushing toilet, shower and electricity. Not having showered for over ten days, we shower, eat and sleep until late the next day.

Directly opposite us is the Guinea Conakry Embassy, a small building for an embassy, with a very helpful security guard, who, assuming David is a Police Officer, put us at the front of the queue. Being familiar with the requirements for visas, we're fully prepared, with spare passport-size photos and photocopies of everything. We wait the few hours for them to be checked, then go away to wait a few more days for them to be processed.

Nothing could prepare me for the devastation of this city, its civil wars and military coups leaving its infrastructure in ruins and the majority of its people in poverty. I'm now not just looking at but living through, an apocalypse. Colonial buildings fold in on themselves preventing complete collapse, their twisted remains bleed red, as internal steelwork rusts. Vultures sit squaring up to cats on the piles of rubbish, which seep a black treacly putrid liquid. Plastic tarpaulin tied to shattered buildings become homes, the black acrid smoke from fires burning everything and anything, confused in the absence of any breeze, becomes a smog. Streetlights, their mangled mess of wires spew out like Rasta dreads, minus any red and yellow hats.

Women carry the water, tend the children, wash the cloths, sell the goods, men mostly chew sticks under trees, or, in this case, beneath the rubble. I was not prepared for the feelings of despair this aroused in me, almost a sense of drowning. I can imagine these once proud hunter-gatherers, as stealthy as any leopard, as strong as any ox, as fearless as any lion, out on the plains but like all those animals and their habitats, they are long gone, along with their purpose. Brought up in a country where everyone has access to education and medical treatment, rich or poor, faced with the reality, I have a sense of hopelessness.

For now, we focus only on the logistics, a constant concern is getting local currency for the country we are in, or about to enter. Each border crossing has hordes of moneychangers waiting in no-man's land, where we change the last of the currency of the country we leave, into the currency of the country we are going into. It keeps us going until the big cities where usually we can find a cash point. In this city, there are no such luxuries as cash points but do find a bank, amazed, once inside, to find a smart air-conditioned building, complete with a ticket queuing system. Our intention is to change Euros to the WAF (West African Frank) on reaching the counter; apparently, we need to fill a form out and take another ticket. We're in this bank nearly two hours, it's just wonderful to be in the air conditioning, watching what should be something so simple, be so farcical.

David becomes sick, sweating, sleeping and shitting through the next few days, at least I can keep on top of the washing. It's slightly cooler now but the humidity is so high the clothes I'm wearing are as wet as the ones I wash. In one of David's lucid moments, I drag him along to the internet café, it's not safe to go on my own but it's terminally slow and so very hot inside, we give up on it. The UN (United Nations) has a very high presence here, evident in all the white Land Cruisers and the shop specifically catering for UN employees, it even has a bakery which sells treacle tarts. Oh, what joy, David, still with no appetite, cannot eat the treacle tarts. I eat them both with a mug of tea.

We're now both full of cold and sickness, not daring to leave the room and its toilet. This might seem very hard to believe but I've always been incredibly private and modest as far as bodily functions go. I'll admit, I lost some of that modesty when David had to dig my toilet holes on Varela beach but what I find most difficult is being faced with the noise and smell of someone else's, specifically David's. I'm so weak-stomached, it makes me even more nauseated. Despite this, we just have to push on if we're going to get to Ghana and a flight back for the wedding. Having retrieved our passports with their Guinea (Conakry) visa covering another full page, we buy a case of beer, purely for medicinal reasons and head off for Gabu, a little closer to the border, ready to cross into Guinea.

On reaching Gabu, supposedly prospering from trade from Senegal and Guinea, again find buildings little more than rubble, without electricity, the broken tarmac road becomes craters, almost impossible even for Lizzybus to get over. Book into a run down but clean hotel, Lizzybus will be watched over by the night watchman and his hand pistol. David spent the night on the seatless, doorless toilet, I dream of a bathroom with a door, to not be subjected to the sounds, as well as the smells, of David and his squits. We're both ashen under our African tanned skin; for breakfast David has a can of coke, I eat mango. We're both losing an alarming amount of weight, know we have to eat but neither able to keep anything, not just down but in, focus for now on drinking.

Despite being in sight of the border, the road is almost impassable; we engage low ratio and crawl over the obstacles, this with constant police and military checks, progress is terminal. Until, at one checkpoint, we're told it's the boarder, an hour later with everything stamped, drive through what we think is no-man's land, to hit a river. It has a ferry (a floating flatbed pulled manually across by chains) but it's on the opposite bank. David is taken across to it in a dug out wooden canoe, to negotiate a price for the crossing. I sit in the shade guarding Lizzybus, trying not to think of the fact I'm a woman alone in no-man's land. Finally, the 'ferry' with David aboard is being hauled back, aboard it is a rusted windowless taxi, hardly visible under its humongous cargo strapped to the roof. When at last it reaches the shore, it won't start. Getting it up the muddy steep bank even with its eight passengers pushing proves impossible: we're marooned. It's like time stands still; cattle drink, women wash children and clothes, men sit in the shade.

It's time to get pro-active if we don't want to end our journey here on the riverbank, get out our recovery kit and tow the taxi off. With Lizzybus and us now aboard the ferry crossing the river, the captain demands double the negotiated fee, we have no choice other than to pay. Once off the ferry, we face the familiar piece of rope strung across the road with shredded plastic bags and a very intimidating, very black soldier with his AK47 strapped across him and a group of soldiers to his left, demanding five dollars to let us past. We try to laugh and joke with him, saying they should pay us for towing the taxi off and keeping the road open. For some reason, I show him Sid (our plastic black mamba donated to us in Marrakesh) he is terrified and backs away. David takes a deep breath, thinking either me or Sid are about to get shot, it's a very tense time.

One thing we know, no matter what, is to always be complicit, we are in the wrong for just being here. Finally, a compromise is reached, we will take the two wizened old women, complete with a year's shopping, which when tied to the roof rack, makes Lizzybus look just like the taxi we towed off, to the next town, where we're assured the immigration office is. Squeezed between our kit on the back seat, I give them a bottle of ice-cold water, they stroke the blond hairs on my arm, wide-eyed and giggling like teenagers minus any teeth. I love them and want to keep them, as they make me forget all about feeling sick or finding the immigration office.

It took the whole day to get where they wanted to go and complete the long, drawn-out process of finally, officially getting stamped into Guinea-Conakry, the second of the six countries we have to get through before reaching Ghana.

Guinea is full of cultural and natural riches (we're yet to be convinced), with one of the world's largest reserves of bauxite aluminium ore. We feel on edge in this country and decide not to bush camp but always look for a hotel (I use the word 'hotel' in its loosest form). At Koumbia in an assortment of decaying buildings viewing a room, I'm trying desperately not to laugh, as in semi darkness they point out the fan, toilet, double bed and the fact that we can park Lizzybus right outside the door, both agreeing its most suitable. There might have been a fan and toilet but no electric or water; we are given two buckets of water and a candle, I don't care—Lizzybus is safe, and we can rest.

By morning, the buckets of water are so hot you could say we had a 'hot wash.' We have bucket washing down to a fine art: wet the body, soap up, scrub and rinse, making sure you don't rinse back into the clean water for the next person, which is always David, the used water is then used to wash clothes, which, strung over the back seats, dry during the day. Finding internet to check the situation in the countries we are heading for is our next mission, push onto Labe, where we're told they have mains electricity and internet. The broken tarmac roads make for a long slow day, before we realise it dusk is settling around us. Despite the perils of bush camping, we know driving on in the dark is as bad and decide to risk it and bush camp.

Pulling well off the road into the bush, there is a swarm of persistent flies. David hates flying things, flies being only second to moths in his repulsion, locks himself inside Lizzybus, sweating into the already sodden seats. Before the flies clock off, to be replaced by mosquitoes, I strip off and bucket wash, applying a liberal coating of one hundred percent DEET, to dress in long trouser, long-sleeved shirt and socks.

It's morning, we're still alive and not robbed, raped and left for dead, the aroma of fresh coffee brewing makes everything better, we even manage to eat a squishy black banana each. Back on the road the terrain becomes hilly, which, due to the lack of back breaks (sheared yesterday) makes the going down bit most unnerving. It's a barren landscape where only smouldering stumps of trees remain from the slash and burn, along with gigantic mushroom-shaped termite nests. A method used to allow grass to grow for cattle but overgrazing causes the thin fragile earth to wash off in the rainy season, leaving acres of barren dust.

Crossing a wide bridge, get out to take some photos, the exit to the bridge is manned by soldiers, a motor bike drives over, demanding we follow him to his commandant. The commandant, outraged at our audacity to take photos, confiscates the camera. Now surrounded by soldiers, becoming more and more animated, the commandant asks why we think we can take photos in his country? Assuring us we would never be allowed, or do it, in our own country. If this was not so real, so dangerous, we would laugh, take our camera back, tell them to, 'get stuffed,' and that in England, anyone can take a photograph of anything, even of our queen!

But we don't, we just say how stupid we have been, how sorry we are, ask for our camera back, so we can delete all the photos off it, right here, right now, right in front of him.

David and I, if nothing else, are very good at reading situations, even situations way outside our experience; we both know it's all about them not losing face. By admitting how stupid it was, how sorry we are and deleting the photos, this shows his authority: we're in Africa, these are the rules.

At Hotel La Campagne, described as a chic, modern hotel, a shabby two-storey building, us its only guests, it does feel opulent, with water, electricity, even a mosquito net over the bed and safe parking for Lizzybus. The staff live in a little brick built shed in the courtyard, in the evening they're squatting around a large metal dish, their dinner of rice and 'maafe' a groundnut (peanut). They signal for us to join them; it smells so good and we're so hungry having finally got our appetites back. Being English, one thing I have found very difficult is getting over my English reserve, the polite side of me wants to say, "Thank you but it's OK," but I really want some.

So, we accept, sitting crossed legged around the pot, form rice into little cups to scoop up the stew. To make sure I eat only with my right hand, means sitting on my left. Knowing how poor people are here, how precious food is, we eat very little, filled not by the food but their warmth and kindness. I realise sharing their food is as special for them, as it is for us. I'm going to work on my English reserve.

We're told about the street food from the 'atieke ladies'—still hungry, go off in search of them. The electricity does not run to street lighting, we stumble around in darkness blinded by the occasional glare of car headlights. It feels so normal, walking back to our hotel with a takeaway of meatballs in a sauce and fresh baked baguette, in black plastic (poo) bags. Today we have to address the battering Lizzybus is taking and give her some much-needed care and attention. Unloading the kit and inch thick layer of red cement dust to get at the new brake pads, filters and seals, a little party of onlookers surround us.

David, having stripped the brakes, is using a long metal pole to push the pistons back. Sweating and cursing, it's not long before others help, pulling on the bar, laughing and joking. It's moments like this, when our life merges with local life, that make the journey real. Several hours and lots of smiles and laughter, Lizzybus has new brakes, new oils and filters to everything and not only greased nipples but a new nipple. We all know how David loves his nipples.

Before moving on tomorrow we go shopping; at the local market the rickety wooden tables are so close, you have to shimmy, hip to hip, bottom to bottom down its isles. For sale are individually wrapped small bags of pasta or rice and single maggie stock cubes, a reflection on the poverty here. We want the peanut paste used to make 'maafe' we had last night and 'fufu,' a mash made of tubers. Vegetables are sold stacked in pyramid piles, we buy pyramids of potatoes, carrots, tomatoes, onions, bananas and oranges, fresh bread and plastic bags of peanut paste, the whole lot less than three dollars.

Finally, get a chunk of what we think is lamb but might be beef, hoping the guy has successfully swatted all the persistent flies off it, feel almost victorious walking back to our hotel with our goodies. Not wanting to risk the meat with our dickey tummies, give it, along with half the vegetables, to our wonderful friends. The rest gets shoved into the pressure cooker with two packs of scrummy peanut paste. Once cooked, it will be kept in the fridge, to keep us going over the next few days on the road. Tonight, we're off out to get our last take away from the 'atieke ladies.'

Driving through The Fouta Djallon region where major rivers cross is spectacular, as the soft sandstone weathers to produce towering spires and deep canyons, we're so happy having brakes. By its very nature it's wet, the day ends in the middle of a downpour, we need to find shelter. Lizzybus has a complete external roll cage, welded to her chassis, this makes a perfect climbing frame to carry passengers externally. We now have two guys clinging on, taking us to what is the 'Best Hotel in the region.' A large two-storey, almost derelict building, we're put in the main reception area and left. An hour later, worried we're being set up for an ambush, leave and go in search of our own Hotel.

The Oberoi—you could see it once had a charm but plant and insect life have made it rustic to the point of derelict. Still, it's drier than outside and Lizzybus is guarded by a night watchman. I continue to live in a world I no longer recognise, without infrastructure, electricity and at times water, where shops are little more than shacks, their metal grills protect the produce of a single egg, sachets of Nescafe, or maggie stock cube.

Arriving in Conakry, the capitol of Guinea, once known as the Paris of Africa, now a broken city with few graces and morbidly dirty. Having been warned about the kilometre thirty-six checkpoint, existing solely for the purpose of maintaining the officials who operate it, does not really prepare you for it. It's a complete roadblock, of gun toting soldiers, intent on one thing, to get money from you. It took hours and more searches than if crossing a border, keeping our eye on kit whilst staying together is impossible.

David and I are still weak and nauseas, the noise, the heat, the fumes, are taking us to breaking point. Finally, with the misunderstanding David is an officer of the law, they let us pass.

Against our wishes, we are forced to follow the local policeman astride his Honda to a hotel of his choice; he negotiated the room and then asked for money for taking us. It was good to have a 'police escort' as in that it spared us the constant stop and search of soldiers but, even knowing David was a comrade in law, didn't fob him off. First though, we have to get local currency, from the bank two kilometres away, when for the fifth time we're stopped and even though I am driving, being a woman, they address David. I get out and walk around to the soldier, smile and look directly into his eyes, to ask "How can I help you?"

It takes a few minutes for him to collect himself, before telling me undoing my seat belt is violation number one, not reaching number two, I just shake my head, get back into Lizzybus and drive away. At this point I don't care, I think shoot me if you want, I've had enough, David sits in silence waiting for the shots. I'm desperately homesick, yes for my family but a deep gut-wrenching ache, for fairness, for honesty and for rules I recognise. I'm English for god's sake, it's just not Cricket! I'm having a meltdown. David realises he has to get me out of

Guinea, specifically Conakry, right now before I abandon ship and find the nearest airport.

Leaving the city of Conakry is as difficult as getting into it, at one point, with me driving, I'm told I can't drive in 'flip-flops.' What? Most people don't even have shoes, at this point, David and I are stood outside of Lizzybus. I looked at David wearing his Land Sandals and said, "No problem, Officer, I will swap shoes with David." Holding my nose in a charade, showing how smelly his sandals are, we change shoes. Again, it's about us being complicit, for them to not lose face, it's a moment that hovers, for a split second they laugh, enough for us to get in Lizzybus and piss off.

Driving away, we can almost see the funny side but it will take a lot more than this to bring me round. Fortunately, as Conakry is close to the border with our next country Sierra Leone, we can get to it today but first we have to get out of Guinea. It's a border with no offices, just desks outside, under tarpaulin, immediately our documents are locked in a drawer, as apparently, we don't have the current 'Typhoid certificate'—it's a scam. It's too late in the afternoon, we just cannot be bothered with more lengthy negotiations, accept the five-dollar fine and cross no-man's land. Sierra Leone, an African country rich in diamonds, became its downfall; during the eighties and nineties these diamonds were used to finance conflict and war in Sierra Leone, Liberia, Angola, Cote d'Ivoire, Congo and Zaire. A time of mass murder, rape and mutilations, to become known as "Blood Diamonds."

A once British Colony, it won its independence in nineteen sixty-one, what joy, they speak English and they drive on the right-hand side. Welcoming us, they ask for nothing other than for us to enjoy our time in their country, no searches, no documents locked in drawers, just big smiles and handshakes for us both. We are asked, not ordered, if we mind giving a lift 'down the road' to the local Police Inspector, his month's shopping and two chickens. Still reeling from the constant roadblocks in Conakry, think it will make life easier, if we have our own Policeman on board. We're stopped just as many times but only for a chat and to welcome us to their country.

Also, our Police Inspector wants to catch up with his 'friends' along the way, which as it turns out, is everyone.

Several hours later, heading for Freetown, still giving a lift 'down the road' to our Police Inspector, David driving, I'm wedged in the back, the chickens held by their feet break free. Even scrawny chickens are massive when flapping and clucking inside a Lizzybus, and their claws are something else. Once caught, they are silenced by being sat on. David is very happy, the chicken feathers sticking to his sweaty bald head make him re-live his youth when he had hair. At last, as dusk falls, we arrive at a small hut with Police engraved on a board above it, the half-suffocated chickens spring back to life, clucking and fluttering their indifference. A few kilometres down the road, pull over into the bush to set up camp. Throughout Africa, wherever, or whenever, no matter how remote, when setting up camp, locals will appear and just stand watching, two white people, in a big green Land Rover, going about their evening rituals, it's something we accept and at times even enjoy.

Sierra Leone, with eleven long years of a brutal civil war and political unrest evident, we can actually feel it taking a huge deep breath. Arriving in Freetown, the capital, an aged crumbling tumble of sagging streets, at its centre the 'Cotton Tree.' Slavery in the British Empire was abolished in eighteen thirty-three, whilst 'Domestic Slavery' (outside Crown Colonies) persisted. Around seventeen eighty-seven, the British helped four hundred freed slaves, from the United States, Nova Scotia and Great Britain to return to Sierra Leone, to settle in what they called the 'Province of Freedom.' This is significant, as right now, we are standing dwarfed by the most magnificent Cotton Tree (Ceiba Pentandra—Kapok) its exact age unknown, other than it's older than the town itself and taller than any other building. Here, beneath it, shackled and manacled slaves were sold, I feel their being, as a stillness.

Chapter 8
The Respite

I am awakening from my nightmare, pyramid piles of rotting vegetables become an abundance of fresh vegetables, brought to market on proper roads, by laughing, smiling people. Like a broken arm having had its plaster cast removed, I'm able to wiggle my fingers once more. I am again in the back of Lizzybus, after the policeman we asked if he knew of a cheap hotel is in the front, minus any chickens, directing us. We're shown a shabby rundown Hotel; Lizzybus, we are assured, will be fine, as they will get someone to sleep in her overnight. We know we need to base ourselves in the city to get visas for Liberia but it's so hot, manic and noisy, decide to head for the beaches. It's stunning, as dense green jungle frames snow white sand, crunching underfoot. It's quite magical, despite having to wash in the sea and clean teeth with water from our Jerry Cans, which David hates, so is Mr Grumpy.

Treating ourselves to a delicious meal of Barracuda and rice at an adjacent beach hut, chat to two Canadian aid workers. They are disillusioned by the practice still enforced for female circumcision, the removing of testicles to cure ailments, the accepted 'person per day' mown down by motorcycles. An insight for us, from people living here, into the 'now,' that disturbingly has not managed to break free from the 'then.' I get news, my mother, still in hospital, has taken a turn for the worse. I just want peace and dignity for her, where pain and intrusion stand.

Shopping, at the local village, I realise how life now, bears no resemblance whatsoever to my old one. When going to the supermarket involved slinging everything and anything, wanted, needed, or just fancied, into a trolley. To now, chasing scrawny chickens around, who will need their necks breaking and plucking, leave with six eggs. How precious are these six eggs, fry onions with curry powder, add a tin of tomatoes, add a boiled egg and rice, then head to the beach for a 'Curry night' under the stars. It's getting complicated, David suggests we cross back into Guinea which loops over Liberia (Guinea, that torturous corrupt country I never want to see again) so we can go straight into Cote d'Ivoire, saving the ninety dollars-each Liberian visa fee and time, as our deadline for getting to Ghana looms.

At the British and French consulates, it's made clear the Cote d'Ivoire visa cannot be issued in Senegal, as it has no French Embassy, we have to go via Liberia. I'm so relieved, the thought of crossing back into Guinea filled me with dread. It's wonderful, as at the Liberian embassy, just an hour later, our passports have another visa covering another page. We're also going to get our Ghanaian visa here, leaving just the Cote d'Ivoire visa to get in Liberia. You keeping up? Sierra Leone is gridlock, park Lizzybus and walk to the embassy, past the 'Cotton Tree,' where fruit bats hang from its branches like giant rugby balls, sleeping and squabbling oblivious to the traffic chaos below them. Past the once impressive Law Courts, where trials of captured slave captains and crew took place and the imposing 'Slave Gates,' where liberated slaves walked into an unknown future in Freetown.

We eventually find the Ghanaian consulate, shut as it's a Bank Holiday in Ghana. The last few months have been so overwhelming, weak and sick, living in a world we don't recognise, where everything always hinges on everything else, all out of our control. This idyllic little drive around the world is becoming a nightmare, an ordeal, just getting through each day is a struggle. David scours maps, guidebooks, cross-referencing information, in dodgy internet cafes and just when we sort of have a plan it all falls to pieces. Of course, it's not just that this embassy is closed, or the next, or the next, it's just, in our weakened state, it's overwhelming. Neither of us have ever dared to ask ourselves, or each other, the question, if we really think, or ever thought, we have, or had, a hope in hell of making it. It was just a sentence we spouted out, a sentence that is beginning to feel like an actual sentence we have served on ourselves. To even voice our fears might be a step towards giving in to them; we're not ready for that, ignoring them is far better.

I think what keeps it real, is the routine, whether you live in a roof tent, or a two-bed semi, washing, shopping, even disposing of the rubbish, bringing a sense of doing, to the days nothing gets done. I drift through these days with moments of pure magic, to moments of pure hell, the security I once had of knowing when I am right or wrong, all gone, replaced with rules I don't understand. It's much harder than I ever thought possible. At times, I feel I'm floating above it all, looking in. I laugh at her, I feel sorry for her, I'm incredulous at the naivety of her but most of all I'm proud of her.

David and I have sort of become a team, Team Lizzybus and in an odd way, it works most of the time, as I see everything so differently, helped by my lack of mechanical and logistical understanding. If we both thought of worse case scenarios, we would have imploded long ago. Change in us, like in life, is imperceptible but changed we both are, as we push relentlessly on, in our quest. Focus for now on getting to Ghana, one thousand two hundred kilometres and three more countries, away, to store Lizzybus and get flights back to England for the wedding.

Back at the Ghanaian consulate, we're invited into the consulate's office for a chat, we're given tea and handshakes, along with assurances he personally will be processing our visas, which will be ready first thing in the morning. Today on the hour drive into Freetown to collect them, the roads are blocked by queues at all the petrol stations—there is a fuel strike. With only a quarter of a tank and an empty spare tank, knowing we leave tomorrow, we join the queue. Three hours later, with both tanks full, finally head off to the consulate, where waiting, as promised, are our passports, adorned with another beautiful visa covering another whole page.

Liberia, here we come, queuing for diesel yesterday was a good idea, as today, all petrol stations have completely run out of fuel. Along the way, people living their lives pound rocks with hammers until split into a fine gravel, groups of women heat flat irons in coals 'ironing.' Giving the now customary lift to a local Police Officer, 'down the road' there is an old Mercedes truck upside down in a ditch. Warned never to stop at accidents, as you will be guilty by association, figure having our on-board Police Officer as a witness, we will. After checking no one was dead inside or underneath it, winch it out, to notice Lizzybus has a flat tyre, ten minutes later it's changed. It crossed my mind, that perhaps David and I almost know what we are doing.

Liberia, capital Monrovia, part of 'The Pepper Coast' (Grain Coast), a name given it by Europeans trading in 'melegueta,' a type of Capsicum chilli pepper. In the early nineteenth century, the American Colonisation Society (ACS), believing black people would face better chances for freedom and prosperity in Africa than in the United States, helped them relocate to Liberia. It still suffers from systemic corruption, petty and violent crime, has one of the world's highest incidence of rape and most worryingly of all, the majority of its escaped prisoners remain un-captured. It's so odd, sitting here writing about these countries like this, countries I can honestly say I had never even heard of before this journey, it almost feels like I'm being a traitor to them. But unlike me, who never read, or let any of this information into my head, I feel it's important now to have a little understanding of what we're facing and our actual reality.

The landscape flattens out to coastal plains, the years of slash and burn have left massive scars upon it. We're at the end of 'Harmattan' season when a constant dry and dusty wind, driven in by the trade winds, makes it hot in the day and bitter cold at night. At a town forty kilometres short of the Sierra Leone border, we're stamped out; when we reach the actual border, we're searched again but nothing is needed to be, or is, stamped. Cross a no-man's land, where people live, the persistent groups of 'money changers' and beggars block our way. At what we think is the actual Liberian border, decide to pay a 'fixer' to take us to the different offices. It's still a long drawn our process, we feel on edge here, unlike Sierra Leone, try our best to stay together.

Heading for the capital Monrovia, one hundred kilometres away, as dusk settles know darkness will soon follow. Seeing a Police car and a hut, realise it's the 'Police Station' pull over to ask if we can camp behind it, which they agree to. Setting up camp with our now customary gathering of fascinated onlookers, desperate for a pee, I head off into the bush. On hearing footsteps behind me, turn to see a snaking line of women and children following.

Now I don't have the strongest of bladder at the best of times but when it thinks it is going to be allowed to pee, it's a done deal. There is nothing else to do other than pull down my trousers and pee. I realise the group, having formed a circle around me, have all bent down: they're checking to see if my arse is as white as my face. Once I've started, I cannot stop, so they have plenty of time to reach a conclusion. Right here, right now, in the middle of the jungle taking a pee with my audience, I close my eyes and imagine being at my friends or family, using their bathroom, in complete privacy.

If anyone then, had even hinted at my predicament now, I know it would have been so far outside of anything I could ever have imagined, to ever be of concern. I figure, if I can pee here in the Liberian jungle, behind a police station, to an audience I know, I've got this, I've arrived, I'm African.

As darkness falls, we're besieged by a biblical plague of moths, if you held your hand out and shut it you would have a handful of them. I feel a breeze and the soft velvet touch of flapping wings on my face. With David's repulsion to flying things, specifically moths, he is now in the tent, not just zipping the internal moggie net up but the outer skin of the tent, I know it will be a torturous hot sweaty night. Hearing gunfire, we're told there is a disturbance in the village, the two police in the only police car, drive off leaving us all alone. I get in the tent with David, sweating or not.

Back on the road we face many roadblocks, each one requires our fixed smiles and for now an explanation as to why we have a 'Carnet De Passage' and no 'Laissez-Passer,' for Lizzybus, which apparently is something needed in this country. David knew and asked about this at the embassy but was assured by the very nice embassy official, it's not necessary for them to issue us a 'Laissez-Passer' as the 'Carnet De Passage' supersedes it. Yeah, right, try telling that to all the drunk, gun toting soldiers we face, who are insisting we go back to Sierra Leone to pick one up. David starts shaking, his nerves are in tatters, the only reason we are able to continue, to get through this nightmare, is with the beautiful, wonderful, glorious, West Midlands Police Crest and the assumption David is a very important man. We have no idea how any other travellers ever make it through without this assumption.

Being stopped twenty or more times a day, on trumped up 'charges' like: no yellow fever certificate (we have one), having only one fire extinguisher (we have two), having five doors, when the Logbook states four (it was referring to the cylinders), etc. etc. etc. It was a game to start with but has become sinister, serious and very wearing, David bears the brunt of it. I have found getting out a chair, sitting on it and reading as if we have all the time in the world, sometimes helps. It is not specific to us (but we are targeted)—the poor locals are subjected to it, too. Knowing it is an accepted part of life in this part of Africa still doesn't stop the injustice of it and makes progress terminal.

Monrovia sprawls across a narrow peninsula, during the last two decades of war and civil unrest, of the many thousands of soldiers disarmed, almost half of these were children, children under fifteen years old. 'The Child Soldier,' unable to return to their villages, their families murdered, or displaced, live on the streets here in Monrovia.

Independent charities and the United Nations are working to support these boys and girls, with shelter and education. The high United Nations presence forces up hotel prices; as we're here for the Cote d'Ivoire Embassy, it's here we need to be.

At Hotel Metropolis, for forty dollars we get a musty, dark, damp broom cupboard of a room, Lizzybus parked on the street, we're assured will be safe, as they have three-armed security guards on duty at all times and it includes breakfast. As darkness descends, with nothing other than a small amount of local currency, go out to find food. Only husks of buildings remain, to realise anywhere with a blasting television, a few benches and tables built into their remains, is a café. Iron grills protect the cook, a small boy serves us a tiny plate of spaghetti with a meat sauce, followed by a creamy sweet and quite delicious bowl of oats, for a couple of Liberian dollars.

It's JJ Roberts' birthday today, an African American merchant who became Monrovia's governor after independence, it's celebrated with a Bank Holiday, processions and closed Embassies. We cannot move on until we get the visa for Cote d'Ivoire but being Friday, it will be Monday before we can apply. On the edge of panic with our deadline looming, decide to drive over to the embassy today, so we know exactly where it is for Monday.

The traffic is crawling, having the loudest horn in Africa is essential and blasting it continually is a must, leaving a constant ringing in our ears. We're forced into the gutter as police outriders clear the route for a cavalcade of white United Nations vehicles and blacked out vehicles with the flags of office on. I can't help wondering why they all drive virtually brand new, top-of-the-range vehicles and the United Nations headquarters is a large sprawling building, with roof, windows and immaculately laid out gardens, even fountains.

Tonight, back at our café, a ten-inch Father Christmas is on the table, its once glittering tinsel tarnished, an indication the vast majority of Liberians are Christians. Walking back to our hotel, we're tailed by young men, they appear from the shadows, the displaced child soldiers. On crossing the street, a young guy with no arms walks out to stop the traffic for us—a taxi knocks him down. Our instinct is to help but it's too dangerous, it's so distressing. We head back to the hotel.

We're on the move, it took three days but finally another page of our passport is filled with a wonderful visa. Stationary in the gridlock traffic, my arm resting out of the open window, a young guy strokes it with his stump asking for money. It's incredibly soft, like the skin of a newborn baby, his eyes so full of despair, this moment haunts me now and will forever more.

Finally, having made it out of the city our progress is good, seeing a Motel sign pull over to find Aaron and Nick, volunteer teachers working for the

American Peace Corps. Chatting to them over an ice-cold beer, they invite us to camp at the back of their house in the village. A tiny mud-built hut, with no mains electricity or water, they are provided with a generator but have run out of petrol. Although Lizzybus is diesel, we have petrol for our Coleman cooker, it feels good to be able to fill their generator. Over a bowl of spaghetti, made with my last tin of corned beef, the conversation turns to what they miss from home, mainly girlfriends. Each 'volunteer' period is three months, this is their second trip, the first was before having girlfriends and both agree it has made it much harder.

Before pushing on today, visit the school Aaron and Nick teach at; although financed by the government, most of its teachers are volunteers. A basic concrete block building of five classrooms with over forty students in each, you cannot move between the desks they're so tightly packed. Aaron & Nick have a two-foot square space at the front with a black board they have to stand sideways to write on. These boys and girls are eager to learn, they walk miles each day to attend school, their white shirts as dazzling as their smiles. Armed with our maps, it's wonderful showing them our route, talking about the countries we have passed through and those we are heading for, ending with a tour of Lizzybus.

In England, I had a complete set of vinyl credit card-sized flags made of all the countries we think or thought we might pass through; when entering each country we have the 'Flag sticking-on ceremony.' I also have a world map in silhouette on the door to mark out our route. They have become a visual triumph, a common language, as each flag has the name of the country written on it, we can cross-reference them to the world map. My daughter, working in the corporate world, had donated bagsful of merchandized pens, I give a handful to Aaron and Nick to distribute amongst the students. Like the rain after a drought, this is the tonic we both needed. The helpless despair I saw in my Boy Soldiers' eyes, replaced with hope in these students. Of all the people we have met and will meet on this journey, working for, or in aid of charities, we have found and will find the American Peace Corps, one of the very best.

Heading for the border at Danane, face a torturous bone shaking ripio road (gravel road). A well-maintained gravel road is far more acceptable than a broken pot holed tarmac road but they are never well maintained. The washboard ripples in the surface vibrate through every nut and bolt of Lizzybus. Go too fast, you fishtail and the rear wheels lose traction, go too slow and the vibrations take your fillings out. Along with thick dust, from us and other vehicles, it's torturous.

Ahead is a jack-knifed lorry on its side blocking the bridge over the river, its cargo, sacks of grain, spread out like a rice pudding. We're advised, even if the road is cleared, which could take days, the bridge is too dangerous to cross; seeing the long drop, huge rocks and river below, we know it's too risky. This leaves us no choice, other than to head back into Guinea (Conakry), the country I found so threatening. For some reason when David applied for the Guinea visa, he had opted for multiple entry, as it cost the same. I love David. Will we ever get to Ghana?

Leaving Liberia took longer than getting back into Guinea, which after the first time, felt relatively easy, I think I'm just getting immune to it all. The border into Cote d'Ivoire is only fifty kilometres away but with darkness settling around us, the road ahead being a potholed broken tarmac, pull over into the jungle to bush camp. Due to insect life, eat our dinner of boiled potatoes, carrots and a fried egg in the roof tent. Sweaty and stinking from the lack of any form of wash, utterly exhausted, leave the dirty plates at our feet and pass out.

Woken by a tapping, find we're in a small clearing where locals with hammers are busy making gravel. They look on incredulous as we go about our morning rituals of cleaning teeth, flannel washing and putting down the tent, before heading for the boarder.

Stamped out of Guinea, cross no-man's land to the Cote d'Ivoire boarder, immigration is a painted brick shelter, manned by two French women who do all the paperwork but it's an hour before the commandant arrives with his rubber stamp. Just as we're leaving the police call us over, asking "What is our mission?" When we say tourism, it's met with hostile disbelief, asking how it's funded. Being self-funded is not acceptable, they demand to know who we are working for. We consider making up something but it's hard enough for me to remember the truth, let alone a made-up story.

Next, customs (Douane): we were expecting a few searches and to be on our way but wedged into the back of Lizzybus is now the biggest, blackest, most intimidating soldier with his AK-47 (Avtomat Kalashnikov) taking us to the Military Commander. We are driving through a jungle swamp, constantly having to get out and re-build the road as the wooden poles balanced over crater-sized holes have been washed away or rotted. Our escort never offers to help, just sits inside Lizzybus watching. Poor Lizzybus groans through mile after mile of this swamp with the extra weight, I'm having an outer body experience, the only way I can keep the terror in the pit of my stomach from surfacing.

I take myself to a happy place. It's interesting, if not a little scary, that this happy place is my sister's bathroom, with a shower, flushing toilet and a door with a lock. The only indication there is life are the constant roadblocks (a rope over the road with plastic bags), fortunately with our on board man mountain escort, we are waved through them. I begin to think we are voluntarily driving ourselves to our own kidnapping, even if we are, there is very little we can do about it. David and I don't look at, or speak to, each other—actually, breathing is not a regular thing either.

Three hours of this torture, our ordeal is not over; exhausted, arrive at what we're told is Customs (Douane). Here, face hours of interrogation, together and separately on what "Our mission" is?

We admit, the "It just seemed like a good idea to drive around the world" explanation seems pretty lame, even to us. Then the searches of Lizzybus start, I couldn't care less what they take, my 'mission' is to stay as close to David as possible.

They tell us of the temporary cease-fire between the Government held territory in the South and the Rebel held territory in the North. We're not sure what side they're on but we're constantly asked to donate to their cause. Exhausted, I sit in the dirt, propped up against the tyre, head in my folded arms ignoring the lot of them, poor David is left to it. I think they realise we are who we say we are, apart from twelve dollars paid for our 'escort' everything, including the Carnet De Passage, is stamped and we are free to leave.

Cote d'Ivoire, its political capital Yamoussoukro, its economic capital Abidjan, were in the middle of the twenty ten, twenty eleven, Ivorian Crises, due to the first vote in ten years for president. This all makes sense now, our main concern now is carjacking, a real risk here. Feeling we've already been carjacked and survived, head off for Man, "la city des dix-huit montagnes" (city of eighteen mountains), supposedly the most beautiful location of any Ivorian town. It's a landscape stripped of forests, smouldering stumps fill the air with smoke, ash floats on the breeze. A broken city, devastated by years of conflict and neglect, mostly abandoned. We book into the only hotel still open, with secure parking, water, electricity and an included breakfast.

This morning, after our basic included breakfast of omelette, bread and coffee, we're charged sixteen dollars, more than the cost for the room, as they have our passports, we have to pay. David and I are exhausted, we really need to rest but with four hundred kilometres to Ghana, our final country, flights and storage to arrange, we have to push on. I have been keeping count of the amount of times we are being stopped, sixteen so far.

No longer go through the farcical process of showing documents, in their vain hope they can find some trumped up reason to fine us but immediately flash the West Midlands Police Crest. Assuming David is an officer of the law, they all, bar none, allow us to pass unhindered.

The main road is little more than a track, until, like a mirage before us, is a three-lane highway, leading to the Yamoussoukro Basilica (Our Lady of Peace) modelled on St. Peter's in Rome. At an estimated cost of three hundred million dollars, under the presidency of Houphouet-Boigny, you cannot deny its beauty and magnitude, or the complete lack of understanding to his country and its needs.

Arrive at Abidjan. When under French rule, the Vridi Canal was built, connecting it to the Atlantic, to become a major trading port. Like all port towns, in the suburbs are the dispossessed, beggars and street hawkers; at its centre, smart hotels, boutiques, with chic Ivorian ladies, click-clacking along in heels wafting of French perfume. To us, an industrial city, heavy with pollution, we find a cheap hotel to overnight.

We need cash, apart from Mauritania and the Guineas (Bissau-Conakry) we have been able to find cash machines, they are heavily guarded and access to them restricted. It's incredible, when putting our English bankcard in, it churns out wads of local currency, connecting us to our past. I always imagine it's the girl at my local bank, not a machine, I can even hear her telling me, "The weather's good today."

Back on the road, David asks if I have my phone? Shit, I tucked it into the pillowcase last night and that's exactly where it is. We just have to go back for it, passing the same checkpoints but on the opposite side of the road, with no pleasantries, flash the Crest and drive through. David got to the room first, to find the cleaner, who assures us there was no phone. I join him, on seeing the pile of laundry on the floor, rummage through it, to find tucked into it, the phone. I'm not sure if they genuinely had not found it, or if it was put with the laundry to take with them, it matters not, we have it, so give her a reward.

The landscape changes, huge logging lorries thunder past, clearing the way for Palm Tree plantations. Millions of acres of forest cleared for the production of palm oil, effecting local communities, wildlife, water supplies and inevitably climate change. Since being separated as a twin and put into the lower class, my education, based on that decision, was of cookery, needlework and art. To now begin to understand the world, it's like pouring water on a flower, I feel nourished, whilst resentful of the effect their decision had on my life. My mind can't soak up the information now it could have then, it's learnt to be lazy and uninterested, the bastards, I feel wronged.

Chapter 9
Falling at the Last Fence

After all the corrupt hostile checks endured throughout our time in Cote d'Ivoire, we leave unceremoniously and almost hassle free. Crossing no-man's land arriving at the border, Lizzybus is checked, rather than searched, all our documents, including the Carnet De Passage stamped without question. Ghana, about the size of the United Kingdom, English its main language—as West Africa's golden child, of course, it's all about comparison. So, compared to its neighbours, it's stable and prosperous, has miles of beautiful coast and ruined European forts. The significance of getting to Ghana is quite overwhelming but somehow, we made it.

David, the confirmed bachelor, never wanted children, will, by default, be writing the 'Father of the Bride speech.' It makes me smile, thinking back to when David first arrived on the scene, with my son Ricky flat sharing with friends, Adele and I were just Adele and I. I got Adele a Saturday job doing general office duties with me, including answering the phone. As there were two David's at the solicitors David worked at, David Turner and David Fisher, my David was D.T. the other D.S. Answering the phone at work Adele was most polite, at home, Adele would shout, "Mom E.T. is on the phone," as opposed to D.T. loud enough so he could hear. When he visited, she would sit between us, arms folded, or stomp off to her room.

That was until in the early hours of the morning at work, I got a call from Adele, she could hear someone in the back garden. A lone parent with a mortgage to pay I had to work, leaving Adele was always a worry. As coordinator for emergency call outs, I couldn't possibly leave work; knowing David was out at a local police station, I suggested him going over to check. Adele considered this for a minute, before agreeing, this for them was the turning point, the beginning of a friendship. The next day David bought her a 'Rolling Pin' to keep under the bed, I was not that impressed but it became a standing joke, one I'm sure will be in his speech.

We can't celebrate just yet, we still have to get to Accra, the capital, book flights and find secure parking for Lizzybus, a simple enough task, surely? Not wanting to be in Accra longer than needed, we follow the coast road to Green Turtle Lodge. Passing mile after mile of headless coconut trees with 'wilt disease' causing the crown to yellow, shrivel and drop off, they stand as decapitated skeletal stumps. A disaster for the local communities, these trees provide food, fuel, building material and income. Disease-resistant trees are being developed, to one day replace this very important crop for Ghanaian farmers.

At Green Turtle Lodge, owned by an English couple, built entirely of local material with solar power and composting toilets, we will rest. All things considered, Lizzybus has been holding up pretty well, David's vigilance in his maintenance, specifically the greasing, the reason. But, little things, like the inverter died two weeks ago, which we charge stuff with. Living through the journey is far easier than being family back home worrying about it, we don't have a satellite phone but a 'Synchronized Pre-deployment Operational Tracker' (SPOT). Sounds hard core but is pretty basic, something most travellers now have. SPOT uses GPS data to track you, it sends your location as an email through a satellite network, to family and friends.

You cannot make or receive calls on it but it has an emergency button, that if pressed sends a distress signal to a centralized centre, who in theory, set in motion a rescue mission. It's not permanently active, each evening we switch it on to send our position to the four nominated people via email. Seeing us moving is confirmation we're still alive, a small comfort, so it's essential we keep it charged.

At Takoradi, a deep-water port, the commercial centre traffic is at a standstill, as the central circular market areas huge mountain of refuse is being loaded onto lorries. The stench is nauseating, putrid liquid seeps from it into open drains. It's vital we get up-to-date information on flights and storing Lizzybus but failing to find any internet cafes, we go shopping. A few hours later, victorious, head back to Turtle Lodge with a crate of beer, bagsful of vegetables and a new inverter.

I know I am prone to the drama queen syndrome but being here writing this is a small Jayne miracle. Here on the Atlantic Ocean, the second largest and I might add, second most dangerous ocean in the world, we decide to take a swim but change that to a paddle, on seeing all the warning sign to watch out for 'Rip Currents.' A huge wave knocked us both off our feet, dragging us out to sea, surfacing I know I need to swim to shore but am gripped with terror and only manage an ineffective, useless form of doggie-paddle I learnt when I was ten. David, surfacing beside me, tells me not to panic and swim for shore. I wish he were closer; I could sucker myself to him and we could drown together. My attempts are futile as the shore gets ever further away, I become a dot in the vastness of ocean, that may I remind you, is the second most dangerous ocean in the world. I have a very calm feeling that my travels will end right here right now, until I hear someone screaming 'Help'—it's me!

David through the crashing waves orders me to shut up, stop panicking and swim. I momentarily consider this, to disregard it and scream louder, rewarded by the owner and the waiter on paddle boards heading to my rescue. Just seeing them calms me, giving back my ability to swim, make it unaided to shore. The humiliation, when all around are signs warning of rip currents, doesn't bother me one iota, I am not dead, I'm rescued and apart from a gallon of swallowed salt water, alive.

I am going to be a Chief Nanny, I say Chief Nanny as I'm already a Spare Nanny, to Jenny's two grandchildren but now I will be a Chief Nanny and she will be a Spare, take that Jenny! It's only taken my son and daughter-in-law ten years and me to be halfway around the world but finally I will have my first Grandchild. I thought this would really make me homesick but knowing I will be back in a few weeks with them has made it extra special.

Camped ten meters from the ocean, the humidity is a constant eighty percent, the 'Harmattan' wind blowing in from the Sahara brings a fine dust making it constantly hazy. I visit the kitchen ladies and ask about getting my hair re-plaited, last done in Senegal. Along the beach is a collection of huts making up the village, where I'm told is a woman who can "Do it." At eight the next morning, walk along the beach to the village, to be sat on a plastic chair surrounded by women and children. It's toe-curling embarrassing but I remind myself, at least it's only for hair plaiting, not for peeing.

Two hours later all the old plaits ripped out, apparently the price does not include re-plaiting, (exactly what happened in Senegal). I'm told to return tomorrow, with more money. Pissed off, walk back along the beach, looking just like Tina Turner on a bad hair day.

One of the hardest things of travelling like we do is not meeting other travellers but Turtle Lodge is a meeting place. A German couple arrive, journalists in a Nissan Patrol Car, having shipped their vehicle to Dakar, Senegal, will document their journey to South Africa for the twenty ten Football World Cup. I'm just relieved they don't want to film me with my Tina Turner afro frizz hair.

It's seven thirty, strolling along the beach munching my apple on the way to my hair appointment, I imagine sealed with a piss Gayle, at her Salon, sipping coffee, wrapped in clean, fluffy, white towels, with hot water, shampoo and conditioners. Five hours of torture later, interrupted only by breastfeeds, I'm shown my hairdresser's cracked bleeding nipples. I remember breastfeeding my son, the array of soothing creams I had—I give her my tub of Vaseline.

It poured down last night; Lizzybus leaks like a sieve, all the books in the passenger foot well are sodden, with the humidity everything is mouldy and stinks. With what look like magical blocks of yellow soap, the locals scrub children and clothes until they sparkle and I want some. With my block of magical African yellow soap, tackle the stinking pile of bed linen but what I failed to realise was a vital part of the soap's magic is hard graft. Pounding clothes on rocks, or scrubbing vigorously, for a very long time, is knackering. Once washed the locals lie them directly in the dirt to dry, how they don't end up as filthy as they started, I've no idea but they don't, I peg mine to a washing line strung between the trees. Preparing lunch is equally as exhausting, pounding cassava to a very sticky near solid glob, then building fires to prepare the peppery groundnut oil sauce. I'm far too knackered after all the washing to do this, buy a 'poo bag full' off the locals. We're expert now at forming the sticky globs of fufu into balls and scooping the sauce up. Camped out on the beach, pounding clothes over boulders, eating with our hands, sat in the village having my hair plaited, all feels so normal now.

A Dutch couple, on a three-month trip, are looking for someone to travel South with them through Angola. Years of civil war have left this country littered with unexploded mines, along with the corruption and security issues they don't want to go alone. It would be great to join them but for now it's not an option.

Sat on the beach in the morning sun, transfixed with the army of little sand crabs living in the swash zone, like an orchestrated symphony they appear from holes, to rise and fall with the tide. I put the butt of a roll up (knowing they will compost) in one of their holes, fascinated as it's turned into shredded paper and ejected, I'm sorry Mr Crab, I promise I won't do it again. The solar panel, with such overcast days, is not keeping the Lizzybus batteries charged, the new inverter squeals its alarm, like a runt of the litter piglet pushed away from the nipple. One thing that David can and does dwell over, constantly, are batteries, it becomes almost an obsession and the main topic of conversation.

Knowing we will make our deadline for the flight home, the urgency has gone, we relax through the days. At the end of the 'Harmattan' season, the first glimpse of an uninterrupted sun appears, allowing Lizzybus to dry out, the only danger we face now is from falling coconuts and dying palm heads. Strolling along the shore to the headland for a lunch of boiled egg sandwiches, we sit on smoothed weathered rocks forming a half moon, looking out to a nothingness of everything you want nothing to be.

The sun becomes fierce rising high above us, bathing naked in a crystal-clear rock pool, I try to avoid the sea urchins, treacherous to a bare arse. I plait fronds to make a hat to shade me from the midday sun, time evaporates. David, who hates seawater and sand when he can't wash it off, goes back to camp. Alone here in my rock pool, conjure up my very own man Friday, with me his Jayne Crusoe.

It's time to push on, the stop over at Turtle Lodge was exactly what we both needed, we're refreshed and ready for battle. Ghana has a far more relaxed feel, with good roads, as roadblocks are few and far between, begin to enjoy the drive. Heading for Accra and Kotoka, Ghana's biggest airport, spirits high as we dare to believe, we might actually complete 'our mission.' Along the way visit Cape Coast and Cape Coast Castle, the once capital, now a fishing town, with crumbling colonial buildings, haunted by the horrors of its past. My story is not a history lesson but a journey but as history effects it, I have to include it, this is my understanding of it.

Cape Coast Castle, built of wood by the Dutch for trade in timber and gold, expanded by the Swedes, changed hands five times, until captured by the British. During the two centuries of British occupation, it became headquarters for the colonial administration until Accra became the capital. A centre for 'trafficked slaves' captured from as far away as Niger and Burkina Faso, we're shown the dungeons, where shackled slaves awaited their fate, before walking through the huge ebony arched 'Gates of No Return' to waiting ships and a future life in slavery. It's been extensively restored and very white, I feel it stands defiant of its enforced past, in memory of all those who endured it. Stood on the smoothed foot-worn cobles outside the 'Gates of No return,' I no longer hear the droning voice of the guide but see the 'free' fishermen making a living from the very same ocean that took the incarcerated away never to return.

Leaving the coast, head inland to Kakum National Park and Hans Cottage Botel, built around a murky green pond full of crocodile. Book into one of the candy-striped beach huts, just like in the English seaside resort of Brighton, with a few crocs thrown in. At Kakum National Park, one of the last unspoilt lowland rainforests in Ghana, if you go early, from its cable walkway high above the forest floor, you can see elephants, colobus monkeys, antelope, many species of birds and varieties of butterflies. (David's pet hate).

That, of course, is if you're not on a guided tour but as it's the only option, herded to specific lookouts, with a squawking group of tourists, will and does, alert any animal of your arrival, we see jack shit. What is magnificent, is being in the canopy of the statuesque trees, their crowns flattening like lily pads on reaching the sun. Back at our Brighton Sea Hut it's party time, I join the locals in the pool. The four door-sized speakers blasting out music encourage bottoms to sway and hips to gyrate, which in turn produces a tidal wave. As for some reason Ghanaians seem unable to swim, they cling tightly to their bright orange life vests: I just loved it.

Last night, chatting to three middle-aged English guys with their African 'Girlfriends' wrapped around them, doing something with Palm Oil, agreed to winch their truck out but as there is no sign of them this morning we pack up and leave. Pushing on towards Accra at Winneba, a large town perched between two lagoons, now dried-up water holes, full of mosquitoes. It's Easter Sunday, along the dusty potholed road, from houses little more than shacks, families resplendent in traditional dress of cotton and silk, typically woven by men, Kente Cloth, are off to Church.

Booking into a room, on the bed is a small packet of complimentary Chocolate Chip Cookies, David tells me to make the most of them, as it's the nearest thing I'm going to get to chocolate. I miss my children utterly today, a day we would be boiling eggs in a rainbow of food dyes, writing little notes for the Easter Bunny, the family together tucking into roast chicken, laughter, conversation but most of all hugs.

What has been very special on this journey is getting to know my children through the written word. My son, writing every week, gives me an insight into the man he has become and soon the father he will be. Whenever I say, "I'm homesick, I'm missing you," they say "Mom, you said you were driving around the world! Now shut up and get on with it!"

It's their way of supporting me, giving me permission. It matters not, a student on a gap year, a parent or friend emigrating, or just moving away, it's a type of abandonment and edged with guilt. I know of many journeys delayed, or postponed due to family needs and opposition, until ill health, or the ultimate of death, destroyed the chance and the dream.

Finally arrive in Accra, to arrange flights but far more importantly, to find secure storage for Lizzybus. When leaving Lizzybus in the guarded, secure area in the Gambia, returning to find the slashed roof bag with most of the winter kit stolen, it's vital. I expected Accra to be in the middle of the country but it's on the Gulf of Guinea, part of the Atlantic Ocean. Here at 'Big Milly's,' something of an institution for travellers, I see its attraction, with concrete-built huts covered in thatch giving character and twenty-four-hour bar.

Although adjacent to the beach, it's set back, all cooling sea breeze, lost behind high walls. I see the warning signs, to not walk late at night along the beach with valuables, as my most valuable thing is David and he is not one to stroll along the beach at night, I'm good. As its mid-afternoon, figure we're safe, decide to go for a swim, what we find is a heaving pulsating gyrating mass of people, filling any and all available space, as far as the eye can see. It's Easter weekend and party time, the blasting music and laughter drowns out the ocean, an ocean as full of people as its beach. As soon as dusk descends, they disappear, replaced by an army of scavenging crabs, clawing their way over the mountains of discarded polystyrene food trays, plastic bags, empty gin pouches and human waste.

This morning another army arrives, this time of locals, digging massive trenches, to sweep this slick of garbage into. Accra, from the word Akan, meaning ants, specifically soldier ants, is a reference to all the anthills in the surrounding countryside. The city has its own form of anthills, in the concrete and glass self-important buildings and Universities. A few days ago, at our candy-striped hut, we met Naomi Ethiopian and Janik Danish with their two children, a diplomat working for the European Union. They offered to let us leave Lizzybus in the grounds of their house situated in the diplomatic area of the city.

Wanting to make sure Lizzybus will be safe and it's a genuine offer, today we are visiting them.

It's strange to be going into the diplomatic area, not in search of the Embassy of our next country, trying to secure ongoing visas but to meet someone we know.

Everything is pristine, lush green carpets of lawn sit below manicured hedges, sunlight shimmers like a thousand rainbows through fountains. First though we have to collect Janik from work at the European Union Delegation office. Janik jumps into the front seat of Lizzybus, followed by an intoxicating waft of aftershave and clean. David shuffles kit and the empty bottles we're trying to find a bin for, to sit in the back, I drive. I'm suddenly aware of our smell, baked earth and gear box oil, I'm willing David not to lift his arms, so as to not add stinking pit aroma.

Janik is everything I think of from a modern-day Norse Viking Warrior, he is tall, blond haired, blue eyed, he becomes my fantasy God. The imposing gates open to reveal a winding drive, cotton white villa, trampoline and swimming pool. Sitting in the shade on the veranda, being served tea in hand painted China cups, I try to conceal my broken dirty fingernails under the tiny handles. I remember the single China cup and saucer my mother drank tea from each morning, raising her pinkie with each sip, leaving a perfect bright red lipstick transfer upon its rim. Everything on this journey never ceases to amaze me, from peeing in the Kenyan bush with my audience, to sipping tea from China cups with my Viking God. Did I mention my English reserve? This truly is pushing it to its limit.

It's confirmed. Lizzybus will stay on the forecourt of the four-car garage, on the night we return they will let us, complete strangers, sleep in their home with them. I'm so relieved I can scrub and clean every inch of me at my sister's before arriving and drench myself in 'products' in a vain hope I will no longer smell of Africa. I've got such nervous anticipation in the pit of my stomach, it's no longer dread but excitement, as on the way back yesterday, we booked our flights for two weeks' time.

Between us we have lost over sixty pounds (twenty-seven kilo). This and, along with the heat, I'm beginning to have blackouts, moments in time I can't remember. With flights booked and safe storage for Lizzybus, decide to head to a campsite further up the coast. It's good to be back on the road, there are constant checks by military and police, for now, just checking documents. Until David driving, we're pulled over and shown a hand-held radar gun reading fifty-seven kilometres, in a fifty zone. David points to our speedometer reading miles, to be lectured at length on the differences between kilometres and miles.

Looking through our documents, seeing the West Midlands Crest, assume David is a comrade in law, the already written out ticket is torn up and we are waved on our way.

Arrive at Hideout Lodge, tucked down a rambling dirt track open to the sea with tree houses and mud huts. The water here is desalinated, a process similar to distillation, taking out all the minerals, even my magic soap won't froth up in it. I soak the clothes and bedding in the last of our biological powder, add a sterilising tablet and go for a walk whilst it does its own magic, minus any arduous scrubbing from me. The same treacherous rip currents are here, lurking beneath white crested waves, I have no intention of swimming, walk along the endless beach followed by a ragbag of delightful smiling children.

Mosquito life here is something else, despite all my precautions I'm constantly nursing golf ball-sized pulsating bites. Even David, who is their last choice, is being bitten but for him they're only little red, itchy for ten minutes, dots. David spends most of his time tinkering with Lizzybus, I accept and understand this but it's very isolating—the times he does join me, is at my insistence and this takes away its pleasure. Taking a walk along a beach to watch a sunset is not his thing. What he does do, is research and I know we will never miss anything of any interest and this makes up for it.

Today we are off over the rickety bleached bridge spanning the estuary of the River Butre to a spit of forested headland and old disused fort. Following the shore to the village, we pass the most magnificent trees spanning fifty feet in diameter, roots like coiled serpents anchor them to earth. The smell is stomach churning, a young girl squatting tells us it's the toilet area and pile after pile of human excrement confirms it. With the ruined remains of the fort in sight, we're engulfed by a thick blanket of moths brought out by the rains, rains that have turned red baked earth into a slithering, sliding, gelatinous snot, treacherous in my flip-flops reducing me to a snail's pace. I cannot stop laughing at David, with his T-Shirt pulled up over his head, using the armpits as eyeholes, protection from the moths.

Sitting here in the shade, restless to continue our journey, whilst excited by the prospect of a visit home. I'm reading a Ted Simon book, of a sixty-thousand-mile journey on a Triumph motor bike. David is also reading, his book, *The Music of the Primes*, a mesmerizing journey into the world of mathematics and its mysteries but of course it is. I look up to my life now, the ladies with children tied to their backs, large steel bowls effortlessly balanced on their heads, used for everything from washing, cooking, bathing children, carrying produce. Today overripe burnt yellow mangos, vivid green cassava leaves, plantain, peanut paste oil and tiny dried fish; children too big to be tied on backs trail behind carrying bunches of wood. Such a simple life and one we both are beginning to feel a part of.

Amanda American and Wills English arrive, doctors working in Ghana as part of their four-year training. David mentioned how he fancied surfing, something Wills wants to try. With loaned body boards, as stiff as Wills' abs, they hit the surf, in an ocean that is the second most dangerous in the world and David now wishing he had kept his mouth shut. Not long after, a half-drowned David appears, alongside a laughing Wills. Sat on the beach, under a kerosene lamp giving more black smoke than light, the words making up conversation kidnapped by the sea breeze, ends a magical day.

Surprisingly I was up first today, David eventually shuffled down the roof ladder, apparently the body boarding has left every one of his muscles complaining loudly. David and I might not read the same books or listen to the same music but we will and do, have a go at anything.

Surfing with a fit, toned, twenty-five-year-old is now off the list, just hysterical. It's not just his muscles that have suffered, David now has an ear infection and is taking a course of antibiotics. Living like we do, in such a confined space, everything we have becomes vital, as replacing it is near impossible. With the abuse our kit takes, the wear and tear, things are breaking, wearing out. The strap on my flip-flops, the zip on my rucksack, two spoons snapped, a cup cracked etc. But most importantly is the need to re-stock our medical kit, with anti-malaria Lariam tablets, antibiotics, bandages and my EpiPen.

We get news of an erupting volcano in Iceland, the resulting ash is grounding all fights in and around Europe and has been, for the last week. It's a crushing blow, having got Lizzybus through Guinea Bissau, Guinea Conakry, Sierra Leone, Liberia, Cote d'Ivoire and Ghana over one thousand kilometres, to fall at the last hurdle is unimaginable. The immediate concern is if Adele and James will get a flight to Vegas for the actual wedding but more importantly, get one back. It's announced the air space will be opened for twenty-four hours, mainly to get the planes back where they need to be and reunite the disengaged pilots to their planes. Adele and James are on a flight to Vegas.

From Hideout Lodge you can take a coastal path through the bush to the next village described as "A very pleasant walk but take care as several muggings have been reported, possibly take a guide." It's a beautiful walk, once over the rickety bridge spanning the river, you climb the cliffs to be rewarded with a spectacular view curling the eye in all directions, to jungle, to tin roofs, to blond sand and sea. As I'm lagging behind, due to being in land sandals which are rubbing my feet to blisters, David for some reason decides to hide.

I begin to panic, as I can't see him. I'm not sure whether to shout or go into stealth mode to keep my position secret. After the warnings of muggings and the need to take a guide, I imagine him lying dead in the bush. I semi jog to the end of the path and down the cliffs the other side. David had not seen me pass and thought I had gone back, hot, thirsty, with bleeding blistered feet, I go back. I don't know who is more upset, him or me.

Lizzybus needs new tyres, we are told of a contact Mark, a guy who travelled overland in a Defender four years ago to Ghana and never left. He doesn't have the tyres but invites us over to use his washing machine, shower, drink beer and eat. As I'm getting better at letting go of my English reserve, to try to accept hospitality and not squirm under its glare, we agree. At Mark's gated four-bedroom house, with housekeeper and twenty-four-hour security, we drink an iced beer before going over to see Mark's Land Rover. It's in a sorry state; unable to source fuel injectors, all work stopped on her months ago. Mark goes off to work, David with his set of fuel injectors from his 'spares' (knowing we can replace them) spent the afternoon with the mechanic fitting them and putting her back together. As the batteries had been kept on a trickle charge, she fired up a treat.

It's another one of the strange things about travel, your paths cross with a guy who needs the very thing you have. It's a way of giving back to the unconditional hospitality we receive and it feels good. Mark is just as fascinated to hear about our journey, as we are about his and, after a delicious meal cooked by the housekeeper, we look through all his old photos. Mark and David go to 'the pub,'

I luxuriate in the most amazing rain shower, before getting into a bed with crisp white bed linen, the cook washes up and the guard guards.

Today we're going into Accra to pick up the flight tickets waiting for us at the Travel Agents. David has been violently sick all morning, put it down to too much alcohol last night. I'm driving, when I look across to see him shaking uncontrollably. Putting my hand on his arm, despite the heat, I feel he is clammy and cold. Sitting in the shade, David holds his arm saying it feels numb. At these times, the enormity of where we are, of what we are doing, is utterly overwhelming. I just want to get him to hospital but I don't have a clue where it is. I take David's temperature, it's normal, he drinks water, we're now surrounded by concerned locals, who I feel are taking what little fresh air is about and stifling him.

David asks, "Why the hell does this have to happen to me now?" saying, "Do what you must Jayne but make sure I get on that flight!"

I wonder how you get a body onto a flight. I have visions of propping him up in a wheelchair in dark glasses, only to be discovered when they can't find a pulse. There's a desolation to this moment, a physical pain of helplessness, being sick is a luxury we don't have.

Back at Big Millie's for our last night, what should be a night of celebration, is clouded with worry for David and for the Icelandic ash, still causing havoc to flights. It's out of our control, all we can do is hope. The travel agent had assured us, priority is being given to passengers with tickets, not to the huge backlog of passengers whose, flights cancelled, were sleeping at the airports.

With Lizzybus secure and safe, I have another 'pinch me' moment, gliding along in the back of Janik's chauffeur driven limousine on Diplomatic Plates, straight to the main airport entrance. The chauffer jumping out, opens our door, before handing us our luggage, one tatty old rucksack. People stare, wondering who we are, I feel I should be giving them the royal wave. This is where the preferential treatment stops, inside its utter chaos, with people stranded for over a week trying to get new flights. I'm not sure how much more we can both take.

On our limited budget, David booked the cheapest flights which just happens to be Afriqiyah Airways, a state-owned airline based in Libya. Its revolutionary leader Gaddafi, took 'responsibility' for the Lockerbie bombing, killing all the passengers and crew on board. Abdelbaset al-Megrahi, convicted of this atrocity, who, having just been released on compassionate grounds, Gaddafi flew on his private jet to collect him. This, along with a plane crashing on its approach to

Tripoli airport last month, killing all on board, except a nine-year-old Dutch Boy, is all information David keeps from me, for now.

With the check in desk opened early, it was just a case of finding the end of the queue and holding firm our position. We're checked in, have boarding passes and better still, the plane is flying but we can't relax just yet, as it's not a direct flight, we have a transfer at Tripoli airport, Libya. What we find at Tripoli airport is utter chaos, a country that runs on corruption, even paid and booked for flights have and can be, sold on, fights break out and riot police are called in.

For pity's sake, I hadn't even flown until my late thirties and that was only to Spain, how the hell am I here, in Libya, in the middle of all this. We both start to panic, it's looking most likely we will miss our connecting flight and be stranded in Libya, with Lizzybus in Ghana, Adele in Vegas and our family in England. Our nerves are in tatters, after queuing for a further hour, at least get our boarding passes, it's a hollow victory, we know we have missed the flight anyway. With all hope gone, overwhelmed, I sit sobbing tears of frustration, exhaustion and defeatism. I think I'm hearing things, as over the Tannoy, an announcement is made, the flight has been delayed, it's still here, we can make it.

Against all the odds, we're here at Victoria Coach Station London. If they had even a tiny inkling as to what we have gone through to get here, they would applaud us but they haven't, so instead, they charge us five pounds each for missing our coach to Birmingham! Without further fuss or bother, we're put on a bus to an alternative depot, for the next available coach to Birmingham. David and I sit opened mouthed at the simplicity of this, to be looking out of the cleanest shiniest windows, to a life that was but is no longer; where at pedestrian crossings people wait, there are no beggars or people selling packs of matches or tissues, there are rubbish bins and children in prams.

You could say it's 'only been,' or it's 'already been,' over ten months since setting off on this journey but one thing is for sure, Africa has changed us physically and mentally, pushing us to the limits of our endurance and expectations. To a life we could never ever have imagined and things we didn't even know existed. In one day, one long stressful day, we're back to where it all started: Birmingham, England, forever changed but forever the same. Will we ever return?

Chapter 10
Where Is Home?

How different it is on leaving England, than from arriving a few short weeks ago, with only a single rucksack, faced then with cancelled flights, selling on of tickets and riots, to be standing here now, at Afriqiyah Airways check in desk in one orderly queue. As the baggage allowance is forty-eight kilos, plus ten carry on each, it occurs to me, it's almost the combined weight of me and my sister, I wish she was in my bag. The meter, by half meter, aluminium roof box (to replace our slashed roof bag) stuffed with Lizzybus spares, needs both of us to lift it, along with three, bought from the charity shop, tatty old suitcases.

I feel sure they won't let us check them in but looking around, know we have no worries, African's take half of England back with them. Trolleys loaded with televisions, food processors, microwaves, lamps, laptops, box after bag, after box. No designer suitcases but taped up blue and white plastic bags, I'm catapulted back to the life I left, children no longer lounging in pushchairs but strapped tightly to mothers' backs.

Waving goodbye to my sister, it takes everything I have to suppress the voice inside me, wanting to shout out, "I'm staying with you Jen," but my feet continue to shuffle forward. I'm secretly hoping they won't let us check in with all this stuff, to have an excuse to stay but they say nothing. I look back one last time, Jenny has gone, it's as painful for her, as it is for me.

I take with me the vision of my daughter, walking down the sweeping stairs of her now mother-in-law's house, her aqua blue eyes reflected in the bronze and ivory, shimmering in the sunlight, dress. In shoes that only her adoration of could ensure she kept on all day (plus the extra inches given to her petite stature), her husband James at her side. I felt the pride from my son at the prospect of fatherhood, the incoherent mumbles from my precious mother. Enjoyed barbeques with friends, evenings at the pictures, hot showers, the joy of language and a life that once again we knew all the rules of.

I think about when we first set off in Lizzybus, driving away on that typically English rainy day, with no fanfare, no big goodbyes and no idea what lay ahead, to now, knowing exactly what we're facing. What has not changed is, not knowing then and definitely not knowing now, what is making us do this? Other than this driving around the world malarkey, it's more like a chore, than a choice, a chore we just have to get on with.

Initially, the responsibility of a vehicle, Lizzybus to be exact, as opposed to just travelling with a backpack, was huge, it felt restrictive, rather than freeing. The fact neither of us, specifically me, had any off-road driving skills, nor any idea of how to get Lizzybus across borders, the constant fear of breakdowns, or worse, break-ins, made it impossible to relax or enjoy it. Slowly Lizzybus began to grow on us, with experience, came confidence, giving us the freedom to challenge us and her, in getting to the most remote, magical places. We're now in Ghana, halfway down the west coast of Africa, our goal for now is South Africa, the very bottom, twelve countries and almost eight thousand kilometres away.

Ghana, Togo, Benin, Nigeria, Cameroon, Gabon, Republic of Congo, Democratic Republic of the Congo, Angola, Namibia, Zambia, Botswana, South Africa, a rough plan, to be changed as and when dependent on the stability of the countries, availability of visas and surviving it and each other. I have not even heard of most of these countries, David has long since given up trying to educate me on them, as my brain would implode at the enormity of it all. We all cope in different ways, too much information or advanced warning of what I face is a definite 'no' for me.

I'm thinking of the first time I saw the film Born Free, based on Elsa, an orphaned lion cub released back into the Kenyan wilderness. Watching it with my sister at our local cinema in glorious technicolour, I was transfixed, not just by the roar of the lions but the magnitude and beauty of the country and the look and sound of the vehicle they were in, a Land Rover Defender. Kenya is where it was filmed, and although Kenya will be a country we should pass through after South Africa, its wildlife and plains are very similar to those of Namibia. I have every intention of driving through it with this vision in my head singing my heart out to the theme tune from Born Free.

David and I are on the same but such very different journeys, the most important person in David's life is me and I'm with him. He is used to not seeing the seniors (his parents) as for the last ten years they have been driving around North America in a huge motor-home towing a little car, now having bought a park model, are holed up in Mesa, Arizona. For me, family, specifically Jenny, have been a huge part of my life, I've felt overwhelming loneliness and isolation, particularly around Christmas, Easter and birthdays, family times, on these occasions I miss them all terribly.

Of the few short weeks back in England I realised, us and our journey, with no real understanding of its reality and what we actually faced, was given the polite amount of time and interest, before focus was back on weather, work and the daily slog. A stark reality check of our life as it was and our life as it is now. We no longer knew the price of bread, last week's traffic chaos, the freak snowstorm, royal divorces, gaffs made by hapless politicians, or the must-have latest tech gadgets, felt alienated, off-kilter, askew.

I don't journey through life, it's captured in the moment, until the shutter closes moving me from one picture to the next. As Janik came personally to pick us up from the airport, my resolve to accept hospitality with the hand it is offered failed immediately, when trying to force the alarming amount of luggage into his very shiny vehicle. Having spent the night in their beautiful home, we're back sitting on the veranda sipping tea from China cups, only this time I can hold my very nice, clean, manicured little pinkie proud. The shutter closed firmly on the last few weeks in England, of life that was, to the life that now is.

The noise from the tropical rainstorm makes for a shouted conversation, whilst watching, me fascinated, David repulsed, thousands of moths, emerging from the lawn, take flight. Not the small sugary dust coated winged variety, found amongst musty clothes locked away in the cupboard over winter but the long bodied translucent double winged variety, more likely to be seen hovering over stagnant ponds. A phenomenon, we're told, that happens after heavy rain, the moths take flight to avoid drowning. David just wishes every last one would.

Wanting to push on and not prolong the agony of this hospitality longer than necessary, wedge the enormous amount of luggage into Lizzybus, who fires up first time to head back to Big Millie's, as a base for sorting ongoing visas and getting the new tyres we failed to get before leaving. It's a relief to have Ecowas Brown Card Insurance, covering fourteen West African countries but we know it's a paper exercise only, as any accident here in Africa will be our fault by association and claiming on it would be nigh on impossible.

Ghana being tropical pours rain upon us, with Lizzybus leaking both oil and water opt for a room, into which we pile the mountain of much needed equipment, all we have to do now, is fit it. David starts with the 'lightweight' aluminium roof box (that weighs a ton), I take out the Engel Fridge to fit the insulating cover. Not yet acclimatized to the oppressive heat and humidity, dizzy with all this physical labour, sit in the shade.

David is a different man, back where he feels he belongs, to the life he, we, made happen, wants to get on with it and get moving. It's such a change in him, from the first few months when trying to adjust to no salary, no focus and the most difficult, no respect, in and for the job he did.

I watch, as like a man possessed, he fits the cooker housing, made for us by our engineering friend Andre in England, drilling out old pop rivets, removing the backwash wipe motor, fitting hinged arms, locking devises and a metal plate. All this so we can store the cooker off the back door, freeing up internal space. It's amazing what a difference it makes. Continuing as the sun sets, replacing the wing mirrors, drilling out old, rusted screws, until darkness and mosquitoes force a stop. It's a side to David I have not witnessed and one I think I quite like but it comes with consequences, every tool will be used, covered in grease and left exactly where it lies.

For now, I figure it's a trade-off, as I'm better at cleaning and organising anyway. Eating a takeaway from the local ladies in our room, shrink wrapped bags are stacked in the corner like alien pods awaiting birth. I thought I was at peace with the importance of spare parts but the amount of them makes me panic, how the hell will they all fit in.

I'm incredibly irritable as two-day old washing hangs lank on the line, I'm covered in mosquito bites, our clothes cut in and chafe every time we bend, clinging to us with a mixture of sweat and rain. I know all this stuff and us, will not fit into Lizzybus, my home, I question this driving around the world fiasco, as not being the incredible liberating adventure, it might seem. It's true, you don't need designer shoes and handbags, a twelve-piece matching dinner service, or fitted kitchen but you do need shoes, plates to eat off, a knife and fork, a bowl to wash up in, toiletries, a towel and it has to go somewhere. That of course is just for us, Lizzybus and her tools, spares, oils, are a whole lot of other.

Forget all about it and address the more important issue of getting a Nigerian visa, it's not our next country but three countries away, however the visa can only be got here at the Nigerian Embassy.

Driving to Accra, the familiarity of it feels comforting; at the few remaining working traffic lights, bodies are draped with every conceivable item, car accessories, plumbing, electrical, food, clothes and of course the Ghanaian football kit, as the World Cup will soon be underway in South Africa. First, we need photocopies of all our documents, in gridlock traffic, wedge between overloaded tuk-tuks and lorries, think we see a sign for a photocopiers but it's hard to make out, as the rain digests the black clouds of emissions, making a hazy grey fog. It's on the opposite side of the road, I remember I'm in Africa, so cut across the five lanes of traffic, on the two-lane highway, whilst the traffic threads its way around us: it's so good to be back.

At the Nigerian Embassy buried down a back street we're dog tagged, and our phone confiscated, to be told the only person who might be able to accept the application is not available. It's gone thirteen hundred hours, the embassy closes at two hundred, twenty minutes later a man arrives who can accept our application. He insists we need a letter of introduction (LOI) confirming our status and purpose of the visit, not wanting to insult his understanding of his own system, suggest the 'Single Entry Transit Visa' we require does not need a letter of introduction.

Grudgingly he accepts this, along with the one hundred and thirty dollars each fee, instructing us to return in two days. Still hurting after the wrench from home I distract myself dancing with the children in the turgid pools of water in camp, trying not to think of what else it might contain.

Leslie arrives with her eleven-year-old son Tom. Leslie is a midwife who worked in Ghana twenty years ago—larger than life, vibrant, opinionated and just what I need. The hospital she now works at back in England are updating equipment to conform with European Union regulations, making the twenty, almost brand new, digital baby scales obsolete. Through fundraising and her own money, Leslie is here to donate them to local hospitals, having donated the bulk to the hospital she worked at, today the remainder will be donated to the local village clinic and I am taking her.

Lizzybus slips and slides her way down almost impassable forest tracks, until we reach a whitewashed building funded by the government and charities, the local community clinic. Not just for the delivery of babies but for everything, including malaria and aids. At its entrance, two old but immaculate Honda motorcycles, used to take the doctor and midwife to patients too sick, or unable to get to the clinic. As there are no 'live' deliveries (ladies ready to give birth) today, we're shown around the wards. It's not exactly big, with the women's and men's ward having four beds in each, a delivery room and double bed recovery room. I donate a tub of multivitamins and sachets of re-hydration salts, which diluted with clean water can be as effective as an intravenous drip. I can't help questioning how useful digital baby scales are, when batteries are scarce and expensive, even though Leslie has bought spares. I'm sure any African midwife dangling a baby by its feet could tell you to the last ounce the baby's weight.

Driving back to the Nigerian Embassy, having taken out all the mats, which have been dumped in the room next to the alien pods, I put my feet on the dash to avoid the sloshing water in the foot-wells. The main road is a rutted mud river, littered with broken down or just stuck vehicles, I forget about my wet feet on seeing the poor buggers, bent double against the torrential rains, trying to sell their stuff. It's thrilling to have another page of our passports with its impressive Nigerian visa, it marks the start of this journey again, into the familiar of the unknown, just the Togolese visa to get, as the Benin one we can get on the border.

We know exactly where the Togolese Embassy is, as its opposite where we picked Janik up from work a few weeks ago. Our applications, we're told, need photocopying but they have no photocopier, it's a relief when they say, don't worry just complete two forms, they will sign and stamp them both. Handing them back along with the thirty-dollar fee, say they will be ready later today, we not only can't but don't believe it.

It's time to sort out new tyres, at a garage recommended by Mark, get five beautiful, wonderful brand-new BF Goodrich Mud-Terrains. The problem is they only sell them, they don't fit them, with the tyres now tied to the roof rack head off to a garage that can. On the way pass the Togolese embassy, call in to see if our visas are ready, to be totally amazed they are! A few hours later, Lizzybus not only has her tyres fitted but as we paid extra, they all have new valves. Spirits high, I'm no longer bothered by the slopping foot-well water, the crappy Lizzybus wiper blades, with the Nigerian and Togolese visa, new tyres, the adventure is about to begin again—Africa, we're back!

One last thing to do before we leave is getting my matted hair re-plaited at the 'Salon,' a square wooden shed, little more than the garden shed allotment owners drink tea and store used plant pots in. Once again, it's ripped out, for another two dollars washed in hot water, before I'm sent away to return tomorrow to have it re-plaited. The World Cup has started, tonight England play America; at a local bar, sat on damp cushions harder than the concrete seat they cover, surrounded by locals with magnificent colourful knitted woollen hats containing their dreads, no way near as impressive as my 'fro. The atmosphere is electric, everyone is rooting for the English: it ends in a one-all draw.

Sat back on my plastic chair at the hair 'Salon' a fuzzy portable television blasts out in the corner, today Ghana play Serbia, children sit crossed legged on the floor, women spew outside. As the Ghanaian national anthem plays everyone stands placing a hand on their heart to sing, I follow suit, lip-synching and humming. In one of the two 'client' chairs, each time another 'client' comes in, I get left whilst she is attended to. It goes to penalties, Ghana win, there is a roar, not just here in my salon but throughout the village, the village we are all now running around with my half head of plaited hair, half afro frizz. We're hollering and hooting in joyous celebrations, high fiving each other, defend by blasting horns and ear-splitting whistles, just wonderful.

Something strange is happening, there is a reluctance from us both to get moving, we keep finding more excuses to stay put, we have been in this room almost two weeks. I decide I want to re-wash all the bed linen, that was washed before leaving. Opening the roof tent we're covered in confetti, unlike at a wedding of scented rose petals but shredded tent and mouse droppings. Mice have been living in it, gnawing a hole we can see sunlight through. It's a blow. I feel overwhelmed, almost contaminated by vermin, I want to be back in my vermin-free home, I want my washing machine and hot water, even my vacuum and vast array of cleaning products, to keep me and my home insect and vermin free.

We move out of the room and back into the vermin infested mouse eaten roof ten. I get an email—Jane, a close friend to me and my sister, at fifty-two, our age, had a heart attack and died in her sleep. I want to be with my sister, give her strength, support her, Band-Aid the crack through her heart more painful than any physical injury. Since 'abandoning' Jenny, Jane became her buddy, her confidant, her best friend. It's in moments like this I feel so very far away. My night into day is obscured by this sense of loss, at breakfast we're joined by Deborah and Tazmin, two English girls working for the BBC, not wanting or able to share my loss, it's good to hear of them and their journey, it's just the tonic I need.

'Big Milly' joins us, a slightly built, softly spoken very English lady, six children, a giant of a Rastafarian man and a Ghanaian woman. Milly introduces the man as her husband and the children as her children, born to her Rastafarian husband by the woman, the children's 'baby mother.' Milly, having lived in Africa most of her life, did not have any of the reservations to this idea, let's say, most western women would, not wanting to be pregnant but wanting children, this made perfect sense.

David, for the last two days, has symptoms similar to Giardia being next to a toilet, or actually sitting on one all day is preferable. The doctor at the clinic confirms this, prescribing a course of Metronidazole antibiotics to kill off any possible Lamblice parasites. Anyone who has any thoughts, ideas, or dreams, on how romantic or passionate life would be travelling the world sleeping in a roof tent, I can assure you you're wrong.

Passion is ignited from fresh laundered crisp white cotton bed linen, showers or baths scattered with rose petals floating on a raft of bubbles, not mice droppings and parasitic men, greasy sweaty, with excessive gas farts, eggy sulphur burps, or the prospect you might catch worms. Okay harsh, I'll change worms to parasites but either word or way, romance, or sex of any description, is a thing of the past and likely to continue that way for the foreseeable future.

Camp is filling up: James, an American heavily tattooed guy here working in soil, Margaret a trainee doctor on her way home and Sue an American aid worker with a kitten living in the money pouch strung around her neck. Neither David nor I are real football fans but to be here in Africa in the middle of the World Cup, you just get swept up in it. Feeling connected and part of something, tonight, we all sit together to watch England secure a win against Croatia and Ghana, despite losing to Germany, qualifying for the next round. A very special evening, which for some reason feels like an end; we're ready, tomorrow we're leaving. Togo, we're on our way.

Chapter 11
Readjusting to Life Now

As the reality of sitting in a Lizzybus two foot from David every day for the rest of eternity, joyous as that thought is, finally dawns, I see it not as endless wanderings but with a real purpose, our 'mission.' With no actual time or date for finishing, being governed by the visas is good, as it keeps us moving along. I'm constantly told how lucky I am—luck for me would be buying a lottery ticket and winning. This took years of grafting, guts, balls and determination, hinging on insanity, stepping off the edge of everything we had, thought we wanted, into the abyss of an unknown.

We're meeting many people, travelling alone, originally having set off with a friend, a lover, a husband, wife, partner, etc. found spending each and every minute, of each and every day together, exposed irritating habits, a clash of expectations, to reveal a person they didn't recognise, one they actually didn't like. As these journeys are often a once in a lifetime thing, it's a crushing blow, turning the dream into the nightmare. Having survived over ten months together and still be talking, feels pretty good. With David doing all the planning, I know he will and does find the most adventurous, the most challenging route, I'm the yin to his yang, going with the flow, which works well, for now.

I've begun to find comfort in letting my mind settle where it wants, entertaining itself, pacified by the music of the engine, knowing it's taking us to places we want to be. This as David, not exactly won't let me but prefers not to, have the radio on whilst driving, so he can listen to the Lizzybus engine for any rogue noises. I can assure you, a Lizzybus engine can be heard way above any radio but I grudgingly comply.

We're heading inland to the Southeast Volta Region and the Akosombo (Volta) Dam at Lake Volta, the largest man-made lake in the world by surface area. A hydroelectric project once providing all the electric for Ghanaians but with the growth in the economy and falling water levels, demand has outstripped capacity. It takes a while to relax into being back on the road, sixty tough kilometres later of washed-out mud tracks, call it a day to book a room at Lakeside View. An impressive seventies two-storey balconied building, approached via a tree lined drive, manicured gardens and gazebos. I realise how I'm changing, as I do the negotiating, congratulating them on Ghana getting through to the next round of the World Cup, how much we love Ghana, got her down to half.

Being so tropical, most buildings suffer from mould, as does this huge room with communal bathroom, still, at five dollars, its only guests, it will do. David with his dickey tummy does not want to eat from the fridge, I heat up the remains of rice and beans bought off the beach ladies yesterday. If I didn't know then, I do now, how dangerous re-heated rice is and the deadly toxins from Bacillus Cereus spores. I've been poisoned, my body recognising this evacuates from all orifices, just like a horror movie, with the body of the devil spewing out. Sat on the toilet, the force of diarrhoea made a tidal wave back out the pan, projectile vomit ricochets off the door. David finds me, lying in the foetus position, in the stained yellow shower tray sobbing.

David now driver and navigator, my lolling head rocks between window and seat belt, eyelids heavier than a brick, I know it's bad I am not even smoking! The scenery changes ravaged by man, occasional single magnificent rainforest trees stand defiant and majestic, we start to climb. At Akosombo, the hillside settlement for the migrated labour force for the dam, sold off to developers, now palatial houses sit behind high walls, topped with barbed wire and shards of glass. To visit the dam, arrangements need to be made at the tourist office. I'm so weak, it's all I can do to sit upright, forget it and press onto Hohoe.

The reason for going to Hohoe, are the Wli falls, at a spotless German-run campsite nestled in the woods, I sit in Lizzybus whilst David sets up camp, as soon as the roof tent is erect, I crawl into it and sleep until the next day. Being poisoned doesn't stop after sickness and diarrhoea ends, it effects all of your limbs, muscles, eyes and head for many days after.

Over breakfast we chat to four English trainee doctors on a six-week placement at the local hospital, agreeing to hike together to the Wli falls. I'm still washed out and lethargic but no way am I being left out, eat a banana and grit my teeth. Making it to the fall and plunge pool, to be rewarded by an intricate laced doily hanging of alga, highlighted by shafts of sunlight and thousands of roosting bats. A blasting cold wind chills me to the core; exhausted, I can only sit and watch them swim out to face the full force of its tumbling power. Also, having long ago given up wearing any form of underwear, as it only forms another layer to rot and chafe, either swim fully clothed, or naked, neither seems enticing.

I reminisce to the time my schoolmates stripped off for gym lessons, revealing tiny-weenie much coveted pretty lace bras. As Jen and I still wore vests, we pleaded to have bras my ever-resourceful mother took us, not to the local boutique but the x-army and navy store. We ended up with military spec 'bolder holders' you could perform armed warfare in and your breasts would not move an inch. That was always assuming you had breasts, which we didn't, so we stuffed them with socks. I realise now how fortunate I am, able to let what I haven't got swing braless and couldn't care less about their pretty laced pink ones.

I can't believe we are so close to the Togolese border tonight, as Ghana play America, with our trainee doctor friends actually walk to it. The border, places that cause us so much worry and misery, where now here sitting with Police, Customs and Military, from both Ghana and Togo, watching a fuzzy little television. I gain a whole other respect for football, in its bringing together of people and as Ghana win two-nil, it's a night of celebration. Walking back to camp, dancing and hollering in our little group, have such a feeling of belonging, very special.

Yesterday took its toll, unable to face breakfast, our trainee doctors leave, I crawl back into the tent and sleep. David manages to wake me; we're going back to the border for the England verses Germany match. It's a very different scene, with only two women there, as everyone else is apparently sleeping off last night's victory. Germany win, deflated we walk back to our German-run campsite and grudgingly congratulate the Germans.

Today the journey starts again for real as we cross into Togo, a French speaking comb-shaped slither of a country, less than half the size of England. It's strange, having spent an evening and afternoon at it, watching football, it's like leaving friends. Our documents are stamped without question or searches, we're wished good luck and waved on our way into no-man's land. At the Togolese boarder, you would think, as it's the same two women we watched football with yesterday, the process would be simple. First, we need to wait for the Commandant abreast his Honda with his rubber stamp, only then can the painstakingly slow process of recording our details, in the huge worn ledger begin.

Although our documents are stamped, they need another stamp, which we get in the next village.

A few kilometres later arrive at a collection of wooden huts, it's only the fact they are leaning on each other that they're upright. This is both workplace and home to the guards, inside is a desk, in the corners two beds draped with mosquito nets, a pallet-built table has personal items, like soap and razors on it. Even a pen is a luxury. An hour later the same information recorded by our ladies, is written out again but into their dog-eared ledger, we donate a few pens without even being asked. Once again, we're in a French speaking country, David struggles with his schoolboy French, the flag sticking on ceremony is complete, we're waved on our way—hello Togo and life back on the road.

It's a steep climb that annoyingly produces the same clutch slip that haunts us, lush undergrowth dotted with traditional abode mud brick homes, its occupants holler and hoot greetings as we pass by. Dropping back to the coastline at Chez Alice campsite with rooms or pitches, run by a middle aged miserable German man. On seeing the campsite, basically the car park used to defecate in by all their dogs and cats, we book a room, with an adjacent open-air shower. It's hysterical, David naked, filling the bowl with water from a standpipe, uses a little plastic bucket to pour water over him. It's the first time in ages I have seen him naked, I am shocked by how much weight he has lost.

The ballroom sized, reed-covered communal room is impressive, with carved elephant-shaped chairs, floor-to-ceiling twisted trunks of once living trees frozen in time, with animals and men carved into them. Today is the funeral of Jane, who leaves her childhood sweetheart husband, children, grandchildren and many, many friends, to each miss her in their own personal and shared way.

To distract me, we decide to visit Akodessawa Fetish Market, in my subconscious I associate it only to voodoo dolls you stick pins in, black witchcraft, perverse sexual preferences and sacrifice. Skulls of everything sit with skins of everything, endangered or not, along with lotions and potions of unknown origin. Tables groan with flagellation equipment, facial masks and restraints, I can't help feeling a little disturbed by it all.

Taking a walk along the beach, locals shovel, sieve and stack, into neat piles, shells to be loaded onto wooden carts; these heavy wooden carts, with totally flat tyres, are dragged to the waiting trucks. I just wish we were in Lizzybus, so we could inflate the tyres for them with her on-board compressor.

As I collect the washing in the early morning sun, I'm watched over by two tiny chained-at-the-waist monkeys with the most soulful eyes, at the wrong done to them. I convince myself that this wrong was done before any right was known.

It's the weirdest thing, we're already at the Benin border, the visa we were told would be available is not. It's not a complete disaster as Togo is such a tiny country, the Benin consulate in the capital Lomé, is only a twenty-minute drive away. The problem is, the only road to and from it passes the port and is blocked by moving trucks but mainly broken down abandoned stationary ones, it's gridlock at all times of day.

By the time we get to the embassy, we have twenty minutes before it shuts for lunch, completing the forms with five minutes to spare makes no difference as the cashier, the only person who can take the fee, has already gone to lunch and won't be back for two hours. Africa and its rhythm has got to us, this does not bother us one bit, it's what we have come to expect, Inshalla. Two days ago, we met Olly, a quietly spoken English guy serving on Mercy, a ship docked at Lomé. This ship travels the continent with a cargo of twenty Land Rovers and volunteer doctors and nurses, performing life-changing operations, such as cataract, cleft lips and other debilitating conditions. We want to visit it.

Olly left us the details of the Seaman Mission hotel, where he and the volunteers are based. A two-storey concrete block building adjacent to a very pea green swimming pool. Disappointingly, Olly and all the volunteers are all out, the contact number he gave us just rings out, so spend an hour being thrashed at table tennis by the local children. Back at the embassy, the cashier finally arrives, pay the twelve-dollar fee, to be told it will be issued tomorrow. Which also happens to be Friday, the day large scale protests are planned against government petrol price fixing. Olly had mentioned this, telling us to stay put as it could get messy, resign ourselves to the fact it will be Monday before we can collect them.

As there is no imperative to be somewhere for a certain date, look on it as a weekend break, in Lizzybus head for the beach, to pump the flat tyres up on the carts loaded with sieved seashells. Checking back in the room we had just checked out of, get a phone call from Yvonne the Embassy receptionist, saying the visa is ready today. The high commissionaire and his daughter, having heard of our journey, had processed it personally for us.

Did I mention my English reserve, well it also covers one's exaggerated importance. From behind a huge desk, the commissioner, resplendent in full uniform, his daughter at his side, offers us coffee or a soft drink. I shuffle in my chair uncomfortably, in our Embassy outfits, the white shirts, despite being kept in a plastic bag, tinged pink from red earth, once black trousers, a faded dull grey, hanging off our hips. My afro frizz hair, at least, is in neat plaits from my recent visit to the Ghanaian hair salon, David has a full beard of steel grey. I have intoxicating wafts of cologne and see painted manicured nails, with matching lipstick.

But how we're dressed is so irrelevant, I don't even have to be clever, or intelligent, which is a good job, as I'm not, I just have to talk all about our journey and what we have faced driving to Togo, from England, alone, just the two of us. And I love to talk! It was like a revelation to me, I even felt a little pride in us both, at having made it this far and when I said we are driving around the "Whole World," I said it with a conviction I had never really felt before but now, truly believed.

The idea to spend a few days at Lake Togo is dismissed, having been stationary for so long in Ghana, we just want to get back out on the road and unanimously decide to cross into Benin today. Back on the only road, realise the graveyard of broken-down trucks, draped in sun bleached shredded sheets of tarpaulin, have become homes to whole families. Following the taxis, weave in and around them to reach the border post at Hila-Condji. Getting stamped out of Togo is simple, the no-man's land is lined with stalls, on top of them are overripe avocado, mango, bright green potatoes, peanut oil, fish, chicken and flies, underneath families in makeshift homes.

Benin, another French speaking country, a friendly and welcoming country, petty theft and scams are to be watched out for. The border crossing was good, with the customs officer's stick another flag on Lizzybus. The world has shrunk, we cross a whole country in half a day, to arrive at Awale Plage, a Pirate-themed resort, before even the sun has set. Tomorrow, we cross into Nigeria.

I'm not sure how I'm feeling about Nigeria, as the most populated country in Africa it has a history of military coups, civil wars, terrorism and violence. Corruption is systemic, security is dire, infrastructure non-existent. We decide to cross at Porta Nova border, to avoid driving through the reportedly dangerous city of Lagos, arriving at thirteen hundred hours, feeling very on edge and vulnerable.

Once stamped out of Benin there seems to be no no-man's land, you fall straight into a two-storey concrete building, full of military and police, all wearing dark shades. Just inside is a very high bench desk running the length of the room, manned, surprisingly, by women. They laboriously look through all our documents before taking us into the main body of the building. A single hanging light bulb illuminates its middle, the collection of desks around it are in semi darkness, to the back I make out cages, inside men sit on the floor, who I presume are prisoners. I'm ordered to go with the two guys who will search Lizzybus, David is taken off for interview.

Out in the blistering heat, I'm told to put up and take down the roof tent twice, each time they search it and Lizzybus. With the physical effort and heat, having eaten only a banana for breakfast, I'm feeling dizzy and lightheaded. Back in the building no one seems to know where David is, I'm overwhelmed and scared, remembering the bag of disposable lighters with built in torch I brought back from England, decide to beguile them with 'gifts.' It's important not to give money, although bribery is not a crime just an accepted fact but once you give money, it's a point of no return, everyone will need paying.

It works, David appears, I can see he is shaken, he is giving me the look, to just get out of here. I don't need to see it twice, saying nothing just head for the door. It's taken over five hours to get through this ordeal, I know it's bad as even David is shaken by it all, both incredibly relieved everything that needed stamping had been stamped. It would seem that once again, only David's alter ego got us through.

But this is only the beginning, Nigeria is a very different country and not in a good way, every few kilometres we face intimidating roadblocks, I really don't know how we would have got through it without Police Constable Turner. Dusk is settling around us, it's dangerous to be out on the road after dark, at the last roadblock we ask where the nearest safe hotel is, to be directed to a 'Very fine hotel.' A derelict building, the entrance barricaded and locked, back on the main road, see and follow a sign for a hotel, find it behind ten-foot-high concrete walls, topped with razor wire. I'm thinking at least it will be safe for Lizzybus.

Understanding the need to negotiate hard, doesn't mean we do, settle far too easily on a price, just relieved to have got through a shit day and at being able to park Lizzybus right in front of the door and of it supposedly including evening meal and breakfast.

Of the four plastic tables making up the restaurant, sit at the only empty one, to realise the others are occupied by the same police and military guys who manned the last two roadblocks. Without any invite they drag their chairs over to our table, propping their Kalashnikovs against the wall and proceed to tell us they are three beers into the ten they consume each night.

We're served some sort of meat stew with okra, after only a banana each all day, it's just good to get food in us. From the shadows appears a traditionally dressed middle-aged man, he insists on buying us a beer and paying our food bill. We give up trying to explain it was included in the room price and donate a West Midlands Police patch.

David and I have touched on the subject of flight or fight moments, both agree it will always be flight, as fight for us inevitably could mean death. I wanted a covert signal between us to synchronize our flight, settled on raising one eyebrow. I'll admit it's not a failsafe plan, have you ever tried raising just one eyebrow? It's a skill, an art, one that took me many hours in front of a mirror to perfect and one David gave up on after the first attempt.

The neatly stacked Kalashnikovs alarmingly now lie in disarray amongst broken glass and spilt beer, our loud animated and wildly gesticulating dinner guests are on the ninth of their ten beers, I raise my eyebrow to David saying, "I need the toilet!" He follows.

Back in the room, lock it and leaning my back against it, slide down holding my head in my hands sobbing. This is such a low point; I'm feeling scared, vulnerable and overwhelmed, right now if there was a fairy godmother and she was to grant me a wish, it would be to transport me back to a life I felt safe in, away from all this chaos.

David makes the morning coffee off the back of Lizzybus, it's eerily quiet, with no sign of breakfast share a handful of dried apricots. Wonder how we will get out as the gate is chained and padlocked, to notice the sleeping security guard in his hut. Shaken into consciousness, he opens the padlock and removes the chains, with trepidation for the day ahead we leave. We're heading for the capital Abuja, six hundred kilometres away, to get visas for Angola: it's not our next country, in fact, it's five countries away but Nigeria has an Angolan Consulate.

Mercifully today, clouds billow above heavy with rain, keeping the full searing glare of sun off us. On the gridlocked broken tarmac highway, huge crater sized holes bleed with African red soil. Overloaded trucks, cars, motor bikes, tuk-tuks, belch out black toxic emissions, it's impossible to pass, we're almost at a standstill. This with the frequent roadblocks, where every document is laboriously rechecked, an ever-present feeling as to what we could, or should give them, average less than twenty kilometres an hour. Dusk wraps around us, follow a sign for the Daslat Hotel, driving down the dirt track, we're greeted by waving arms and smiling locals, pointing the way to a low strung single-storey salmon pink building, the years of neglect giving it a blistered sponge paint effect.

We realise hotel rooms, as is this one, are either windowless, or the space windows would be, are boarded or covered in rags of once brightly woven cotton. Lighting is a single hanging central bulb, illuminating only the circle of concrete floor below them. Running water is never a thing but buckets of it provide a flush for the toilet and some for washing. It would be far preferable to be sleeping in Lizzybus but we need the security, rate them only for how close and how secure, Lizzybus is, a few cockroaches, lack of light, or water insignificant. Outside the room set up our table and chairs, David makes up a packet soup, adding a tin of tuna, we laugh as locals drag out white plastic chairs and prop a three-legged table on the pile of rubble to do the same as us, their English guests.

Back on the road heading for Abuja, a boiled egg and dried apricots for breakfast as the fan lay idle overnight due to the lack of electricity, the clothes I washed, whilst still damp, are no longer stiff as cardboard with sweat. It's difficult to put into words the chaos around me, a huge country rich in oil, just broken. The once working train track used as a dumping ground for rubbish, goods can only be transported on treacherous broken tarmac roads, littered with overturned burnt-out skeletons of vehicles. Traffic like a poisoned snake inches its way across mile after mile after mile of it. The Angolan visa office is only open Monday and Wednesday, we know it will be Thursday at the very least before we will make it.

Tonight, to a setting sun, no longer able to stomach another hotel room, set up camp in the bush, on opening the table that is stored on the roof rack, smack myself in the nose. Checking the damage in the Lizzybus wing mirrors, I see blood dripping down my chin into the creases of my neck, the creases have a dark grey scum. Examining my other creases, they all look the same, I'm grimy, dirty, sweaty and ashamed. Sheltered by a group of trees, leaves rustle in the collecting breeze, an optimistic moon blacked out by gathering rain clouds. After a delicious dinner of fried onions, corned beef and rice, it's wonderful to be back in the roof tent, with our own illuminations courtesy of the sheet lightning, grey grime creases or not.

Rain pelted down all night, I thought we were on board ship as gale force winds buffeted us, the gaffer taped mouse hole no match for the downpour, we're as wet inside as out. I left the bowl out last night; I'm thrilled as it's full of water, at least we can have a proper strip wash. I have found having two sets of clothes only is the way to go, one to wash one to wear, anymore and you end up with a bag of stinking washing that rots and goes mouldy. Along the way if we find rivers, or streams, or any form of water, I wash us, well not exactly us, David washes himself and our clothes with the magic African block of soap, to hang it on the makeshift washing line strung inside Lizzybus to dry on the way.

David is never too hot, I am, his arse is never hurting from being sat on all day, mine is, he couldn't care less about being stiff with sweat or dirt, I do. What does bother him but not me, is worst-case scenarios, as I refuse to think about them. I know and understand this level of responsibility would overwhelm anyone but it sits like a cloud above him, colouring the mood. Any rattle or rogue noise from Lizzybus can and is, pontificated on all day, I get agitated and annoyed listening to him, going over and over it, not understanding the full implications but sick with worry. Until, unable to contain my worries any longer, I ask what will actually happen when it does break, dismissed with, "Oh, it'll be fine."

So just like coming to terms with our very different driving styles, David is now only allowed to say once what might be of worry to him, then it's either on the list to be fixed if and when, or it is forgotten. This sort of works but he has started muttering to himself, so worry is replaced with irritation.

    The rain has made treacherous roads even more treacherous, only we realise this, as traffic at the same death-wish speed, slides and slithers past us. On the next bend, a lorry and its two trailers are on its side blocking both lanes. The white sacks of grain spread out like a bowl of the disgusting sago dessert, resembling frogspawn, I was forced to eat by the school dinner ladies. We should have known better but take a photo—this before smartphones came along, with their incredible cameras, you can now take a photo discreetly, ours was a huge great big in your face, obvious brick of a camera. Once again, we're surrounded by police, who take the camera off us, agree to give it back only after, in front of them, we delete all the pictures off it.

Chapter 12
Capital Cities and Embassies

On approaching the city of Abuja a criss-cross of expressways, the raised sections used as drop offs for dumping rubbish, to stink and fester. It's testimony to us both, of my driving skills and David's incredible sense of direction, to somehow find ourselves at African Safari Hotel. A three-storey hotel on the outskirts of the city, still, it's expensive but we take it to hold onto any bit of sanity left. A big room with garish seventies décor, en-suite with flushing toilet, hot water, soap, towels, it has electricity and television.

The first thing I do is strip off to shower in oh-so-hot water, the water running over my body is sensual, a physical pleasure, I want this moment to last forever. Blocking the drain in the shower tray, dissolve biological washing powder and a sterilising tablet, to wash our clothes in. Treading them like you would grapes, to make the finest wine, has the added bonus of making my feet so clean I can't believe they are mine.

It's early evening, we're cautious walking through the communal park, where even in England you might expect to find glue-sniffers and alcoholics. It's alive with friendly smiling families, an old fishing net makes a badminton net and net for the rusted basketball hoop, bricks mark out goals on the rubble football pitch. Along the road, steel drums are barbeques, dubious looking animal intestines sizzle, they smell delicious, we're so hungry. With two stuffed pitas of it, wrapped in old newspaper, a slice of melon for dessert, head back to our luxurious room. With washing strung everywhere, lie on the bed watching Spain beat Germany, most rewarding, as they beat England and it's the first time Spain get to the final. We're in a hotel room in Abuja, the capital city of Nigeria, eating a dinner of pita stuffed barbequed intestines, watching football, drinking a beer, you can't make it up.

What a difference hot water and soap make, we feel re-born, in the parking area Lizzybus is trapped between several clean shiny vehicles, we're parked in the 'car wash' area. One thing Nigerians love, actually Africans in general, is scrubbing, scrubbing cars, scrubbing clothes, scrubbing children, anyone and everyone with a bucket and access to water, be it a tap, a murky stream, or a puddle, scrubs. The main thing they scrub after children is vehicles, every single time we stop, at roadblocks, traffic lights, or to find our way, we are inundated with people wanting to wash Lizzybus. It has taken us ten months, on some of the toughest roads in Africa, to get this glorious rust red patina, something we both love but today give in, she gets washed, or should I say scrubbed, inside and out.

Driving into the centre of Abuja heading for the Angolan Embassy, it seems it's not only us and Lizzybus who have been reborn but life: this city is incredible. Framed by nature's wonder Aso and Zuma monoliths, to man's own wonders, the magnificent Central Mosque, crowned by a huge golden dome and fairy tale minarets, beside the Neo Gothic Ecumenical Cathedral (National Christian Centre), are glass, slate and marble buildings, picturesque parks, fountains and tropical planting, it's quite unbelievable. It has working traffic lights, junctions manned by traffic Police in little wooden booths, in high visibility vests, white gloves blowing whistles. It has rubbish bins, which people actually use, this city is glistening and impressive.

With the help from the guys at the local Fire Station we find the embassy, shut, as expected, the security guard assures us it will be open tomorrow, Friday. Not wanting to waste the day, head over to the Congolese Embassy (Republic of Congo), the next but two countries away, as apparently you can get same day visas. When submitting applications, you lose your passport for however many days it takes, no matter how many embassies there are in a city, you can only get one at a time. Embassies are always in the heart of the city, driving around one with no passports is not a good thing but we have no choice.

The Congolese visa can be issued today, for an extra twenty dollars, we pay it, so we have our passports for the Angolan embassy tomorrow. I always thought actual border crossings would be the most challenging but just getting the required visas is close, as without them you won't be crossing any borders.

Getting the Angolan visa will take several days, submitting it on a Friday, know it will sit on someone's desk until at least Monday. We cannot afford to stay at our hotel, so go in search of a budget hotel room. This might be an impressive city but like all impressive cities, scratch its surface and the same poverty exists. Eventually we find a cheap hotel, with en-suite but most importantly secure parking and the added bonus, it includes breakfast.

Up early today, on a mission to get to the Angolan Embassy, the receptionist tells us breakfast isn't served until nine thirty, it's going to be another banana breakfast. I think we will end up looking like bananas, bought from the roadside, 'Lady fingers' or sugar, fig, or date, bananas, are tiny, they look overripe, verging on rotten but are quite delicious, sweet with a lemony aftertaste. At the Angolan Embassy we are checked in and dog tagged, full of hope we might actually be able to submit the applications today. What we failed to ascertain when asking the security guard when the embassy will be open is if on this day you can submit visa applications, which you can't, it will be Monday.

Asking the secretary, I mean security guard, if we could at least have a set of application forms to fill out, to make sure we have all the relevant information, as often applications are refused for things like no paper clip, or needing four copies not two etc. This request needs permission from the top, not something our secretary/security guard can authorize, we wait. Two hours later, summoned personally to the blanked-out counter with six-inch-wide hatch, ensuring even the smallest person has to bend double, a set of applications are silently posted through to us. We now realise how we are treated at an embassy is a direct reflection on how we will be treated in their country. I'm already not looking forward to Angola.

Drive around this city because we can, although the police and military presence is high, we are not stopped or interrogated once, just waved on our way. Lush green lawns, trimmed hedges, blocks of communal housing, with roofs and windows, sit alongside opulent gated housing complexes. Roads are swept by an army of road sweepers in uniforms, no bodies strung with the weekly shopping at the working traffic lights.

Hummers, Bentleys, Jaguars with blacked out windscreens, cruise the streets, even the standard puke green-coloured taxis all have windscreens. It's just as if someone has plucked us right out of the African jungle and plonked us here in the middle of this urban sprawl. Even ever upbeat David is getting bored, it's raining and miserable, stuck in our room on the tiny fuzzy portable television minus any sound, watch Spain win the twenty ten World Cup. It's nowhere near as electrifying as sat in my Ghanaian hair saloon, or on the Benin Togo border but it fills an afternoon.

For the third time, we're off to the Angolan Embassy, taking from the room everything of value, we ask for it to be cleaned. Navigating is so easy on the vast highway, arrive long before it opens, as there is already a queue, know it's going to be a long day. The huge metal doors have a small door and window in it, this is where the secretary/security guard takes names. It's closed now but David stands directly under it, making sure our names will be one of the first on the list.

Once dog tagged, our phone bagged and confiscated, sit in the familiar resplendent air-conditioned waiting room chatting to two English guys, Simon and Sam heading to South Africa in a Land Cruiser. Having already completed our application along with all the supporting documentation, we just need to submit it. Two hours later, feel a little triumphant that they're accepted, with no further requirements, it will be ready for collection Wednesday. As internet access is a massive problem, Wi-Fi not a thing, spend the rest of the day in the dodgy internet cafe, with the normal broken keyboards, keys so worn the letters are illegible and in French. It's torturous, I can see precious emails from home but just can't open them.

Getting the key from reception takes ages and a lot of shouting amongst themselves, almost like they are trying to delay us. The door to our room is already open, we can see it's been cleaned, with fresh sheets and towels, even a spare toilet roll and bar of soap. On the floor at the side of the bed is a used condom, all I can think about is aids, it's a huge problem here—I feel a little sickened by it. David pacifies me, by saying "At least they are practising safe sex." I no longer understand my life, or the people in it, or in fact me, as I actually see the funny side.

Cotton wool clouds float above the razor wire-topped wall, our view for the fifth day in this room. I join David in the car park making coffee off the back of Lizzybus, the chained up and caged black and white Staffy recognises us and wags his tail. David works on Lizzybus, removing (with my help) the spare wheel and bonnet, I allow him for now to waffle on about adjusting the push rod on the master cylinder, allowing for fluid expansion to the clutch but it's not long before I start to get irritated, as he goes into detail about the amount of oil and grease around the drive shafts, of cleaning breather pipes etc., so leave him to it.

Back at the Angolan Embassy it's like having a morning out with friends, sitting in the air-conditioned room chatting with Simon and Sam, Justin a German guy on a Yamaha and John and June a Kiwi couple. The hours pass far too quickly, all too soon the Angolan visa adorns another page of our passports, we say our goodbyes, knowing our paths will cross again as we're all heading South. We have some invaluable first-hand information on the southern border crossing into Cameroon, our next country, at Mamfe. A sixty-kilometre dirt road, impassable during the rainy season (now), just might be doable, as the Chinese have upgraded the road.

Taking this route would save almost a thousand kilometres and avoid the reportedly notorious northern crossing at Mora but it's a gamble. Talking about used condoms, breather pipes, impassable roads and border crossings has become the general chitchat, I don't understand most of it but it's beginning to feel right and at times even interesting. Who needs to talk about feelings anyway?

Our next country is Cameroon; we submit the application along with the eighty-dollar fee. Visas really are the curse of any traveller, not least the cost, getting them is a drawn-out process and they fill a whole page of your passport. David back in the England had sheets of standard passport photographs printed, along with photocopies of passports, driving license, international driving license, even photocopies of vaccinations and any documents relating to Lizzybus. Despite this there always seems to be one more requirement, one more forgotten hoop, or needed item, we see it as a victory if and when, we have everything required.

It seems hardly possible but we have been in this room a week sorting out visas, it's a city with lots to do but on a budget, the cost of the hotel and all the visas our choices are limited to walking around it and picnics in the park. Speaking to Simon and Sam, they tell us about camping at the back of the huge Sheraton hotel for free, we're going to check it out. On arriving the security guard takes all our details, before directing us to a piece of land behind the main car park. It's amazing, huge trees provide shade, you have access to the pool and shower block but best of all we find John and June the New Zealanders, Justin the German on his Yamaha and Alex and Felix, two young Germans in a knackered old Mercedes Sprinter van—and yes, it's free.

It's one of the strangest things about this journey, this hotel with over five hundred rooms, in the heart of the city of Abuja, Nigeria, allows over-landers, not only to park here but protects them. Alex and Felix have just crossed at Mamfe, saying the road to it is not too bad but of course it's all down to definition. Simon and Sam are not convinced, they decide to take the longer route north, David and I, being the idiotic 'intrepid explorers' just can't wait for some proper adventure, we will cross at Mamfe.

Our focus is on getting to South Africa, as an old commonwealth country, it's visa free and English speaking. Unsure of the exact road conditions ahead, the possibility we might end up having to take the alternative route north and the real risk of overstaying our Nigerian visa, decide to leave in the morning. It feels good to be getting back on the road, there is always a little fear of the unknown, as to what lies ahead, we do know the border crossing into Cameroon will be a tough one.

It's incredible the city just stops, it looks like a mural painted on the wall behind us, we're back on broken tarmac with the African red soil bleeding from it once more, straw and mud replaces glass and concrete. A few kilometres in, with a demonstration completely blocking the road both ways, follow the taxis through the bush. Back on the main road, conditions worsen, we're constantly getting stuck, swallowed up in the quicksand lurking in huge open craters, we're already questioning our decision. Ten gruelling hours later, I'm negotiating a room, David is being guided under the brick built arch entrance by a load of locals.

I find him under it, the arch is now a broken pile of bricks on the Lizzybus bonnet, the new top box dented and split. I cannot believe he would accept their word, to not have checked for himself, or at least wait for me to guide him. I do love that Lizzybus has some more war wounds, reminders of her travels.

I can hear my name being called, slowly I make out a fuzzy David but I can't focus, I begin to feel excruciating pain. Going to the bathroom I had fainted, falling forward smacked my nose on the sink and my head on the concrete floor. David, hearing the thud, found me there, on the bathroom floor, fleetingly thinking I'm dead. Through the night he puts cold compresses on my head, making sure I'm still breathing, my pulsating twisted thumb, blocked nose from congealed blood and egg forming on my head, brings me in and out of consciousness.

As this is happening more often, decide it's got to be the heat, the lack of water or salt, from now on we will monitor our water intake, add salt to our cooking and as for the heat: it's Africa, what do we expect? I'm severely concussed but we must push on, leaving the room I can't even walk in a straight line, once in Lizzybus it's only the seat belt keeping me upright. I feel incredible sorry for myself, with two black eyes, a bloody nose and the most painful of all, a twisted thumb. I do however feel relieved on realising you can only feel one hurt at a time, so my pulsating thumb distracts me from my throbbing head. I snooze and moan my way through the kilometres, until David pulls over to check the spray of oil covering the back window.

I'm told it's the differential plug sucked into the housing, which if we continue on will cause us problems. I help with taking out all the boxes to get at the tools, with my one good hand, along with passing tools to David spread-eagle under Lizzybus trying to unbolt the axle pan bolts. As the last 'bastard' bolt refuses to move, it's being heated with our little gas blow torch. Now, I'm sure all this is fascinating but right now I'm resentful of Lizzybus getting all this care and attention, I sit on one of the kit boxes in the shade feeling utterly dejected.

I look up to see a man with his four children squeezed onto his little scooter, speaking pidgin English he tells me his children have never seen a white person. I'm not too sure how to respond to this revelation, getting up parade my 'white' self about, feeling a little disappointed I can't show a proper specimen of white, as my eyes are blacker than theirs. I had a bag of the little toys you get free inside chocolate eggs, give them one each, whilst popping a sugar lump into each mouth. I'm so cheered and comforted by this; I want them to stay forever but all too soon they are gone.

It's a tough day, digging and building the road ahead, using sand ladders, shovel, or just driving off-road through the bush, somehow, we make it to within spitting distance of the Cameroon border. Exhausted, book a room and evening meal, Lizzybus resplendent in African red earth, looks real hardcore once more.

Cameroon, bringing us past halfway down West Coast Africa, its best kept secret its corruption, which still exists but without it being a secret anymore. A dramatic diverse country, from dry grassy plains to volcanic crater lakes, mountain ranges, beaches and wildlife parks. Is this going to be what I naively thought Africa would be like?

Knowing the process for border crossings makes it easier but we're still wary, you get an immediate feel for the country, by your treatment at them. Faced with a very intimidating, very big military police commandant, with facial tribal markings, we're taken aback on realising it's a woman. Chatty, friendly, interested in us and our travels, it's not long before all our documents are completed and we're on our way. It's getting late, the road cuts through a single track, with drop offs either side, Lizzybus makes a loud clonking noise from the front, whilst the fix to the back axle is no longer fixed but spraying oil back over the rear window.

A motor bike pulls adjacent to us, we ask about camping or a hotel, the two guys on it indicate for us to follow them. Heading deeper into the bush, leaving any form of civilization or the possibility to turn back, feel a little alarmed. Then a clearing appears; it's a village, at its centre a compressed earth square. Due to Cameroon's colonial past, French and English is spoken along with many versions of it and other native languages. The 'chief,' in good English, tells us we can camp here, in the centre of the village. Unlike Nigerians who are animated and gesticulate wildly when speaking, Cameroons are softly spoken and timid. I can see they have dressed in their finest, old waistcoats, suit jackets over faded shredded T-shirts.

The whole village forms a circle around us. I invite the children to climb up into the roof tent, they are cautious at first but after the first one does, they all climb up, even the women. We're invited on a tour of the village, abode built single storey tin roofed homes, perch above the washed-out mud streets. Some of the houses even have electricity, there is a single room school and tiny church, we're introduced to the pastor and teacher. Sitting in the classroom on the laptop, show pictures of our travels, pointing the route out on maps, donating a bag of pens to the teacher. It's getting dark and late. From past experience of peeing with an audience I have taken to wearing long skirts, so I can stand in the bush peeing without exposing my arse.

Mosquitoes here are on steroids, even putting on long trousers under my skirt my legs resemble the trunk of the African Baobab tree, my skin stretched and swollen, it's so painful.

Back on the road progress is slow; at the petrol station, ask for a mechanic, specifically a Land Rover mechanic. We're directed down a potholed dirt track, at the end is a graveyard of rotting vehicles, two of which are shells of Land Rovers, this apparently making the mechanic a Land Rover specialist. Lizzybus had her axel removed, the drive shaft flange replaced (from David's spares) and everything, including bearings, greased, with lots of other things but we're at the point of not going on about them, just getting them fixed, all for eighty dollars.

Camping at the back of the Presbyterian Mission, it's immaculate with access to a flushing toilet and shower but what is quite incredible is being given the code for the Wi-Fi and getting my emails. A great night becomes a great morning, when invited to join four Americans on a seminar for breakfast, our shrunken stomachs complain when stuffing them full of the most delicious pancakes, boiled eggs and fresh baked bread. I want to take some for later, slathered in butter and jam but it feels wrong. David asks about the challenging three hundred and sixty kilometre 'Grassfields' ring road, through some of the finest scenery in Africa, of lush pastureland, thundering waterfalls, volcanoes and crystal-clear crater lakes.

Setting off, what we both choose to ignore, or give any thought to whatsoever, is waterfalls and craters are formed in mountainous regions and nature loves keeping them top secret. 'Grass fields' for me conjures up images of vast savannahs, full of elephants, giraffes, zebra, buffalo, prides of lions and tigers. This might be true but for now, the vivid green pasture grass is higher than our roof, we see only a few meters ahead.

Occasional wispy tails of smoke from the wood and dung fires rising through it, the only sign we are not alone. Our steady climb circling high into the Cameroon northwest highlands becomes mountainous, the road little more than rubble, needing one of us outside of Lizzybus, 'spotting,' the rock sliders, fuel tank and rear diff pan guard are a triumph. Pressing on hear the roar of water, well before seeing it, Menchum Falls, one of the many tumbling, cascading falls in the area. Strip off, swim, wash, scrub us and our clothes, filing the two Jerry Cans. Boulders washed down from the highlands make the road more like a riverbed than a road, we're proud of Lizzybus, she is strong and right at home here. Today, having only managed sixty of the three hundred and sixty kilometres, know it's going to take a week to get back to exactly where we started from but for now we're enjoying the challenge.

At Lake Wum crater lake, the villagers tell us we need permission from the Senior Divisional Officer to camp but no one knows where he is. Head off down little more than an old cattle trail, to a small walled area with concrete seating and corrugated roofed pagoda, two locals are scrubbing their motor bikes. Set up camp, permission or not, crack open a beer, illuminated by head torches, in the inky blackness of a moonless sky, serenaded by a chorus of birds and insects. Pretty chuffed we have made it this far, dismiss the other three hundred kilometres ahead.

It was cold last night; we grit our teeth and swim in the crater lake, wrapped in towels watch the rising sun with a mug of hot coffee. The road is good in parts but almost impassable in most others, crossing dilapidated bridges is a leap of faith, not only that they will hold our weight but that the 'spotter' does his job. With most of the planks missing, dropping a wheel through the huge gaping holes is a real threat. Hit a long wide section of almost vertical soft clay, I hike to the top, David makes a run at it, the front end of Lizzybus lifts, she slides sideways, then slithers back down. I have visions of David and Lizzybus tumbling over and over to become a square box, spat out of the crusher at the bottom.

It's during moments like this you realise how utterly alone and defenceless you are, how ridiculous you were to even think you could do this but knowing you got yourself into it, know it's up to you to get yourself out. Even with a full external roll cage welded to the chassis, somersaulting to the bottom is outside its functional capacity.

David releases the thirty-meter winch line, I drag it to the top, securing it to a heavy boulder, telling me to put a blanket over it in case it breaks free and decapitates us. You are kidding me, I just wanted to see a few animals, okay, forget the lions and tigers, how about an elephant or a giraffe, I'll even settle for a few zebra, actually watching a David Attenborough documentary will do just fine, take me back!

We're at the top, in Lizzybus, in one piece. I want to go back but we're at the point of no return, a small victory, in what feels like a war. When in the grasslands, I wanted to be able to see, now I can, I wished I couldn't, ahead, as far as the eye can see, the road is little more than a boulder field. I'm now learning about jacking, when wedged on rocks, you have to jack Lizzybus up, to fill the gap with rocks. I'm knackered, even my short nails are split and broken, my legs scraped and bruised but in an odd way, I'm sort of enjoying this and still amazed I've not asked, "Why?"

As the sun sneaks off to bring daylight to another continent, we see civilization ahead at Millennium Start Hotel, built of black painted melon sized boulders, held together with beige cement, like the mighty Cheetah. It's been an incredible day, we're amazed at ourselves and Lizzybus, proud and relieved it's over for now. Justin the young German guy on his Yamaha is here, who we first met at the back of the Sheraton hotel in Nigeria. Justin is also doing this road but in reverse, we decided not to tell each other what we face, what's the point, we still have to do it.

We agree the road is punishing for his bike and our Lizzybus, the most significant for Justin is his back brakes, or lack of. As David has an extensive set of tools, unlike Justin whose kit carrying capacity allows only for a very basic 'get you home set,' and as Justin has a spare set of brake pads, they set about changing them. A five-minute job takes the whole afternoon, I don't ask about it, on a 'don't need to know basis,' but it's not just the brakes that get fixed, a load of other stuff does too. I make us dinner, frying the green spongy potatoes with a tin of sweetcorn and tuna. It's a fabulous evening.

Woken by a tap on the door, find two buckets of hot water waiting for us, it's such a treat. I make a six egg, cheese and onion omelette, (cheese spread triangles) for us all, with bread, still warm bought from reception, it's delicious. These pockets of normality lift us, despite being alone, you are part of something greater. It's tough for us in Lizzybus but at least we have each other and, although small, a home, to shelter from the elements, can filter our own water and carry enough food for a week, it makes me feel incredibly spoilt. There is something about people like this that intrigues me, I'm beginning to realise, we are also the people who intrigue. Justin, like us, can't really answer why, or what drives us on, what makes us all, essentially, give up everything, to do this. But what we agree on is, whatever it is, it's not an actual choice, it's just what we have to do.

Scenery that was spectacular three days ago loses its appeal, it's becoming a relentless ordeal, between spotting, building, winching and criticizing, tempers flare. David shouts, "Just shut up, woman."

Amazingly, I do just that, sitting with arms folded, not only shut up but refusing to help in anyway whatsoever. For David, it's impossible not to speak, like Donkey in the film *Shrek*, who keeps asking, "Are we there yet?" on being told to "Shut Up" lasts five minutes. He speaks, I ignore him, so continues on with his one-sided conversation, this infuriates me even more, until eventually I do speak, telling him to, "Shut the f…up!" I shock myself with this potty mouth but it feels good. Six days after leaving, totally exhausted, make it back to the Presbyterian Mission where we started, this time given a room at the back of the main building, with two bunks, a toilet and hot shower but joy of joy, directly opposite is a laundry room. On a particularly bone jarring section of road, the lid on the new bottle of gear box oil came loose, leaking all over David's bag of clothes. Having, after nearly a year, almost got rid of the reek from the last exploding bottle of oil in Morocco, it's frustrating. I put the whole stinking mess and two biological tablets into this wonder of man washing machine.

After the most wonderful night's sleep, we're gently roused at six in the morning by soothing lullabies, rejoicing the glory of God. It's the weirdest thing to be sat here, having breakfast with the Americans still here on their seminar, just as if the last six days were nothing but a bad nightmare. Our room, or any other room, is not available today, we're taken to another of their 'houses' in town. Steep hills envelop this town, the large concrete gullies running either side of the roads also serve as urinals for men, who stand directly in full view urinating. It feels poor, livings made from selling barbequed sweetcorn, tiny fish and peanut oil in plastic bags. Pollution coats everything with a sooty black, rotting wood shutters, rags or plastic sheeting shut out any glimmer of light to breezeblock-built houses.

We're given a room, on the top floor of a three-storey concrete building, a big room with access to hot showers and the use of a communal kitchen. Back on the streets, buy a bag of delicious beans and stewed potatoes, we eat them back in our room, watching a film on David's laptop. The walls are so thin, I use earplugs to block out the noise of our neighbour clearing phlegm and spitting through the night. In the morning, the owner of the Mission is waiting to take us back to the main building for breakfast of boiled eggs, fresh fruit, cake and jam. Our Americans have left, we eat alone, after living off mainly bananas it's too tempting, stuff two boiled eggs in my trouser pockets, with four slices of cake liberally spread with jam wrapped in serviettes in David's, a special treat for lunch, as we're back on the road today. I know I'm never going to heaven.

It rains until midday, turning the road into gelatinous snot, the signs and billboards are now all in French—Southern Cameroon is mainly French speaking. There are many roadblocks (pieces of string across the road) but for us, they are lowered with no questions, no searches, just huge smiles and friendly waves. We're heading for Yaoundé, Cameroon's capital, for the last of the visas, the mud road changes to tarmac, progress is good, slowed only by the hidden sleeping soldiers, made of compacted earth, which set like concrete. After the ordeal of the 'Grassland,' it's like a day out, stopping to have our picnic of boiled eggs and jam-slathered cake.

David, being shown the tiny, mould ridden, water-less, electricity-less, stained mattress room, says, "Very good." I agree, it's only for the night anyway. Sitting in the morning sun eating an apple each for breakfast, knowing the road ahead is good, confidant we will make it to Yaoundé today. We're heading for the Internationale de l'Eglise Presbyterian Mission, which is to be found between two concrete chimneys and the local police station. A sprawling city, roads deteriorate into wheel eating potholes, signs or road markings are non-existent, we're totally lost in the heat fumes and mayhem. Asking for directions at the local police station, even when showing them our map, they have no idea.

We now have a Fireman sitting in the front seat, this is most agreeable. I've realised part of the universal job description for Firemen is that they are drop-dead gorgeous, as is this one, I'm hoping it takes us quite a while to find our destination. Yaoundé, suffering from severe flooding, which destroys industry and homes, causing death through water-borne diseases like typhoid and malaria, has started a flood reduction project, roads are almost impassable with under construction drainage systems. Still, all too soon we're at the Presbyterian Mission, perched on a hill between two water towers and police station but on the opposite side of town, there are two sets of towers and police station.

We're greeted by a large African lady, draped over a skinny old Swiss guy, apparently the owner, her husband. 'She' allows us to camp in the grounds for not much less than the cost of a room. John and June (the Kiwi couple) are here and Justin, all needing ongoing visas. With John and June, we walk to the Gabon Embassy, it's surrounded by a high wall, with a pea green iron gate. Three hours later, all the applications in, pay another seventy dollars each, they will be ready to collect Wednesday afternoon. We ask if we can collect them Wednesday morning, so we can at least get our applications in at the Democratic Republic of the Congo Embassy but it's non-negotiable. John and June head back, we go off in search of a cash point, dodging men pissing and choking on the dust and fumes. There are long queues at sheds selling beer and whisky, consumed in paper bags, along with many drinking houses, set up amongst broken shells of buildings, it feels like a city that's lost itself, a life of struggle.

Back at camp with a carrier bag of overripe tomatoes and chunks of some kind of meat, I cook dinner off the back of Lizzybus, as we're not allowed into the main red brick building to use its communal kitchen. Our facilities are an external shower, a pipe sticking out of the wall dripping cold water and a single toilet you need to fish in the cistern for the plunger to flush. Drinking water can be bought from the main building, David fills Jerry Cans from the outside tap and filters water for us all, for free. She is taking the piss, if it wasn't for being perfectly placed for the embassies we would leave, realising this, access is given to the hot showers and toilet morning and evening.

Back to the Gabon Embassy, David is full of cold, that, regardless of being in Africa or England, is man flu, it makes him unbearably miserable. Sitting in the shade I question this travel stuff, the adventure and excitement of it all. The reality is days and weeks of waiting, hanging around and when you do achieve something, it's just a personal achievement, there is no fanfare, or reprieve, the struggle and yes at times it feels like a huge struggle, continues. Looking across the road I see a half dead, tied at the feet animal, hanging from a rope—'bush meat' for sale. I know it's part of life now, buying a filet of something in a polystyrene tray shrink wrapped at your local supermarket would seem far more acceptable but it's no better, in fact worse, as you don't give a shit how it got there but it still makes me a little queasy.

The shutter of my eye closes, re-opening I see smartly dressed people in suits and dresses, an intoxicating aroma of aftershave and perfume fills my nostrils, the queue of hopeful people all waiting for visas. The iron door inches open, I can't help sniggering as the robust security guard has to turn sideways to get him and the now squashed cardboard box full of passports, out of it. At random he takes out a passport calling the name; as ours is the only British passport, David stands right beside him making sure the security guard does not give it to anyone else, who might claim it.

David still sleeping, kept awake through the night with his hacking cough, aching bones and the ear-splitting high-pitched squawking from the resident roosting fruit bats, directly above us. I go alone to the local patisserie for some delicious croissants as a treat with our morning coffee. It's the strangest thing to be out alone, I feel like an escaped prisoner, walking back in the sunshine I'm so chuffed with myself and can't wait to tell David. I'm crestfallen, waving the bagful of still warm croissants under his nose, the coffee brewing, he has no appetite for pastries, turns over and goes back to sleep, I stuff most of them into my shrunken stomach.

John and June invite us for a traditional New Zealand beef stew, apparently what makes it traditional is the three spoons of the two, half kilo jars, of Vegemite they brought with them, I just hope it doesn't include any 'bush meat.' Tomorrow I am making dinner, living in Birmingham close to what is known as the 'Balti Triangle' with more Bangladeshi curry houses than fish and chip shops, we like a good curry. As Vegemite originated from Australia, not New Zealand, we're sticking to our curry as traditional English, originating from Bangladesh Birmingham.

Arriving at the Democratic Republic of the Congo Embassy (as opposed to the Republic of Congo, a country we already have visas for), we're invited into the huge airy waiting room with leatherette settees and fancy curtains. With the applications filled out and accepted, despite being told by the embassy staff it is a one-day process, the security guard insists it will take three days, not counting today, or the weekend, it will be at least another five days.

I've got David's man flu, with a blinding headache, aching bones and a throat full of thorns, not willing to give up, or believe the security guard, head off to the Democratic Republic of the Congo Embassy. I don't know if the security guard remembers what he said, or why but an hour later, we're triumphant to be walking out with our passports complete with the visa. It's an evening to celebrate, now having visas for Gabon, Republic of Congo (Congo), Democratic Republic of the Congo and Angola, taking us to the penultimate country of Namibia, where the visa is available on the border, then South Africa which is visa free. South Africa, the very bottom of Africa, our final destination on this leg of the journey; it's just thrilling, whilst utterly unreal—how the hell did we even make it this far?

Back in camp Lizzybus has everything greased, oils change, the air vents sealed with sealant, which I didn't want done, it might stop the leaks but it's our only form of air-con, and a new fuse to the horn and clock. I wash clothes, bed linen, the inside and outside of Lizzybus, even take out and air the mattress. It's a strange evening, sharing the remains of last night's curry and four cartons of Sangria, we're all sad to be leaving each other but ready to move on. We could go in convoy with John and June, it's hard to explain why we don't but this has to be something we do alone, face alone, learn alone. How many kilometres a day we do, or don't do, when we stop, or don't stop, needs to be entirely down to us.

Being on the move heading for another country, as exciting as it is, there is always a sense of trepidation to what lies ahead. The distant horizons call to us like the beautiful but dangerous 'Sirens' calling ships onto the rocks. Gabon here we come. Reaching the border early afternoon, we're stamped out of Cameroon, with no no-man's land, we're directed to a concrete building, acting as the Gabon border in name only.

Here we're given a signed piece of paper in French, to take to Bitam, thirty kilometres south, where the passports and Carnet De Passage can be stamped. Again, even though no no-man's land, the difference in countries is immediate, children are no longer bound tightly to backs or clinging to breasts but slung on the hips of both men and women. Wrought iron grills, faded shredded curtains, corrugated iron, blocking out all light are no more, homes with shuttered windows are open to the sun, revealing concrete floors and bamboo beds.

Gabonese are communal people, personal space is neither needed, nor given, they stand almost touching us, calling us the 'white man' ask for any of the things they want, even the clothes we wear. At the beginning of our journey, this would have been incredibly uncomfortable, an invasion of privacy, of personal space but just like our English reserve, we now understand and accept our differences. In fact, it's amusing and not an intrusion at all, it's non-threatening, almost child-like and a trait we like in them.

Arriving at Bitam late afternoon, armed with our piece of paper, it's time to get the passports and Carnet De Passage stamped. The Gendarmeries (police) want not just a photocopy of our passports, which we have but a photocopy of the page in it with the Gabon visa on, David is sent off to the 'photocopiers' opposite. I go to a hotel over the road to negotiate a room, it's fully booked due to a local festival but they are quite happy to let us camp in the car park, use the showers and flushing toilets, for free.

Police here are suspicious of foreigners, especially ones in big green Land Rovers, the "What is your mission?" Question is real, to become another interrogation, our genuine reason, of it being a good idea, is just so lame. The idea of making up a humanitarian aid relief story, or of being writers on some fact-finding mission, knowing how seriously they take this question, is forgotten, stick to the truth of just seeing the world. It's nowhere near as threatening crossing into Nigeria, with none of the searches, it's more about them trying to understand why we would do this?

We trundle on in our 'mission' through forests of bamboo that form soaring archways over the road and the impenetrable jungle of grasses, ferns and dense oak shrub. It's late afternoon, follow a Lizzybus wide path into the jungle to a pylon, knowing they have clearings around their base that make good bush camping spots. Its David's forty-ninth birthday, I kept secret the tin of Heinz baked beans, packet of instant mashed potato June and John gave us and the two sachets of butter I had bought at the deli. What you do for your birthday is not what makes it special but where you do it is. Baked beans, instant mash potato with butter, in a bamboo forest in Gabon, makes it very special, even the humongous ants and razor-sharp bamboo can't spoil.

Driving completely alone along roads cutting through majestic bamboo forest, passing small villages of picturesque shiplap houses, each with neat stone-edged gardens, can't distract us from Lizzybus who keeps losing power. Once more David stands looking into the engine, or lying prostrate underneath, as my education as to the importance of everything, not only having oil but specific types of oil and the consequences of it not all being terminal, continues: we press on.

Chapter 13
Milestones: Vous Franchissez L'équateur

It's been almost a year since we left England, the sat-nav reads 00°00, to our left is a sign proclaiming we are on the Equator, dividing the Northern and Southern Hemisphere. It's a massive achievement, standing here alone but together, one full rotation more of the wheel, cross the equator, we're in the Southern Hemisphere. What we have faced, feared, overcome, even a few times enjoyed, on this journey, a journey so far removed from anything I had ever known or imagined, has been incredible.

Taking us both to the limits of our endurance, with moments of utter joy, loneliness, dread but most of all awe, I'm so proud of us both, that despite it all, we persevered and just kept going.

Through the canopies of forest, we see glimpses of the imposing Ogooue River, the soaring forest trees send out fingers of roots breaking the tarmac into a bitumen ice field, almost impossible to navigate over, progress is torturous. As the sunsets admit defeat, knowing we will never reach the city of Lambarene, set up camp at the foot of another pylon. It's amazing how noisy a jungle is, alive with insects, birds and other things I can't let myself think about, the forest floor is a carpet of dried leaves, the noise of anything crawling in, over, or under it, amplified, at times so loud I think people are here.

David since dawn has been working on Lizzybus to discover the accelerator pedal is not engaging fully, tightening it up we have everything crossed this could be the cause of the lack of power. It's not! I drive, David reads through the build-your-own Land Rover files off his laptop. We're in mountains and valleys, with endless ups and downs, freewheeling as fast as we can down, to get some momentum to get back up. It looks like the Turbo is knackered, Lizzybus could not pull the skin off a rice pudding. One thing that makes this journey unbearable, is having a sickly Lizzybus, when one of us is sick we can still make progress but with Lizzybus its game over, it colours the mood, filling the day with worry and stress.

Crossing a very long, single lane British built Bailey bridge, in the middle of it realise we have a flat tyre, on inspection, find one of the new valves had popped out. In such a tight space, trying to get at the tools and the spare wheel off the bonnet, we're sweating with the effort. Sitting on the bridge trusses, like little birds on a telegraph wire, are a row of fascinated children, to the front and rear of Lizzybus stand the drivers and passengers of the vehicles we're blocking in. Where they need to go, or to get, is unimportant, they stand in the midday sun watching us, without a single complaint, fascinated.

With the tyre replaced, we fire Lizzybus up and drive off, to a huge round of applause and cheering, it feels great. Talking of tyres, we have two spares, one on the bonnet and one on the swing away back door carrier, David has a tin of most excellent 'tyre string' great for nail in the tyre type repairs but we don't have any spare valves, or the ability to fit them—we need to find a tyre repair place.

The Chinese have secured contracts for the construction of railways and roads across Africa, specifically Gabon and Nigeria. They bring with them huge earth moving machines and logging lorries, blood red scars cut into the forest far off into the distance, ready to be dressed in tarmac. Lorry after lorry, loaded with ancient forest, force us off the road, on their way to huge storage compounds, where the workers live. With the constant downpours, the rich red earth becomes a heavy clay, progress with a sickly Lizzybus is agonising, bush camping each night, we're beginning to smell like a rotting forest, as washing or drying clothes is impossible.

Somehow, we arrive at The Republic of Congo, Congo, border, caked in mud, stinking from days of bucket washing and bush camping. We almost expect reporters and news crews, telling of the story of the couple lost in the jungle, miraculously surviving, when all hope was lost. Handing over our documents, unable to say where we have been or come from, stand almost silent, the language barrier is starting to hurt in these Francophile countries.

It's a devastated landscape of rolling burnt and burning hills, the air filled with a smog of floating detritus, chalky red roads teeter on washed out huge drop offs. Follow a dirt track to a burnt-out area, Lizzybus now coated in a black soot, giving her a pleasing marbled effect, set up camp overlooking the spectacular remaining forest awaiting the same fate. Sat drinking a cold beer the buzz of one wasp becomes a swarm; we're right next to the hugest wasps' nest ever, having been hospitalized from a single wasp sting as a child, pack up and move on.

The Congo, like a lot of west coast Africa, has suffered from years of civil unrest, corruption and terrorism, resulting in extreme poverty and petty crime, caution is to be taken at all times. Under the glow of a full moon, I sit writing, David is in the roof tent watching *Fawlty Towers*, when I become aware of movement in the bush. Looking up, I'm surrounded by a group of Congolese men, knowing David has earphones in, I figure they can just kidnap, rape and dismember me, leaving nothing but the empty seat I sit on.

Weighing up the options, of the wasps, or this situation, I'm leaning heavily towards wasps. They're workers on the way back home to their village, what I momentarily thought were guns, I realise are hoes. They are as shocked to find me, a white woman, here in the middle of the bush, seemingly alone sat writing, as I am them. I'm smoking roll ups, give them two to share and stick to the handle of one of their hoes, a Congolese vinyl flag. They disappear back into the bush, passing the roll up between them, admiring the flag, David is still in the roof tent, oblivious.

News has spread of our whereabouts, wake to find ourselves surrounded by villagers and the swarm of wasps. The burning hillsides become dense virgin rainforest, it's breathtaking, ascending ever higher through and above the clouds on original forest tracks. Below us through patches of broken cloud, see whole hillsides cut away leaving sheer walls of marble rock quarries. With our lack of power, a fully laden motorized tuk-tuk overtakes us, rounding the bend we find them parked up: a fallen tree is completely blocking the road. The passengers and driver of the tuk-tuk get out, fire up a chainsaw to cut the fallen tree into pieces, clearing the track ahead. It's quite amazing.

A whole day later at our snail's pace, make it to the port city Pointe-Noire, a city of smoke, dust and mayhem, looking for the yacht club, an English guy we met at the Angolan Embassy recommended, where over-landers can camp for free. Find it with the help of police and locals, it has everything you would imagine of a yacht club, once in its life but is now almost derelict, broken yachts with shredded faded sails, buildings with blue painted exteriors, blistered and peeling. The few over-landers here in trucks warn us about the security, having had stuff stolen, as we sleep in a roof tent on top of Lizzybus, unlike a truck you can lock yourself inside of, it's a concern.

In a way it's idyllic, overlooking the harbour but it has a floating slick of oil and garbage, the toilets are locked, plus the two very intimidating, very big, security guards want twenty dollars a night. We're travel weary, exhausted, the time left on our visa is becoming an issue, made worse by the problem with Lizzybus, agree to pay but on leaving and only if they unlock the toilets.

It's just incredible to be stationary, parked on concrete with no insect life, from the standpipe fill Jerry Cans which I stand in the sun to warm, used for washing clothes and us. I feel so content, clean washing hanging on the fence, Lizzybus oils topped up, earlier in town, bought onions, tomatoes, eggs, bread, bananas and beer, even found an internet café, after a whole week I get precious emails. Simon and Sam (uncle and nephew) the English guys we met in Nigeria and again on the Congo border, arrive.

Simon having once lived in Africa, a mining expert, is fascinating; they, like us are heading for South Africa.

What a terrifying night, having been warned about security, lock everything inside Lizzybus, including the toilet (shovel), strapped to the front wing. Camped under a twenty-foot halogen floodlight, against a whitewashed wall, with Simon and Sam a few meters away felt pretty safe. In the early hours were both woken by the ladder to the roof tent clunking, through the mosquito net see the silhouette of two men holding knives, their shadow magnified onto the whitewashed wall. I hear David, spewing out expletives, in what he hoped was an aggressive manly way but was little more than a high-pitched squeak, I just scream. For what feels like forever but is actually only a hovering moment in time, we lock eyes, I wonder how my raised eyebrow theory, for flight, not fight, could possibly work in this scenario. The stray dogs that always alert you, along with the security guards, are all missing, we just know we have been set up, pissed off for us not paying up front.

In this moment our fate is decided for us, stabbed and left for dead, or to survive, we're defenceless, possibly knowing there is another vehicle right next to us, they leave. Simon and Sam never stirred, we found out later they both sleep with earplugs and never heard a thing. The reality of our situation cannot be ignored, we are vulnerable in the roof tent, this has unsettled us both. Before dawn breaks, we're packed and on the road, leaving a note for Simon and Sam on their windscreen, heading for the Democratic Republic of the Congo.

Cabinda, an enclave of Angola but separate, surrounded by The Republic of Congo (we are leaving) and the Democratic Republic of the Congo, we're heading for. Getting into and out of this enclave takes all day and uses one of the five days on our Angolan transit visa. Once through, pull off onto a dirt track, as we're about to put up the roof tent a group of local men arrive, through David's pidgin French, understand they want fifty dollars to protect us whilst camping here in the bush. Too tired to argue, or even to be pleasant, drive off. It's a desolate road, dusk has settled, both almost broken from our encounter at the yacht club, a little further on, pull even deeper into the bush to camp.

The whole mammoth endurance of the next few days merges into one, a road corrugated at times or just broken rock, thick dust sticks and coats everything, specifically our sweating bodies. Our crippled Lizzybus reduced to first and second gear, when even faced with the slightest incline, somehow reaches the real Angolan border, not just its enclave. You're given a five-day visa for Angola, one day was used going through the enclave, leaving four to get to the Namibian border. It's a delaying tactic by all involved, leaving us sat for over three hours, whilst processing our documents.

We're dirty, hungry, tired, I haven't been for a poo for three days, my stomach aches, my skin has the greasy black creases back, Lizzybus is sick, for fuck's sake, just get on with it! From the Angolan border to the Namibian border is one thousand and six hundred kilometres—Lizzybus, when well, only averages two to three hundred a day, we need to do at least four hundred a day, it's an almost impossible task, especially as half of the first day is spent waiting.

Angola, devastated by a prolonged civil war, advice is to carry a weapon for protection, David likes this idea far too much for my liking. Knowing Lizzybus needs a new turbo, is something we can do absolutely nothing about, being in Angola with an expired visa would be a whole other world of pain. By the time they have completed our documents (we later realise these are delaying tactics to force an overstay), the blood red road stretching before us through desolate bush land swallows the setting sun. Despite this, we have to push on into its blackness, manage one hundred and fifty kilometres before pulling off to camp. With the tent erect, eating our four egg and onion omelette, hear an approaching vehicle, it passes then stops, reversing back.

David says to switch off our head torches, I've already done this, along with legging it into the bush. Trying not to breath, the hairs on the back of my neck stand up, I'm terrified, wondering how the hell I will survive out here, on my own, what will become of me, the prospect of a gun right now becomes most appealing. I don't know what's happened to me, I'm on the edge, I cope in the only way I can, with make believe. I make a complete film of this scenario, relief floods over me, I'm in my home, safe, clean, eating popcorn, watching it.

I hear David calling my name, is this a trick to lure me out? The last few months have almost broken me, I pick up a rock, I have to get a grip. I refuse to break cover, until David comes to me; apparently, all they wanted was to check we were okay, or if we needed any help. David keeps a brave face but is shaken and ashen, he is feeling this as much as me.

Day one of our three-day push through Angola to Namibia starts at four in the morning, through mile after mile of torched desecrated barren land, a halo of hovering smoke blocks out the unrelenting sun. Occasional collections of reed huts make small villages eking out some sort of existence, children and women carry woven baskets on their backs strapped to their heads piled high with remaining bush wood. A monkey not swinging through the trees but gingerly stepping through its burnt remains, is a sobering sight neither say a word. The landscape changes from burnt nothing, to small enclaves of Baobab Trees, these comical upturned trees sit among forty-foot-high cacti sprouting delicate red flowers. The day ends after fourteen bum-numbing hours in an old quarry, a beer, bowl of couscous and bed.

Day two well before dawn breaks our self-imposed rule never to drive at night, or more importantly, in the dark, like all rules, is one made to be broken when needs must. A few hours later the regurgitated golden ball of sun re-joins us on what is now good tarmac, to heat it to a shimmering haze before us. Running parallel to the coast it's time to head inland and pick up the more major highway to the border, despite the road wrapping around the mountains, Lizzybus still struggles. I'm in my rose printed cotton skirt, as I can pee more discreetly at the roadside, the only reason we stop through fifteen hours of driving. I ache all over, I've got red blotches at the back of my legs from the heat off the transmission box, just like when sitting too close to the campfire; 'toasted skin syndrome,' would you believe there is even a syndrome attached to it. Pull over and camp.

Day three, David insists on coffee before we leave at three in the morning, it was good and comforting, as the world sleeps, we get back on the road. A main road proposed to be excellent, is so only in parts, in others it's broken tarmac, in a way this does not slow us more than the slow we already are, Lizzybus is better in low gear. The clock, unlike our progress, is on fast forward, as the border gets further and further away. I think I've missed a day, or I have chosen to totally ignore it but twelve long hours later it's nothing short of a miracle, as at three o'clock on the afternoon of the last day on our Angolan visa we make it to the border. Totally, utterly exhausted, stinking but euphoric and so very proud of our sickly Lizzybus for getting us here.

Despite the plush new magnolia painted spread of buildings, computers and electricity, trying to get stamped out of Angola is brutal. Into the second hour of waiting for the customs officer, Simon and Sam, who we last saw at the yacht club where we had the attempted robbery, arrive. They knew of our sickly Lizzybus and are totally amazed we actually, not only made it but made it before them. To stamp the Carnet De Passage they want thirty dollars each, all protests are in vain and to make matters worse, we're told we need to pay three dollars each, to keep our place in the queue, the queue with only us in it. These are delaying tactics, which is exactly what they did when entering Angola. The reality is, huge fines or worse, having our vehicles impounded, paying up leaves a bitter taste in our mouths.

Namibia, a peaceful country full of natural wonders, from the desert dunes at Sossusvlei, to the haunting desolate Skeleton Coast and national parks full of big game. Joy of joy the official language is English and they drive on the left-hand side. It's the penultimate country before reaching the very bottom of west coast Africa, South Africa, our final destination for now. Simon and Sam go on ahead, we continue at our snail's pace, find them parked up beside a police roadblock. Slowing down, I thought I was waved on and continued, until I heard 'the whistle.' This whistle sound and the blowing of it, will become very familiar to us as we travel on.

I walk back to the two teeth-sucking women traffic officers, demanding to know why I drove straight past them, explain how I thought they had waved me through and how excited we are to have made it to their wonderful country and how far we had travelled to get here. The chief of police, sitting in his office, came out to see what was going on, it would seem that behind where the traffic cops stood was a waist high sign indicating a stop. Of course, no one could see it, as their fat arses conveniently covered it up but this was no excuse not to stop, still they shake our hand, wish us luck on our journey, and let us go.

Reaching an old pea green metal bridge, realise it's a peage and three dollars to cross, we genuinely don't have any Namibian dollars, having spent almost a year bargaining, we laugh and joke with them, negotiating a fee of two cold beers. Speaking to Simon and Sam later, they were fined ten dollars for not stopping at the stop sign and three dollars for crossing the bridge. We feel victorious but the reality is, even here in Namibia, it's a reminder of how corrupt these countries are, even the peaceful ones.

Arriving at the campsite, the relief is total, the last few weeks having physically and mentally, pushed us to our limits, we're incredulous and triumphant at not having buckled under its onslaught, particularly with our sickly Lizzybus. David, showering first, tells me to watch out for the shower tap, as he got an electric shock off it. It will take far more than this to put me off finally getting clean, I use the plastic soap dish to push it. It takes a moment to realise that water running over the soap dish makes an electrical connection, running into my arm and down my body, I make David switch it off. It occurred to me, it was the first time he had seen me naked for months, I almost felt I should cover up. What is shocking, is having reported this to reception, within the hour a guy fixed it—and we thought we were in Africa.

Today, quite literally we do nothing, despite having the details of a local mechanic, Lizzybus and her new turbo is put on the to-do list for tomorrow. To sit, chat, eat and snooze, washing drying on the line and the damp stinky mattress airing, is far more important.

The mechanic and David give Lizzybus the once over, I'm stood making sure the bonnet is secure on the improvised bonnet stay, since the metal one broke. Being far more familiar than I would like with the layout of the Lizzybus engine, due to the many hours of tuition I have had on the subject. I mention again, about the bend in the big fat black pipe coming from the turbo, to be told again, it's fine. As David and the mechanic piss about with the actual turbo, not convinced I try to unbend the pipe, to find a split on its underside. What! Don't say all this time it was just a split pipe, allowing air to be sucked into the turbo.

David is as gutted he missed it as I am, for him for missing it, it's just one of those things. It's fixed with an old piece of inner tube and gasket sealant. The mechanic having stripped the turbo down and the pair of them pushing fingers into it, says it needs replacing, a new turbo will take a week to get and cost over eight hundred dollars. On a test drive, Lizzybus is perfect but David's confidence in the turbo is shattered, the decision is made to press on and get it replaced in South Africa, where we know it will be half the price.

That night back in camp locals invite us to join them for our first Braai. This is not just a barbeque, it's an institution, a social time, a shared time of cooking around a fire.

We're given a bag of Biltong, dry cured meat, traditionally wild game but it can even be ostrich, now mainly beef. We're given prime kudu biltong, totally delicious and will forever be one our very favourite things to eat. A very special, much needed magical night, spent with friends and strangers, on this never-ending odyssey that has become our life.

Everything clean, including us, say our goodbyes to Simon and Sam once more, head off on our Namibian adventure spirits high, driving on the left-hand side, on unbroken tarmac, on roads with markings and road signs and for now, not a single roadblock. Treat ourselves to breakfast at a roadside café of fried egg on little round muffin breads, with a bowl of pasta and cabbage soup, it's just delicious. Lizzybus who couldn't pull the skin off a rice pudding is now ripping it off, as we head up country on our quest to see elephants, giraffes, hippos, lions, tigers etc. Having been in Africa over ten months and only seeing two monkeys, we can't wait.

Our euphoria is short lived: towards the end of the day hear a whistling noise from the turbo, do we head back, or press on? The capital of Namibia is Windhoek, just over four hundred kilometres away, there we know is a Land Rover specialist. It's decided to press on. David takes Lizzybus failings personally, for now with the pressure off, it leaves him free to focus purely on this, a huge cloud of doom and gloom hangs over his head. I'm furious he is ruining our enjoyment in Namibia, the problems faced over the last few weeks compounded by his dismissal to my concerns of bent pipes, reneging on sticking to our pact, of once the decision is made to fix it, or forget it, then move on. Still not allowed to have the radio on, he listens to every single time the turbo kicks in and the hissing, which to me sounds like it always did but what do I know?

I'm aware that this story is my story, my experience, told from my perspective; for such a long time, I've felt like the passenger, the spare part, not because of how David has made me feel but how I have made myself feel. Slowly I begin to understand my importance, David has got us and Lizzybus this far, in the paperwork, the constant greasing, the process but our roles are beginning to be defined. As I become more aware of the logistics, the mechanics and of what is needed to make it work, I become the negotiator of us, if you like and this is equally important. It's a camaraderie with and in, each other, something at times I feel is missing in David and it's beginning to hurt and isolate.

Setting off early call in at a local 'superstore,' like rabbits caught in the glare of headlights we are overwhelmed by its excess. Aisle after aisle, shelves groan with every food item imaginable. People no longer squeeze between rotting wooden tables selling single stock cubes, plastic bags of pasta, or pyramid piles of rotting veg but waddle past, their expanding waistlines and sagging bottoms protruding from behind piled high shopping trolleys.

At Chameleon Lodge in the heart of Windhoek find paradise, with pool, courtyard, dormitories, private rooms, camping and a huge communal kitchen. Razor wire and broken glass is replaced with shiny neat electric fencing, electricity and hot water. The 'Windhoek' experience, of getting mugged at knifepoint, is to be avoided by not going out at night, showing any visible signs of wealth, or carrying large amounts of money. I am not a jewellery type of girl, I don't own any carat-ed gold necklaces or rings or even a watch, don't go out at night and certainly don't have large amounts of money, so I'm good.

We have an old wallet with expired credit cards, a few dollars and the remaining currency we didn't use in it. The thinking was, if we were robbed at knife, or even gunpoint, giving them this will give us chance to flee. We used to carry it with us but have given up on the idea and leave it in the front of Lizzybus; carrying it made a bulge in David's pocket that looked like a wallet, as it was a wallet. There is lots of advice about carrying fake documents, money belts, splitting cash, having hidden safes and the likes, in theory this sounds great but in practice it's unworkable. The best thing is to make sure you have copies of all your documents and, of course, only have small amounts of cash on you. Our stash of cash, you could say, is hiding in full view but I'd have to kill you if I told you where.

In the communal kitchen the included breakfast of toast, cereals, coffee, tea and milk, on Sundays even a boiled egg, has become my favourite part of the day. John and June, the Kiwis gave us one of the two, five-hundred-gram jars of 'traditional' New Zealand Vegemite. Even if you liked it, which we don't and were to spread it on your toast every day, it would last the rest of your life. But we're gracious in the accepting of their gift to us, whilst waiting for an opportunity to donate it to a good cause. The communal kitchen is just perfect, as it's full of backpackers from all over the world, some familiar with Vegemite, some tasting it for the first time but all ecstatic to have it.

We're given the number of big Ollie, an English guy living here, who runs a garage out in the bush, speaking to him were thrilled to find he just so happens to have a turbo charger and will pop over today for a chat. Big Ollie is, as his name suggests, big, in stature and personality, having adopted the laid-back

African way, it's late afternoon and we're all still chatting. Arrangements are made for us to drive out to his place tomorrow when Lizzybus will get a brand-new turbo.

We find big Ollie off a winding track an hour outside of Windhoek, his home set up in a barn, attached to someone's house. Big Ollie knows his stuff, has a genuine interest in Land Rovers but I feel a distance in him from people, his not lonely but alone, existence has created. I feel like a proud parent, as big Ollie is impressed with Lizzybus overall but before working on her, insists on cleaning the engine. Once the old turbo is removed, stop for lunch, where we see why big Ollie got his name, when tucking into his lunch of eight slices of well-buttered toast, wrapped around chunks of cheese. As we never brought any lunch, or were offered any, David takes this chance to do an oil and filter change. I'm not exactly sure what but lots of other bits have been done to Lizzybus, some of which will need to be finished tomorrow.

Back at the Superstore, with a trolley full of stuff for lunch and a crate of beer, head back to big Ollie's. Lots of bits are welded, replaced, cleaned and greased, from engine mounts, to drive flanges, to drive shafts. All I know is that, with drive-something in its title, it must mean it's most important for the purpose of driving, which is very promising. With her new turbo and other bits and bobs done, Lizzybus no longer belches smoke, okay she still does a little but only on start-up and smells of new rubber and oil. It's an incredible feeling to have given her some tender loving care and to have confidence back in her once more. To us, on our journey alone, this really can be a matter of life or death.

When setting off on this journey, work colleagues, friends and family wanted to buy us gifts to take with us, I insisted they didn't, as it would only become stuff. What I did do is take things of theirs, things that would be both useful and reminders of them and home. One was a towel, embroidered with the name and paw print of my daughter's Doberman, Fudge. As my daughter and now son-in-law, lived next door, I watched as this pissing, chewing puppy grew into a loyal obedient huge part of our family. Today this once black, now grey, loved rag of a towel hanging on the communal washing line has been stolen. I get a message to say Fudge has suffered a heart attack whilst out on a run and passed away.

Chapter 14
The Real Beauty of Africa

Namibia, at nearly four times the size of the United Kingdom, a tortured landscape of rock, open plains and bleak coastline, a hostile environment and the last place on earth where black rhino, cheetah and dessert elephant roam free. Spread out before us the road meanders through swaths of scrubland, even with her new turbo, Lizzybus struggles against a fierce furnace hot, head wind, on our way to the Etosha National Park.

Etosha National Park, translated as 'great white place,' or 'place of emptiness,' is half the size of Switzerland, formed around the Etosha Pan, a huge depression which becomes a lake in heavy rainfall, bringing hibernating catfish and water turtle back to life. For now, it's a blinding expanse of flat shimmering white, with spiralling dust devil whirlwinds chasing each other off to the horizon. Pay thirty dollars each entrance fee, to see tiny bee yellow flowers adorning the hardy gorse along the dusty, well laid-out roads, leading to specifically placed water holes, adjacent to fully equipped camping sites, secured behind electric fences, the only place you can camp at another thirty dollars.

On the evening via floodlight in a secured area, watch the nocturnal animals, seemingly oblivious to the balcony of onlookers. It feels orchestrated and almost sterile, for me one of the beauties of nature is to stumble on it, still, to at last be seeing these incredible animals, is very special. I miss desperately normal conversation, the, "What is your mission?" "What have you got for us?" From military and police, replaced with "Where have you come from?"
"Where have you been?" and "Where are you going?"

Driving through the park I'm eight years old again, watching in glorious technicolour the big screen at my local cinema, as Joy and George Adamson, in their Land Rover Defender, cross the plains of, okay, Kenya but a close second, raising Elsa the abandoned Lioness cub. But now, I'm looking not at a big screen but out of the window of our very own Land Rover, in total awe, alongside elegant lolloping giraffes, black and white humbug stripped Zebra and herds of wildebeest and antelope, springing through butter scorched grassland, it's quite simply, magical.

Press on along the Caprivi Strip, a long panhandle-shaped piece of land over four hundred and fifty kilometres long, in the northeast corner of Namibia, heading in the direction of Zambia. It's the first time I'm sort of aware of the route, thinking Namibia was our last country before South Africa, the last leg of this part of the journey. How exciting, we will be going to Zambia, not just Zambia but Zambia into Botswana, before dropping down into South Africa. This flat flood plain is surrounded by three major rivers, the Zambezi, Kavango and Kwando, forming the boundary to Namibia, Zambia, Botswana, Angola and Zimbabwe. I'm still at the stage of it all being one great big adventure but what has not become fully apparent yet, is that this journey is one David never wants to end.

The rising sun heats up the day, occasional white Toyotas complete with roof tents pass, considering this is one of the least populated countries in the world, bush camping is not an option, as cattle fences secure mile after mile of white Namibian owned farmsteads. Some of these farmsteads offer cheap, immaculately maintained, self-catering huts or camping pitches, with showers and toilets. At the one we're camped at, with the roof tent erect, dinner simmering away in the pressure cooker, the owner asks if we would like to feed the pet lion? We don't but go with him anyway to a football-sized enclosure where a magnificent lion, its two gigantic feet straddling half a freshly shot animal carcass, turns his ash blond mane, crimson red. This lion, rescued as a cub, now domesticated, is unable to be released back into the wild—life is not always like the film.

We hear a high-pitched clipped English voice squawking "Bow-wow, naughty Bow-wow, come here," followed by a panting blond-haired woman, Lucy. Lucy and Australian boyfriend Rob, planned to drive to South Africa from England in a brand-new Discovery Land Rover bought by her father but they couldn't afford the Carnet De Passage bond. The bond, from two to ten times (depending on the country), is calculated on the value of your vehicle, based on the most expensive country you intend to pass through.

Lizzybus being ancient on paper, is only worth a couple of thousand; for them, with such a valuable vehicle being unable to raise the money needed for the bond, shipped directly to Namibia, to drive directly to South Africa, avoiding all this.

Lucy is a breath of fresh air, chaos surrounds her, she asks us to join them later for a Braai, as the Namibians they met on the border are coming to pay her back the five hundred dollars she lent them, basically all the cash they possessed. I'm quite shocked she did this, sceptical she will ever see them, or her money, ever again. But I'm wrong, two white pick-ups arrive, packed full of Namibians. Once paying Lucy her five hundred dollars, they start setting up the Braai. A Braai that takes hours to reach temperature, one where only holding your hand over it for five seconds before it burns is acceptable. As the racks of salted lamb ribs go on, we're shown a video on the phone of their twelve-year-old son, who earlier that day shot, gutted and prepared these ribs.

I can't take it in, firstly that they are here and have Lucy's money but more so of it being outside of anything I used to think of as normal. What happened to the proud parent for the latest school report, or the goal scored, or a painting hung on the kitchen wall, I'm not sure how to respond. Sitting alongside the ribs now are coils of homemade Boerewors, from the Afrikaans-Dutch words, boer and wors.

Learning about making Boerewors is a lot gentler, regulated by the South African government, they must contain at least ninety percent beef, lamb and pork, or a mixture and should not contain offal, or any mechanically recovered meat pulp. Top-secret recipes are handed down through the generations, with annual Boerewors competitions. It's just incredible to be part of this evening, to feel their passion and pride in this tradition, a real privilege and the best ribs we have ever tasted.

At breakfast Bow-wow bounds up with his new buddy, a twelve-month-old pet warthog which rubs up against our legs and rolls over wanting its tummy scratched. I'd say I don't know what is happening to me but whatever it is, has happened, as I scratch this warthog's stomach with one hand and Bow-wow's with the other. Reluctant to say our goodbyes, rejuvenated by conversation and tradition, feel part of something once more, as we continue on along the Caprivi Strip. As evening closes in camp at River Side Lodge, under a new moon, swim in the river, chatting about last night, before tucking into the 'doggie bag' of salted ribs and Boerewors.

We stay three glorious relaxing days at our riverside retreat before pressing on, a few kilometres later cross the 'Red Line,' a manned barricade preventing the movement North to South (you can take it South to North) of livestock, meat, animal skins, horns, trophies etc. in the fight against foot and mouth and rinderpest (rinderpest will be declared eradicated by the World Organisation for Animal Health in another year). The Caprivi is only four hundred and fifty kilometres, just a road to a destination but we're having such an adventure driving along it. A habitat for the endangered wild African dog, a corridor for African elephant moving from Botswana and Namibia into Angola, Zambia and Zimbabwe, it's incredible just seeing these majestic animals, right here in the bush.

At Ngepi Campsite, on the Okavango River, it has a sunken cage you can swim in, to watch crocodiles and hippopotamus. Wooden stumps prevent access to your allocated pitch, we have to park adjacent to it on the path. For people with a pitched tent, this is not a problem but for us with a roof tent on our vehicle it is, the owners know it's a problem but didn't think to mention it. Living on savings and rental income, the budget is tight, the cost of visas and diesel our biggest expense, paying for camping or eating out is at times a necessity but always a treat, having to pay to effectively camp on a path makes us incredibly grumpy.

One of the downsides to the many hours sat in a Lizzybus with no radio on is the freedom it gives your mind to go over and over insignificant shite, such as wishing we had just refused to pay last night. Sat in our silence, hear a hissing noise and steam coming out of the engine, the needle on the temperature gauge alarmingly heads into the red. Pulling over into a lay-by under a huge tree, find the water pump cracked and pissing out water. It's nearly two hundred kilometres to the next small town, we have to change it or do terminal damage to the engine block.

My respect in all the 'spares' David brought along reaches a climax, he produces a new water pump. Three hours later, having removed what seems like half the front end of Lizzybus, in efforts to unbolt the water pump, the two bottom bolts, almost impossible to get at, just won't budge. I wave down a vehicle towing a speedboat, the first vehicle we have seen in three hours, they phone a local mechanic. As its Sunday, a day most Namibians apparently only drink beer and Braai, they can arrange a tow at four hundred dollars and book us a hotel for the night, to fix her Monday.

Thanking them, refuse this offer, they drive off, we're alone once more, nothing more to do than have another go, David sets to taking the small radiator and other things off to get at the two offending bolts. Doing this in your garage at home, with access to any and every tool, knowing help is at hand if needed, is totally different from doing it here, in this harsh, desolate environment, where no help is available, and your life depends on it. David questions his capabilities.

Darkness descends, having finally got access to the offending bolts, they're heated with our mini blowtorch, still they refuse to budge. After checking in the box full of "These will be useful, son" bits that Mr T Senior insisted we took, find two, perfect replacement bolts, David can now resort to the final plan of drilling them out. I hate myself for doubting David but I'm sure everything will never go back together and all the pieces will be lost, we start arguing.

It's a while before we realise there is a group of herdsmen standing silently in the bush watching, stopping us mid-sentence. Through sign language and broken English, they ask if we're staying the night, not wanting to admit we might have to, in unison say "No!" On leaving as silently as they came, warn us to watch out for the elephants. It's almost midnight, having fitted the water pump, unable to see if everything is back where it should be, even with head torches, decide to wait until the daylight of another day to check. Using an old rag, wipe the grease from our hands, saving our precious water to re-fill the radiator, even our bowl of noodles tastes of grease as I used the dish to put nuts and bolts in. Greasy, stinking, worried and totally alone, get into the roof tent.

"Can you hear that, David?" "What?"

My whispered words hang heavy in the rancid roof tent, through the mosquito net, illuminated by the full moon, I see what looks like the floating blobs you get when blinded by a flashlight. Then just like binoculars twiddled to focus, my eyes, without any twiddling, focus. Elephants, not one or two but a whole herd of them, surround us. I watch fascinated as they reach up into the trees breaking off small branches, stripping the bark off with their mouths and tusks. One of the few lessons I do remember from school, was that an elephant's trunk is a fusion of nose and upper lip, used for breathing, smelling, touching, grasping and producing sound. Never did I ever imagine how this lesson would be proven to me and right now, sure as hell it's one I don't want to be learning.

It's with a mixture of terror and sheer awe that we watch; they are so close I see the moon reflected in their swimming pool eyes, under luscious long lashes. Knowing how incredibly inquisitive elephants are, a tusk, a trunk could easily tear through our canvas, overturn Lizzybus, I'm aware now more than ever of how loud David breathes, I want him to stop! In a whisper, ask why the hell we didn't ask the herdsmen what to actually do if elephants come? Slowly our gentle giants move on, looking for fresh bark, drifting off once more, dream of rampaging elephants.

What feels like only seconds later, we're woken by the hissing of air brakes, two gigantic lorries, each pulling two split-level trailers, full of cattle. David got up to speak to them, I stay in the tent, they are two days into a four-day drive, from South Africa to the Congo. It's so very strange, there is no mooing from the cattle, just a steady rumble of shuffling feet like a hushed stampede.

Before even the sun appears from the east, David is up making coffee for us and the cattle guys. We're knackered and still concerned about the new water pump and if Lizzybus is back in the right order. I think I dreamt about last night's elephant visit, until looking around, see the piles of dung and broken bush. We had been noticing many trees along the way, with what we thought were wild cat claw marks, to now realise its cause: elephant tusks. Elephant dung is special, burnt it acts as a mosquito repellent, inhaled a natural remedy for minor aches and pains, you can make paper or even coffee from it, here I draw the line, I don't fancy elephant dung coffee, one bit.

The new water pump shines in the old engine, filling the radiator with the last of our water, clean our teeth with spittle and wipe sweat off with the greasy rag. Right, it's time to fire Lizzybus up, she makes an ear-splitting squeal, the fan belt replaced as the old one had a slight split in it, is the wrong size. With the old belt back on, a bag of elephant dung secured to the roof rack, we're off. With bated breath, watch as the temperature gauge starts to move. It reaches halfway but continues, one blip past half, it settles, it's a euphoric, momentous moment for us both and for the rest of our journey, this is where it will stay.

We're visiting Mudumu National Park, what makes this park so special is there are no boundary fences, animals can migrate between Botswana and Angola, no strategically placed water holes, or viewing galleries behind electric fences, you're on your own.

It's in the southwestern corner of the Caprivi, an area of conserved swampland. At the ranger's hut, adorned with bleached elephant skulls and artefacts, we're given details of where to camp, on the banks of one of the lakes formed by the Kwando river floodplain. Down tracks of deep sand and mud, accessible only by four-wheel drive vehicles, the facilities are basic, a long drop toilet, with reed shelter and fire pit.

Setting up camp, we're concerned about the monkeys eyeing us from the trees; on the opposite bank, herds of elephant wash and play, water gushing from their trunk's cascades over them and their calves. I'm relieved on seeing sets of eyes lurking in the depths, that they also have ears, so are hippos, not crocs. As the sun begins to set, a crescendo of insect and birdlife fills our ears, once again I've been plonked right in the middle some wildlife survival programme. With our bag of elephant dung burning in the fire pit, in hope of distracting the swarming mosquitoes, not wanting to risk swimming in the lake, even though hippo, not crocs, with buckets of water wash us and our clothes, with all these monkeys, string them inside Lizzybus to dry.

I'm a bit of a drama queen I know and you would think by now I'm more than used to a few elephants but when you're in a roof tent, surrounded by these inquisitive giants of nature, a good night's sleep is not what you're going to get. I'm just glad I never left the washing out; I have visions of rampaging animals draped with our washing line and clothes. At ease once more with Lizzybus and life as it is now, full of our African adventure, the sun shines, the road is never ending, the Zambian boarder gets closer. One last night at an immaculate campsite on the banks of the rambling Zambezi River, complete with swimming pool and as there are warning signs everywhere to watch out for crocs and hippos, the pool is the only place we will be swimming. We don't exactly swim in it but sit, as the water has a green tinge but we're at the stage when finding a pool that actually has water in it, in this oppressive heat, is a treat.

Our Caprivi adventure is over, we reach the Zambian boarder, at forty-five dollars for the visa, twenty dollars carbon tax and twenty-seven dollars insurance, it's an expensive crossing but we think it's going to be worth it. Although landlocked, Zambia has three major rivers running through it, culminating in the spectacular 'The Smoke That Thunders' Victoria Falls. A country where the human footprint is rare and animals roam freely. A few kilometres past the border, we hit our first of many military roadblocks, the familiar rope across the road with shredded plastic bags. Confident they will never catch us out on anything, fail immediately as, for the first time, we have been asked to test our horn, which fails, contravening section whatever, of whatever, of the road traffic act. Looking through our documents, once again they assume David is an officer of the law, a comrade, after a few handshakes we're waved on our way.

The Africa we have come to know is back, homes of reed and mud, barefoot children draped in earth-coloured tattered rags, people live subsistence lives gathering wood and working on the land, next to fenced off high class lodges, some complete with private airstrips. Maramba Lodge, offering opulent chalets or luxury tents for the African experience without the deprivation of it, allows us to camp in its grounds and use the facilities, including the pool, for ten dollars a night.

Today we see nature at its finest. At the mighty Victoria Falls, we feel its incredible power and deafened by its noise cascading thunderously into a deep gorge a hundred meters below us, billowing clouds of mist rise from this seething cauldron, shimmering rainbow shafts of light rise with it. Not the highest, or the widest, waterfall in the world but it has the largest falling sheet of water and this is breathtaking. A winding path leads us to the head of these falls, where a vast expanse of river meanders, forming two islands, one known as Livingstone Island, where, in eighteen fifty-five David Livingstone, the first recorded European laid eyes on these falls, naming them Victoria Falls, after Queen Victoria.

I might not have had the education I wanted, or needed, having been born a twin but sat here now with David, feet dangling in the Zambezi River overlooking Victoria Falls, eating cheese triangles with chunks of bread, I'm certainly having my education now. It's a 'pinch me' moment in life and time, one I want to stay locked into for eternity.

We're taking Lizzybus, who I realise has become David's demanding and very temperamental mistress, to Foleys, an English expedition preparation vehicle specialists. For those interested, several things are replaced, firstly the pesky horn, then a ball joint, along with more greasing, tightening and adjusting but overall, they are impressed with Lizzybus and how she is holding up, again we are like the proud parents.

This is a much-needed boost to David, able to talk endlessly about what could, might and has gone wrong, is therapy, a therapy I no longer allow. I know the magnitude and responsibility of Lizzybus stops at David's door, it colours his enjoyment of our journey but the consequences of her failing affect us both equally. I see how voicing these worst-case scenarios help the person, David but the recipient, me, sits in my uneducated constant worry.

This causes tensions between us; travelling like this, you're at the mercy of each other. I also have worries but on a more personal level, like hygiene and intimacy, I desperately need to address and talk over but discussing feelings has never and will never, be part of David. I'm finding at times I just want to gaffer tape his mouth shut, in fact I've gone past wanting, I have moved on to imagining and that's most appealing.

The words, or conversation I never thought I needed but now realise I do and feel pissed with myself for, are telling me he loves me, or how good I look. Yeah, okay, how anyone could 'look good' under these circumstances is a stretch but that's no excuse, he could at least pretend. One of David's go-to responses when asked how he is feeling about life, the journey, me, is "I've not thought about it." I just wished he had 'not thought about all the other shit,' then he wouldn't need to talk about it quite so much.

I know we are both united in our journey, in our new life but are becoming distanced in our personal one, a fact that David is totally oblivious to. Since hygiene has been an issue, any physical closeness is non-existent and has become the norm. Of course, a shower, shave and clipping of toenails, so they don't leave huge scratches down my legs every time he turns over, can easily be remedied. But, for some reason unfathomable to me, David sees grease filled fingernails as evidence to all the hours of greasing.

I understand that hair cannot be cut from ears, nose, head and face, on a regular basis but an occasional one, would be most agreeable. I feel this nomadic existence has released the inner caveman in David, he is becoming almost feral. Just like when prioritising and sorting kit, I have prioritised emotional and physical needs but I have momentary lapses when I become fragile and needy.

From wanting so much to see elephants, we now can't get away from them, still camping in the grounds of Maramba Lodge, we're woken by the staff banging big metal dustbin lids in their efforts to chase a rogue elephant calf out. In the cushioned open veranda of the lounge, we're joined by Charley Boorman and his group of guests, who at great expense, are on a two week, 'Taste of Africa' adventure on motor bikes. Charlie, with the actor Ewan McGregor, has over the years done some of the toughest, most incredible motor bike routes in the world, aided and abetted by sponsors and back up crews The most recent, a twenty thousand four hundred kilometre trip from Scotland to South Africa, 'The Long Way Down,' similar to our route but the first leg of it, becoming a documented television series, with other routes added over the years.

Of course, I've heard of Charley and his accomplishments but I never quite got into him, finding an irresponsibility in his reliance on his back up teams of mechanics, doctors and admin. I never felt the real passion from Charley, just a constant of all the trials and tribulations endured, specifically of being followed by a film crew, a film crew that did as much as he did and filmed. Meeting him has not changed this, I can't help feeling a little judgmental as to his achievements but I can be, with first-hand experience to the realities of it.

It makes me think of all the crazy driven people we have met, along the way, in trucks, on bikes, or just backpacking, who I've come to love and respect. Of course, we all journey through life in different ways, this is his, their journey, although different from ours, it's still an incredible one. Charley, a family man, has managed to turn this love of travel into a career, through books, films and fee-paying guests: now that's an achievement.

At three in the morning in our roof tent realise the removal of the renegade elephant calf was unsuccessful as he is back, only this time with the whole family.

Today we cross into Botswana, one of Africa's most stable countries, relatively free of corruption, its wealth from diamonds used to transform it into a middle-income nation, with some of Africa's largest areas of wilderness. HIV-AIDS is prevalent, despite having one of Africa's most advanced treatment programmes. It's a simple border crossing, straight onto a small ferry, over I think the Limpopo River; if it's not the Limpopo, I want it to be, as it sounds just wonderful when you say it out loud, just as if you have a mouthful of marbles.

The plan, I use that word loosely, as planning is not something we plan, so I'll change it to destination for now, is still South Africa, completing our west coast African leg. I have never really seen this journey as having a beginning or an end, it just began and I'm sure it will just end. But I am realising the longer I'm on it, the more I focus on getting Lizzybus around the world and of it having an end. I'm finding myself looking at the map, having an opinion on where we go—for me it's back to Namibia and directly to South Africa. For David it's the opposite, he never wants to reach any destination, as reaching it is a chapter over, closed, finished. He makes me smile, like a child who wants to keep playing with all his favourite toys forever but I know we need a bit more structure.

The Chobe National Park, Botswana, affectionately known as 'the land of the giants,' the third largest in the world, home to the magnificent river lions, its greatest threat being Namibian farmers who shoot them for preying on livestock. With the concentration of over fifty thousand short-tusked Kalahari elephant, its eco-system struggles, in the rainy season, they migrate two hundred kilometres into northwestern Zimbabwe. The Chobe Park is vast, David has been told about 'The Sand Road' through its heart, so despite everything I said about wanting to get on with this journey, I am excited about this challenge, our next adventure.

Both confident now in ours and Lizzybus' abilities, deflate tyres, fill the tanks with diesel, the Jerry Cans with water, the foot-well with beer and the draw with food, we're ready. It's the softest sand that saps all the power from Lizzybus, keeping her moving is imperative as it becomes liquid. Troupes of monkeys hang out in the trees grooming each other, elegant giraffe stretch to reach the most succulent buds high up amongst the trees, wrapping their snake-like tongues around them. Thinking it will be one main track, find lots of distracting tracks off it, it's a little used road with only the occasional concrete sign, navigation is now based on compass points, we're constantly bogged down and having to dig out progress: it's torturous.

Setting up camp in the bush, David worries about our petrol consumption, how long the water will last and the apparent 'not a clue' situation we seem to be in. The adventure and purpose taken away, it's become an arduous task, although prepared with maps and coordinates, they're not detailed enough. Forgetting I had been excited about this route, now remembering I had not wanted to come this way, I voice my frustrations. So here we are, camped on a sand road, somewhere in The Chobe Park, Botswana, David sitting inside Lizzybus due to insect life and worry, me sweating it out in socks, long trousers and shirt, outside writing my diary.

It's the start of a realisation for me, that we don't actually have to, or need to, do every single challenge along the way, the journey itself is the challenge. Our route takes us through incredible remote scenic desert and mountain roads anyway, without these detours, I feel we should be concentrating more on the progress, not the challenges, the cracks are beginning to show.

A night's sleep has not lightened the mood, David insists we retrace our tracks back to the main road, which of course is the right thing to do. I refuse to drive after his cutting comment of me apparently not letting the engine warm up, compounded by the "So I have to do all the driving as well now," a slight to my appalling map reading abilities. It's a telling sign amongst couples, of something that amused you about the other, to now be used against them and a very destructive path. I'm sitting choking on the 'stupid bastard' words I want to shout at him, let the engine warm up? We're nearly at forty degrees. The day ends more or less as it started, back on the main road with insults slung throughout it, as I still refuse to drive.

It's late when we make it to a local camp site, what we don't realise is how this journey is taking its toll on us both, worn down, travel weary, with no network of friends, family, or work to give us the approval and support needed, we are falling apart. We push ourselves like this, with a stupid ideology of what the journey should be, feeling almost obliged to take the toughest, most scenic route, when in reality the constant of it, is just too much.

David has decided that he is going to get Lizzybus shipped back from South Africa, to be broken down and sold, his mind is made up.

His giving up would be the end for me, it makes me feel incredibly vulnerable, resentful and bitter, to be even put in this position. If ever we were to 'give up,' it should be a unanimous, giving up decision, not a fait accompli. I'm hurting, broken, with no-where to turn, it just seems crazy that with everything we have faced so far, to fall apart now.

We just can't seem to find the strength to support each other and honestly, I don't want to pep talk David, when I feel he has become the traitor.

Despite all this, as we're in the Delta region with rippling beds of water lilies and forests of baobabs, head off to explore it. I drive and for the first time whilst I drive, David, emotionally and physically exhausted, sleeps. In this moment my heart breaks for him. Our heart not in it, it was almost a given, that with the lack of proper maps, a day so hot you could cook an egg on the Lizzybus engine, a sand road disguising itself amongst a maze of dead ends, we would give up. Finding ourselves outside a little whitewashed bakery, buy six gigantic fresh out the oven doughnuts, filled with synthetic cream and jam, eat the lot and head back.

It seems ignoring, instead of addressing, issues will be what we do, I know unresolved they will be back to haunt us, today we hit the Trans Kalahari Highway, known for its monotony, cows, scrub and the odd wild horse back to Namibia. At the border, they are chatty and welcoming; we pay another twenty-dollar carbon tax, even though the one paid for on entering is valid for three months, it has to be re-paid on leaving, or re-entering.

Back at the backpackers in Windhoek having coffee, hear the familiar hissing sound of escaping air, another of the new valves fitted to the tyres in Ghana jettisoned, it's incredible it happened here, where we can get it fixed, not in the Delta or Chobe. We spend a great evening with Clive, an English guy and his latest group of volunteers, paying three hundred and fifty dollars a week to work at the 'AfriCat Foundation,' a non-profit organisation for the protection and conservation of Namibia's wild carnivores north of here.

Namibia is an incredible country, with good roads, English speaking, without the constant roadblocks, it allows us to relax, a much-needed respite, making real progress on our journey, whilst doing and seeing stuff along the way, rather than going backwards. We're heading for Walvis Bay, the largest coastal city in Namibia, which has a natural deep-water harbour, the Benguela ocean current and winds make plankton-rich water that attract the mighty southern right whales, wow, for real, I'm going to see whales! It's bitterly cold at night, our deserted campsite has wonderful hot showers, which I am most reluctant to get out of. It's morning and I'm back under the oh-so-hot shower, I know how very precious water is but I just can't help having a little longer under it to warm up.

The city of Swakopmund, surrounded on three sides by desert, the fourth the South Atlantic just appears from a nothingness. You imagine, having the title of a city, it would be sprawling and congested but it's not, it's pristine and manicured, the turreted pastel-coloured buildings picture postcard pretty. Over twenty-five years, the German Imperial government built extravagant buildings here, which today is the best collection of German Colonial buildings. It's out of season and deserted as we drive through on our way to the Cape Coast fur seal colony. A small marble headstone marks the community graveyard where one hundred and twenty-four people died trying to make a living here producing fertilizer from the nutrient rich guano (droppings of birds, bats, or seals).

A few rusted tracks all that remains of the sixteen-kilometre train track running across the barren harsh salt plain, I can only imagine the hardship they faced. On a wooden walkway over a carpet of Cape Brown Fur seals, the largest of the fur seal family, you are only feet away from them. They are social animals basking together in the sun, heaving their huge bodies around on flippers, raising their heads high, bark, groan and croak, the smell is something else, if I wasn't so fascinated, I'd be retching, quite incredible.

At the local campsite, there is a kitchen area with an electric cooker, it just so happens we bought a big bag of potatoes and a chicken in town, put the lot into the oven, whilst I'm under another, oh-so-hot shower. The smell of roasting chicken and potatoes is intoxicating, two hours later, share with the equally frozen security guard, the most delicious baked potatoes and roast chicken. Fully clothed get into our sleeping bags, it must have been cold as we zip our sleeping bags together for body heat, despite the ongoing tensions.

The set up in Lizzybus, or lack of it, being unable to get inside her, out of the cold and rain is tough, the gaffer taped mouse holes and broken corner (David parking back in Spain), the constant putting up and down, is just not working, not least the security issue of us sleeping on the roof, it has to be changed but we just can't see how.

We're heading inland to visit Clive, who we met in Windhoek, at his 'Paws for thought' cheetah volunteer programme, a part of the AfriCat Foundation, along the Salt Road, its surface hard as concrete, made slippery as ice with the morning dew. Clive met us at the gate on his quad, to take us to the campsite he built himself—it's picture perfect, with open air kitchen roundel toilets, beautiful reed-built huts and communal fire fit pit. It's a wonderful evening, chatting with the latest group of 'volunteers,' hearing about their lives and future plans. It's so very special spending time with people full of enthusiasm for their adventure, exactly what I crave.

The 'volunteers' in the mornings go off on little safaris in search of cheetah, the programme is set up on a two-week turnaround. Speaking to one volunteer staying for a month, he feels the work of 'fence building and hole digging' is created rather than needed. After the morning, the afternoons are free to utilize the pool and siesta in the hamacas in the grounds of the game lodge. The volunteers, in pairs, are rota'd to collect wood, make fires, cook, wash up and clean; they are all given laminated sheets with the duties and how to carry them out, including cooking the evening meal. It's not exactly the work they do as volunteers but more the income generated from their stay, which in turn helps the charity.

We're not invited to go out on safari with them and get on with the odd jobs that always need doing, like replacing three of the four sheared bolts holding the roof tent on, fitting the new windscreen wipers to stop the squeaking chalk-on-a-board noise when we use them.

Once back, their food is budgeted for, we understand us eating it is not an option, put the chicken and potatoes left from last night, wrapped in foil, in the fire pit with theirs, it's still wonderful just eating together around a campfire over conversation.

David donates half his video collection, as they have a video player but no films, still at a time of no internet, it's a real treat. Heading now to the desert dunes of Sossusvlei, on a tarmac road, lost to drifting sand, up, over and around these ever-changing dune mountains is quite magical. Camped overnight in this vastness of emptiness, hear animal hoofs, expecting to see camels, antelope or the like, see donkeys.

Pushing on through headwinds and sand, we're using a tank of diesel a day, finding places to re-fuel becomes an issue, the long-range fuel tank and being able to filter water for drinking has been crucial. We're at a Dam, I'm not sure which Dam, disappointed as its fenced off, so can't swim in it, press on to the isolated outpost of Solitaire, derived from the lone dead tree that stands next to its service station. A dead tree that featured in a Toyota advertisement and title of a Dutch novel, it has a haunting beauty, surrounded by half buried rusted cars, who never made it out, its fame has made it a place to visit, so has a bustling bakery, with fresh bread and pastries.

Facing gale force furnace winds, cracking open the window even slightly sand blasts you, with the air vents sealed shut, it's like being cooked alive. Pull over at a camping sign, we're greeted by the limping toothless owner, as skeletal as the Solitaire tree, he shows us the row of hanger-shaped corrugated and cement block buildings, built by himself, big enough to park double-decker buses in, each with a kitchen and bathroom, it's fantastic to get out of the wind.

We enter The Dune Sea Park, ever-moving, ever-changing, a striking landscape, to Sossusvlei, dead end marsh, or place of no return, where the iron oxides produce okra reds, to blushing pink, undulating dunes, over five million years old. Wind coming from all directions form star-shaped dunes, amongst the highest in the world, a unique 'fog' provides water, supporting plants and wildlife. Before the rising sun burns off the cloud, we climb the snaking ribbon dune of Big Daddy, to its summit for our boiled egg breakfast.

I live in flip flops, drive in them, hike in them but today I'm barefoot, as the sand can reach temperatures of one hundred and fifty degrees, we have to get down before it absorbs the sun's heat. One of the incredible things about sand dunes is it takes hours to hike up them but only a few minutes to get down. Taking giant strides the sand grains support and lower you to the bottom, it's just delightful.

Heading South through sand mountains, ahead a of what looks like thick fog but is a sandstorm, pull over under a lone tree sitting just off the gravel road, adjacent to the miles of fenced off area. The strength of it rocks us, I think we have been buried in our very own sand dune, we see nothing through the windows, sand is forced through the gaps in the doors; a thick coating of sand settles on everything, our faces are gritty, licking my lips, the grains crunch between my teeth. Once passed, there is a calm, a silence, giving us a peaceful night, until the rising sun brings a shimmer back to the desert around us.

From sand dunes to sandcastles, visit the Duwisib Castle, built of local red sandstone, a reminder of Namibia's Colonial past when in the nineteen hundreds an American heiress and her German husband commissioned it. The building materials, like iron, wood, cement, etc. along with all the furnishings, were shipped from Europe before being loaded onto wagons and pulled by oxen through the dessert. Despite being now owned by the government and having been extensively restored, as it retains a lot of the original furnishings and beautiful flagstone floors, it's still impressive. But I am English, a nation known for our castles, I do feel a little, "Call this a castle?" moment.

Driving on to one of the least hospitable coastal harbour towns at Luderitz, along the only road in and out of it, at three hundred kilometres. It's a small town with faded picturesque German Colonial buildings, all but abandoned until in the nineteen hundreds and the discovery of diamonds, the diamond rush began. It prospered for a while when the town of Kolmanskop, ten kilometres away, was built specifically for the mining community. It's here at a backpackers that we call the number on the note pinned to the door, a guy tells us where the door key is and to 'make ourselves at home.' It's a huge place with kitchen, dining and television room, double and six bed dorm rooms. The whole place is ours for eighteen dollars a night—we're to leave the money on the table when we leave.

Today visit the mining ghost town of Kolmanskop where in the nineteen hundreds a railway worker found a shiny stone, claimed by his German boss, who secured a prospector's licence, and the diamond rush began. By the nineteen twenties, three hundred Germans and their black labourers were contracted to a two-year contract, working seven-day weeks on twelve-hour shifts. During this time, they were forbidden to leave the secured fenced-off area, until on their final week, they were imprisoned and fed castor oil, when their faeces was checked for hidden diamonds. At the very beginning, just crawling on hands and knees in full moonlight, the diamonds could be plucked from the surface, until being mined for real.

What a haunting place this is, a once thriving community, complete with bowling alley, gymnasium, concert hall, school, hospital and the first X-Ray machine in Africa (more for detecting diamonds than broken bones). Supplied by ships sailing from Cape Town, every resident was given twenty litres of water per day. It struck me that, when we are on the road, that's our allocation of water. This abandoned town, slowly disappearing, semi submerged in sand, faded shredded remains of silk wallpaper flutters in the breeze, I feel the life that was. In nineteen twenty-eight, diamonds six times the size were discovered at the mouth of Orange river, the great diamond migration began. This very special day ended alone, back at our backpackers, with potatoes and pork chops roasting in the oven reading emails from home, as joy of joys there is even internet.

Reluctantly leave our little home, the distances are vast, the areas all but deserted, we enter the Quiver Tree Forest. The quiver tree is a national monument of Namibia and just like the baobab, it looks upside down, with its smooth bark and strangled branches sprouting grey-green leaves, with pineapple tops. Not really a tree but a succulent plant, aloe dichotoma or kokerboom, it's a unique forest, some trees over three centuries old, it got its name as the Kalahari San Bushmen made arrow quivers from it. It's other worldly and very special, this is what the journey should be, pushing ourselves but not to our limits, a wonderful harmony descends.

In this remote vastness, I actually got stopped for speeding, eight kilometres over the limit. Firstly, we're shocked to find anyone out here, whilst super impressed with Lizzybus and her new turbo. David had a little chat with his comrades and all is forgiven.

We make it to Keetmanshoop National Park and Fish River Canyon, over one hundred and eighty million years, ice ages and movements in the earth's plates have made this the biggest canyon in Africa. Parking Lizzybus, hike to the breath-taking viewpoints, the scale of its ravine makes us feel like little ants on the rim. I've had a thorn in the sole of my heel, which has become infected, walking on tippy toes it's not long before my calves are screaming but I ignore it, as I don't want to get left behind. Camping in the park is allowed only at official campsites, here we find Claus, the German guy in a Toyota we met in Windhoek, who we had made our honorary English man, with his sense of irony and humour.

It's incredible how fulfilling conversation is, especially over a beer and Braai, we make a loose arrangement to meet Claus at Noordoewer, the first campsite over the border in South Africa. Just saying South Africa sends a shiver down my spine, have we really almost made it, have we got where we wanted to go? I'm breathless with this thought, the awareness of it, that we might actually make it, just us two in Lizzybus, might, just might, get there.

Included in the park entrance is access to Ais-Ais Hot Springs Retreat, where hot spring pools of varying heat are housed under a thatched roof and marble building, with crisp white cotton, wrapped around you two times, towels and recliner beds, apart from the lady on reception, there is not another soul here. We lounge, we bath, we snooze, wrapped in the pure white towels, longer than we should, before heading off. The magnitude of the landscape makes little dots of us, two hours later, David driving my feet as usual hanging out the window, I realise the heat of the pool has finally dislodging the infected thorn from my heel, I'm just mesmerised by my clean pinkie toes.

The day ends camped at Orange River; a mighty river, its life-giving water fingers up the banks to the surrounding mountains, turning arid landscape into lush carpets of vivid green. One of the hottest places in Namibia with its abundance of water, many acres are fenced off, given over to grape vineyards, their vines hang with succulent sun-ripened grapes you cannot get at. How I would love a whole bunch of those succulent sun ripened grapes, sat on a cheese board with crackers, right now.

Chapter 15
The Goal Is in Sight

It's just happened, we crossed the border, we are now in South Africa, it was so simple, no hours of writing out information in dog-eared ledgers, no physical searches of us or Lizzybus, our passports are 'scanned,' we are welcomed in, stick the final flag of West coast Africa, South Africa, on Lizzybus. I count the flags: it's our twenty-sixth country.

South Africa, known as the 'Rainbow Nation' due to its diversity of cultures, religions and people, rich in minerals, it struggles with corruption, poverty and petty crime. At five times bigger than England, it's vast, the capital is Pretoria but it's Cape Town, with Table Mountain, part of the oldest mountain range in the world, that is most iconic.

We're heading to Cape Town, stocking up at a local supermarket, something felt wrong, I was rammed with a shopping trolley and forced out of the queue. Looking around realised we are the only 'white people' here. Un-wittingly we're in what was once a blacks-only supermarket during apartheid, when black and white segregation was enforced. It's been over twenty years since this was abolished but despite the massive strides made, for us, here, we still feel a chosen separation. We decide to use any supermarket as we would back in England, whether the preserve of black or white, push our way back into the queue, hold firm and smile.

After our rendezvous with Claus, celebrating over a campfire with beer, of us all getting to South Africa, it's another farewell. We're swallowed up in this immense country, following the Orange River and the Cederberg mountain range, named after the native Clanwilliam Cedar (Widdringtonia wallichii) tree. Not the most spectacular tree, a little stumpy evergreen thing with globe-shaped cones but what makes it so special is how it thrives here in the harshest of conditions. This area of wild wilderness, with dramatic rock formations and San rock art, is where a German couple driving from Cape Town to Namibia broke down, the husband died and the wife, after a week, was found delirious from hunger, thirst and heat exhaustion. We understand exactly how, in this desolate remoteness, this could easily happen and passing or seeing other vehicles is very rare.

It's such a victorious moment today, before us we see, in all her majestic glory, silhouetted against the imposing Table Mountain, to a backdrop of the wild Atlantic, Cape Town, South Africa, the 'Mother City.' Dominated by Table Mountain, the city is outgrowing itself and slowly creeping up the mountain, the outskirts a maze of confusing flyovers, fly-unders and roundabouts. Grandiose Victorian buildings sit against modern skyscrapers, a city apparently worth crossing the world for and we agree. In the streets, it being the weekend, people enjoy the café culture at upmarket cafes, wine bars and restaurants. At Cat and Moose backpackers, for twenty dollars, get a six-bed dorm all to ourselves, the bathrooms, living area and kitchen shared.

What is extra special is the wonderful balcony, overlooking the streets of Cape Town with a perfect view of Table Mountain.

The downside is the chargeable, unsecured street parking for Lizzybus. We're advised not to leave anything on display as vehicle theft is prevalent here, we will have to find more secure parking. Named by the Dutch settlers in the late sixteen hundreds, Tafelberg, Table Mountain, as simply its summit is flat like a table and today we are going to hike up it. Just getting to its base from our backpackers takes an hour through the streets of Cape Town on a steady incline, having sat on our arses for many hours and many days, our bodies are asking us, 'why?' Once reaching the official start of the climb, follow small wooden pointers to its summit. A unique feature of Table Mountain is the tablecloth cloud formation that, just like a tablecloth, drapes over it.

The path becomes treacherous as the tablecloth of cloud sinks into the rising air, becomes rain; both in tee shirts and shorts, I'm in flip-flops, David in land sandals. The path leads directly under the waterfalls, soaking us—we're chilled to our core in the wind. Many people have lost their life on Table Mountain, in fact last year was a particularly bad year, with fifteen people dying. With no intention of helping them break any records, turn back, with every intention of returning tomorrow more prepared. Back at Cat and Moose after a hot shower, hot coffee, steaming noodles, wrapped in our sleeping bags, we're still shivering.

Watch back-to-back episodes of the Discovery Channel, whilst the wind rattles the old Victorian windows, dislodging its yellowed peeling paint.

It's Déjà vu heading once more to the foot of Table Mountain, this time drive the six kilometres to the base, fully prepared in hiking boots, waterproofs, handheld GPS and a picnic, with the added bonus of saving a dollar an hour for street parking. Taking the supposed toughest route, it's just fabulous, at times on hands and knees rock climbing, nose to nose with intricate tiny wild orchids, without the rain we can walk behind the lace curtain of algae, formed over waterfalls, secure in our footing and toasty warm.

Reaching the summit, we're rewarded with panoramic views of Cape Town, its harbour, the surrounding valleys and infamous Robin Island, where Nelson Mandela was incarcerated for twenty years. At the top a huge restaurant and gift shop, where the cable car exits; we eat our picnic, soak it all up, before hiking back down, feeling accomplished.

Back to the reality of travel and the logistics of it, my forty-page passport is full and needs replacing at the British Embassy here. I can't shake this wave of homesickness that's engulfing me, although David and I are back to being a piece of caring kit, the declaration of David's intentions on reaching South Africa to ship Lizzybus back and sell her, whilst I understand it's a process of adjustment, a moment in time we're both entitled to and was not meant, it's made me reflect. I'm so fiercely independent, it's come of having to support me and my children through life, for some stupid ridiculous reason this resurfaces feelings of a very dark time.

My husband was a good man but the world was going through a tough recession, unable to secure a decent job ended up labouring for a basic wage. He just lost his way, started drinking, spending the mortgage money and all our savings on alcohol, even after being sacked, he spent his days at his brother's, drinking.

The bailiffs had taken anything of any value, the local liquor store was knocking at the door for payment, at my local council armed with the repossession order, I was told to come back, with my children, when I was actually homeless. I lied on the mortgage application, forged pay slips, borrowed and begged, to buy my little house, swearing I would never be in this position again.

Of course, this situation is nothing like that now but feelings are hard to control, they get into your head, talking this through, specifically with David but right now anyone, would help. Setting out on this journey was a joint decision, well, joint idea, one we both made happen. People often talk about what you 'gave up' to do it. I suppose I gave up my sister and my children but as hard as it was and at times a real physical pain of missing, it was not giving them up, it was just moving onto the next chapter of my life. But the reality is David could continue on alone, if I gave up, something impossible for me to do if he gave up.

As my level of education was sealed from being born a twin with the policy of separating twins, I was learning nothing academically. With two of my sisters living and working in Canada as nannies by now, Jenny and I had been offered places with other families. But, as on the first of September nineteen seventy-two the school leaving age was raised from fifteen to sixteen, we had to stay on another year. Despite being assured we would still have many more opportunities, I became rebellious, smoking, drinking and playing truant, when reaching sixteen my only thought was not a career but independence and earning money was the only way I thought I would get it.

It was at this point my parents split up, any support we had from either was gone as they tried to get their own lives in order. Jenny and I supported each other, with two children each finally we grew up. Grafters, we worked any and every job until the day we had both bought our own house and had decent jobs. This is what made me so fiercely independent, self-sufficient; I know if, in England, David had said, "That's it, we are selling Lizzybus, it's over." I would have put the for sale notice up myself, I'm definitely a cut your nose to spite your face type of person, a very bad trait in me but I never said I was perfect.

We have something greater than just a relationship, we have a life, a life of adventure, a whole world we both want and need to explore and yes, what has become not just an idea, has now become the ultimate dream and something worth fighting for. I talk it through with David, who is gob-smacked I feel like this, when in his mind he didn't actually mean it and because he didn't mean it, thought I would know he didn't, so any reassurances were unnecessary. This has helped, whilst adding to the void in my feelings, it leaves a bitter taste, I'm finding so very hard to control.

I sit on the veranda with my morning coffee, the sun reflecting off the mustard yellowed, gloss painted balustrades overlooking the streets of Cape Town. I see life as it is in cities all around the world, road sweepers, traffic wardens, police, people on their way to work, taking children to school, walking their dogs. The homeless wave polystyrene cups at anyone walking past, searching through bins, wiping foods slops from beer bottles for the deposit on them, decanting any half-drunk liquid into plastic coke bottles for later. One guy finds a pair of boxer shorts in the bin, pulling them over his jeans, is now strutting up and down the pavement, as if on the catwalks of Paris.

We become domesticated: I get my hair re-plaited at the local salon, buy whole fillets of beef for carpaccio and salad, or fry with onions to eat with buttered baked potatoes. For David, a true carnivore, this red wine and red meat man diet is his idea of heaven. We had become so skinny on our African diet, an almost vegetarian diet, this amount of rich food is too much for us, both end up with terrible stomach ache. A few days later, we're back to our chicken rice and banana diet, with a beer each.

You can't help but admire Cape Town, its historic buildings preserved or restored alongside the ultra-modern skyscrapers and harbour full of multi-million-pound yachts but it's its historic past and struggles that make it what it is. Visit the haunting Jewish Holocaust Museum, beautiful Bertram House, a unique red brick Georgian style house, now a museum, Companies Gardens, an oasis in the heart of Cape Town. Initiated as part of the trade route rounding the tip of Africa, ships after months at sea could stock up on fresh produce grown in the garden. The South African Museum and Planetarium, spread over four floors, with life-size plastic replicas of dinosaurs and extinct sea-o-saurs(?).

In the dimly lit globe planetarium, David has a siesta in the reclining seats, I try to educate myself on star constellations. Slave Lodge, the second oldest building in Cape Town, once housing up to one thousand slaves, disturbing in its sterility with a muddled collection of relics from ancient Rome, Greece, Japan, Egypt, for me did nothing to convey the suffering of its past.

Instead of crossing my legs all night, I make the most of the ten steps and you're their bathroom, no ladder to climb, no hole to dig, no audience, just over polished oak flooring and a little chain to pull for flushing.

Life has found its rhythm, once more we spend the day sightseeing, this time at The Castle of Good Hope, now Cape Town Castle, the oldest existing building in South Africa and home to the Cape Town Highlanders Regiment. Its unique pentagonal shape featured on flags and monuments, at midday, gather on the parade ground to watch the changing of the guard and firing of the cannon. In full ceremonial uniform, in kilts of Gordon tartan, a tiny cannon is carried onto the parade ground, once on the ground they have to bend to prime and fire it. It's just hysterical, I think of the Queen's Household Calvary and its changing of the

Guards, with all its pomp and ceremony but of course they can't let off a life-sized cannon in the middle of the parade ground, it was very special, in that it was so underwhelming.

After breakfast of avocado, lemon and oil on crusty wholemeal bread (you can see how the diet has changed), set off to hike Lion's Head, the mountain opposite Table Mountain resembling a crouching lion or sphinx. It was a challenging hike, pulling yourself up with chains and ropes anchored to the rock at specific points but you're well rewarded with a three-hundred-and-sixty-degree panoramic view of Table Mountain, Cape Town and Robben Island, a splat in the mighty Atlantic Ocean. I liked it even better than Table Mountain, as the physical effort to reach its summit kept it peaceful and quiet, no cable car or gift shop here.

One last day becomes another one last day. At the Holocaust Centre and Jewish Museum, reading the accounts and personal stories is sobering but feels respectful and poignant, that their voices are still heard through their letters. Back at Companies Gardens, eat our picnic watching squirrels, obligatory in all parks. We feel an unrest here in this country, a bubbling undercurrent of unease—it's edgy and not in a good way.

It's said that, over time, 'over Landers' suffer from the 'over-Lander disease' of wanting to stay put, to stop moving, settling in the country they hold up in, to make a new life, never getting to their perceived destination. I can't settle, as my first and, as it turns out, what will be my only grandchild is about to make his appearance. My quiet undemanding son would never ask me to be there with him but as his only living parent I absolutely want and need to. Before leaving Cape Town book flights to England next month from Johannesburg, one thousand two hundred and sixty-two kilometres away. I will fly home to be with my son, my lost to me mother renew my passport, celebrate my daughter's wedding, and get some much needed Lizzybus spare parts This makes me feel all warm inside, I see everything again as it should be, without the compromise of precious family.

We're off along the spectacular Chapman's Peak Drive, a series of hairpin bends cut into the cliffs high above its dramatic coastline, where the aqua blue sea meets ashen white sands and the vegetation of hazy purples and summer yellows colour the cliffs. In the distance amongst the white crests of waves, see vertical jets of water, right here right now, right in front of us, is a pod of nine, possibly more peduncle-slapping (I just love this word) thrashing whales.

I wonder how much more time can be spent and how many more things can be done, on David's ever demanding temperamental mistress, as once more amongst suburbia's pastel iced detached houses with swimming pools and speed boats, a babbling brook, its banks lined with linen white lilies, we wait the day out. At this four-by-four specialists recommended by Lucy Bow Wow, Lizzybus gets new door hinges, a door handle (we could only use the passenger door), new front brakes (from David's kit), oil and filter change, tappets adjusted and lots more. What is important is to have been given details of his friend who has secure parking for Lizzybus in Johannesburg, as David has decided to fly back to England with me.

It's a momentous day on this journey, as we arrive at the Cape of Good Hope, on the Cape Peninsula, where the currents of the Atlantic join the currents of the Indian Ocean. For ships coming from the west, this marks the point they begin to travel east, although Cape Agulhas is the most southerly point. I don't care, to me, for me, for us, it's the bottom, our bottom and a huge milestone on this journey. At the lighthouse protecting sailors, we are and have been for most of this journey, quite alone, eating our picnic of cold sausage sandwiches, its picture postcard perfect, breaching whales, a pod of basking fur seals and beneath the waves, two mighty oceans meet. It's the sixth of October twenty ten, exactly one year to the very day since we first stepped foot, or should I say tyre tread, on African soil.

I have the answer to the question we never dared ask ourselves, 'could we do this?' Two inexperienced, totally alone people, armed only with desire do this, through some of the toughest, hostile, most corrupt countries, on non-existent roads, all the way to South Africa? The answer is, 'yes we can!' and 'yes we did!' It's nothing short of a miracle. But of course, this is not the end, it's only one chapter in a whole blinking saga, just the end of West coast Africa, one-half of one continent, and depending on the route with another five continents, and at least eighty countries to go. It feels strange, as the goal for now was South Africa, I can't think beyond this. We will do it by focusing only on the few countries ahead, anything more for me is far too overwhelming.

For now, our next 'mission' is getting to Johannesburg a vast distance through the very heart of South Africa. At the next town of Stellenbosch, South Africa's second oldest town, book into Stumble Backpackers, a double fronted Victorian building with added to and added to some more, rooms. In the communal area, people hang out on black vinyl settees, their innards of nicotine-stained yellow foam spewing out, in the centre a well-used pool table. Lizzybus is parked on the forecourt in front of reception, although not a secured area, she is overlooked. Around midnight there is a banging on our door, two guys have been seen trying to cut through the bungee ropes securing kit on the Lizzybus roof.

Since the theft of kit in Ghana, with the addition of a metal roof box rather than a material stuff bag, it's secure. They are after the metal sand ladders and Jerry Cans but they are wired and bolted on, who would steal items of equipment that our survival could rely on? It's unsettling everything we have is everything we need, we are vulnerable even in a city, or perhaps being in a city—who knows? I know we are constantly watched, not just out of admiration but for what can be stolen, this of course is the same in every city in every country around the world but when your world is your vehicle and your kit is part of it, it's a worry.

Stellenbosch, also known as the 'City of Oaks' for all the oak trees planted by the Dutch, is surrounded by vast wineries. There are organised tours to visit them, or you could just drive to them in a Lizzybus for nothing. We chose the latter option, as I don't drink wine, David became the official taster, a few hours later, pissed as a fart, David sleeps the afternoon away in our room.

Lizzybus has always been our priority, it's not just a feeling of her not being safe, it's a fact, head off today to a secure campsite with electric fences. Adjacent to the ocean walk along the beach to the local shops for wood and food for dinner, it's stunningly beautiful along boardwalks undulating over the dunes. On the way back, the grey clumps of cloud no longer hang heavy but disgorge rain upon us, the gentle breeze becomes gale force.

Finally make it back to camp, to sit in a leaking Lizzybus, the wood sodden in our backpacks, all possibility of a Braai gone. Not being able to get inside Lizzybus, out of this wet and cold, just has to be changed but how?

As it continued to rain all night, I'm now in the only dry area, the communal toilet block, listening to the rain clattering on the tin roof, humming to myself whilst turning a nice rosy pink, soaking in the hottest bath skin allows before burning. It's miserable as rain drips from our hoods into our morning coffee, chairs too wet to sit on, stand silently, lost in our own thoughts of wretchedness, preparing to put down the sodden wet tent. How long we can keep going with this set up, the pile of shit German Auto Camp tent, its stapled joints leaking even before the mouse attack and no internal space. Here in South Africa, the heart of overland outdoor life, we have seen so many great alternatives, the ultimate would be a roof conversion but even a clamshell tent, although still accessed externally, it would at least be easier to open and close.

It's miserable and cold, for once prioritise us over Lizzybus and return to the dry warm comfort of a room at Stumble Backpackers. We have made a decision, to replace the roof tent, having found one here, not exactly what we want but a clamshell, available in store and they can fit it. A team of seven set about taking off the old roof tent for the, 'one day' it will take. Sid, our black mamba snake, despite assuring them he is plastic, has to be removed and put into a bag before they will work on her. Metal plates are welded directly to the roll cage to take the weight of it through the chassis not the gutters. This African one day, is two, Lizzybus has a night on her own we are taken back to Stumble, at least she is secure locked in the garage.

I just love it here with everyone, listening to their stories of travel, how being alone or school buddies or loving couples or groups, tests their relationships, I feel vindicated that ours is falling to pieces. Always making the most of anything free, on knackered old bikes free from Stumble as the sun comes out in all her glory, we drip sweat, as bottoms turn numb, muscles complain bitterly at the effort of turning the wheels, on the way to the local nature reserve.

I've never really ridden a bike but it seems pretty simple to me, on the flat, on smooth tarmac but I've changed my mind, it's turned into a shale rocky path, with a gentle incline, that to me feels vertical. My attempts to steer around the rocks only means I miss them with the front wheel but hit them with the back, causing pain to shoot through my bottom, right down my inner leg to my ankles…

The surrounding mountains are stark against the crystal blue skies, with the river cutting through cascading over boulders. It's totally, utterly, excruciatingly, bloody painful, I sit my pulsating throbbing butt into the ice-cold river, refusing to move. Had Lizzybus not been in the garage having her tent fitted, I might even have insisted David go get her and pick me up, the pain is so severe. An hour later, the cold has numbed it somewhat and the pain eased slightly, we head back. Had sex been a thing, which it isn't, it would not be a thing now, as the blisters formed start bleeding.

Chapter 16
Becoming Part of Something

I have some exciting news. My old neighbour from England, Eileen's daughter Jackie lives in Cape Town and wants us to visit. Although we have been to Cape Town, it's only fifty kilometres away, I'd love to. Jackie, my once children's babysitter, is now all grown up and runs a very successful business. They live at Pine Lands, a suburb of Cape Town, its name reflects the forests of wind bent pines, it's a thatched burnt orange sprawling house, sitting behind electric gates. We're greeted by three rescue dogs, before shown our en-suite room, its double doors leading to a huge pool. What a wonderful evening; Jackie, just like her mom, is warm and energetic, as is Elaine her South African life partner.

Jackie runs her business with a team of ten from outbuildings adjacent to the main house, aware they are working in the day, making ourselves scarce we take the train into Cape Town wanting to visit Robben Island. A familiar driving route to us in Lizzybus looks so very different seen through the opaque plastic windows of a train. We have been advised to book a first-class carriage as pickpocketing and muggings are a problem. The carriage is rammed, we're almost deafened as through a megaphone a guy bestows the glory of God in all his wonders upon us.

Graffiti covers every inch of the walls, floor and ceiling, people squeeze amongst us selling enormous bags of cheesy puffs, raw meat, a two pack of apples etc. A young girl holds the arm of a wizened old man with opaque eyes, shaking a tin under our noses, a woman blasts out a song almost louder than the megaphone. We're thinking blimey, if this is first class, what the hell would cattle class be like? Before realising we're in the wrong carriage but we're glad, we have nothing to steal and it's part of life, as it is for many here.

All the boats to Robben Island have been cancelled due to the blustery weather conditions and will be for the foreseeable future. Once more fill the hours around the streets of Cape Town to have our picnic at the harbour, people-watching.

Gale force winds continue to blow across the Atlantic, having already spent a few weeks in Cape Town, amusing ourselves every day without spending money is becoming a chore. Go to the pictures to watch *Oceans*, a subtitled documentary, not having been to the pictures for years, it's quite a treat. On the huge screen, with surround sound and glorious technicolour, we're totally lost in the wonder of nature, warm, dry and stuffing our faces with our picnic.

Jackie and Eileen have, or had, every intention of painting this beautiful house, of putting up their pictures but as the years passed, they never 'got around to it,' despite having bought all the paint. With the main house being separate from the offices, David and I spend the week doing just that, painting and hanging pictures. It's something I've always enjoyed, it's familiar to me and comforting in a strange way. It struck me, never, in a million years, could I have ever imagined being here in the house of my grown-up babysitter, in South Africa, painting, life is such a puzzle.

Jackie's mother, my good friend Eileen, is, for the first-time visiting Cape Town for her seventieth birthday in two weeks. Eileen is not in good health, I know if I don't get to see her now, I might never. I really want to be here with them all but feel we have overstayed our welcome, it's six weeks before our flights from Johannesburg, decide to go off exploring, come back and surprise Eileen for her birthday. It's so exciting, like a secret mission.

The sun that hid behind clouds all weekend shines bright, we leave Jackie's heading back along the coast, calling in at Stumble Backpackers to meet up with Claus for the night. I get emails taking me to a life that will be mine again very soon, the dream home, wanted and wanted some more by my daughter has fallen through, a blanket of disappointment engulfs her until day-to-day life problems and pleasures will swallow it back up. It's a boy! My grandson's sea of blue nursery is ready and waiting, Jen is counting the sleeps until my return. I'm asked if I want a 'smoke,' I've noticed but never really registered the borders full of plants here at Stumble. David laughs, knowing they are cannabis plants, just here growing like your prized roses, the smoke I'm being offered is a spliff; thanking them for their kind offer, I refuse.

Claus gives us 'Tracks4Africa,' a programme for our Garmin, what a revelation this is, all the times we had been lost on a sand road to somewhere but ended up nowhere, now revealed to us. It's like someone has opened our eyes, removed the cataract, this will become invaluable to us. Claus is in the middle of arranging shipping to the Americas, a continent we are heading for but not yet. I wonder if we will ever make it, or if we will ever see him again? All of us cling to these moments in our journeys, with the people who have become family, who just understand.

Heading now to Hermanus, 'Hermanuspietersfontein,' shortened because it was too long for the postal service and its calm, warm waters, where the southern rights give birth before taking their calves out into the vast Atlantic Ocean. Along the way visit Betty's Bay, a small reserve protecting the breeding colony of African Jackass Penguins, named because their call is just like the Donkey's Bray. Having fattened themselves up at sea, waddle to shore for the twenty-day malting season and have their chicks, before, once more, becoming slimline waterproof torpedoes, it's incredibly special to see these masters of the ocean, a few feet away with their equally fluffy chicks.

Tonight, we use our new roof tent for the first time. David is animated at how easy it is to put up, the sturdy welded joints, double sown gummed zips and internal LED lighting.

I'm just ecstatic it smells of new, having even bought new sheets and pillows, take deep gulps of breath, of glorious, wonderful fresh.

Leaving Lizzybus at the campsite, walk along the cliff path of pale lemon shale, through strands of Milkwood trees (national monuments permits are required to even prune one if on your property). I feel like Dorothy in *The Wizard of Oz*, following quite literally the Yellow Brick Road, through this spectacular floral kingdom with the most diverse non-tropical plant life on the earth. We see and hear the 'Whale Crier' of Hermanas, unlike the bell-ringing town crier we have in England, he is blowing on a kelp horn, a tradition announcing the sighting of whales.

At Shark Ladies, a huge hand-painted billboard hangs above the door of a menacing whale looking into a cage of divers, we meet Sam, a friend of Jackie's, who offers to take us cage diving with great whites. It's not something either of us want to do, for us it's far more rewarding to see them frolicking in the ocean with their calves.

Despite the sun hiding behind clouds David burns his nose and looks just like Rudolph the Red-Nosed Reindeer. Much to his irritation and my amusement I loop serenade 'Rudolph the Red-Nosed Reindeer' to him all the way back.

The vertical side entry to the tent as opposed to our front entry takes a bit of getting used to, as you have to climb over each other; with my bladder dictating constant overnight peeing trips I have the side nearest the ladder. This in theory should work well but as David always needs to 'check something' the first hour is spent climbing over me to do it.

Following the Garden Route, a jewel of South Africa of over two hundred kilometres of rugged coast, imposing mountains, a protected area through leafy forests and friendly seaside towns. Pull over for our picnic lunch, sat on a bench beside empty pristine manicured shuttered houses, awaiting the return of their seasonal owners, see pods of southern rights frolicking with their calves right in front of us. These gentle giants of the ocean, black with streaks of grey and white, can live up to a hundred years, weigh up to eighty tons, it's truly a humbling, special moment in time, forever mine.

After rain all night, see three wet patches on the sheets, devastated at the realisation the new tent leaks, not helped, when making the morning coffee, realising I had left the coffee pot and mugs at the last camp site. The loss of the coffee pot is a huge blow, how can a morning be faced without coffee but the leaking roof tent is tipping us over the edge. As we're heading back to Cape Town for Eileen's birthday, decide to get the roof tent looked at back in Stellenbosch, the grey skies, heavy with rain, do nothing to lift the mood, hold up at another cheap campsite.

A South African group of dairy farmers invite us to breakfast, which their staff, after setting up their extensive campsite, are now cooking. What a feast, bacon, eggs, mushrooms, tomatoes, fresh fruit and best of all huge pots of coffee. These moments in our journey, afloat in an ocean of land, are life rafts to us. They connect us to the cultures, the lives, the families, confirming our belief that we're all so very much alike but all so very different. We feel a real genuine interest in us, how we prepared for our journey, the challenges faced but mostly of how we fund it? They believe that what we are doing is something to be admired, an accomplished, longed-for dream of many, inviting us to stay at their dairy farm, something we would just love to do but want to get the roof tent looked at.

Back on the main road we see ostrich, these flightless giants amongst birds can kill you with a single kick. Unlike, when told to watch out for the elephants and paying no attention, paid full attention to the advice of lying down if charged by one, from our dairy farmers but hopeful I won't need to try it out. Despite their puppy dog dinner plate eyes as big as snooker balls and the belief they bury their heads in sand when in danger, which they don't, ostriches are to be treated with respect and they have all of ours. We're passing vast Aloe Vera plantations, able to survive desert harsh conditions, nature's miracle plants, used in medicines, creams and cooking throughout the world. With razor-sharp green leaves, which cop like hell if caught on bare legs, a soothing cream would be most beneficial.

What we did expect and are now passing, are cattle farms, it's so very hard to imagine the scale of these places, stating a number in terms of acres would just be a number, it registers for me only by how many hours of driving along their fenced borders we do, as to how vast they are. Cowboys on horses replaced with quad bikes, or even light aircraft, check out the water holes and movement of cattle. But on very special moments, we see them, the cowboys, on horseback kicking up trails of dust, herding cattle.

Life and being on the road, really has found its rhythm, evolved from necessity and need, even on occasions, comfort. I use the word comfort in its most abstract form, in fact I'm not sure comfort has evolved at all, it's just the lack of it has become the norm. David or I cook pasta, rice, sauces, stews, etc. which go into the fridge for the week. The packing and cleaning of Lizzybus is sort of down to me, as I've mentioned, David is not one to put stuff away, or clean it. I try cleaning the tools passed to me when David is scrabbling underneath Lizzybus but with no hot water, or at times no water, it's impossible. Greasy tools, like greasy fingernails, are tangible proof of all the 'greasing' being done, it drives me to distraction, as greasy hands leave a greasy oily scum on everything. David calls me obsessive, I wish I was, how cool would that be, if that was the case, everything would be clean and in its place.

Sticking to the 'two sets of clothes, one to wash,' or should I say, 'swill through in the used washing up water.' One thing that is a triumph is the wooden Ikea shower tray, placed at the foot of the ladder, with the bowl of remaining water, David's minging feet can be washed before getting into the tent. This sounds quite disgusting, even to me but there is an African way to washing in limited water. Scooping water out to clean plates, you leave only clean water in the bowl, then clothes are dumped in it and trodden on like grapes to clean feet. For me, the odour of pits, bits and breath, along with the lack of grooming, is a huge issue. Even the most expensive anti-bacterial breathable garments are overwhelmed and become impregnated with body odour, as David still refuses to wear any form of deodorant. The occasions I find the wonders of man washing machine, to put the whole stinking lot into, is always a very special one.

We're facing days and nights when a cold wind blows and rain falls upon us, now back in our sleeping bags fully clothed, I find most agreeable. We're trying our best to ignore the tent leaking issues, both a little broken by it. The lack of internal space is taking its toll, along with not having fitted the diesel heater, sitting outside, wrapped in blankets writing my journal, I can barely move my fingers. On the plus side, with no expensive visas to buy, using only half a tank of diesel a day, able to bush camp, or find cheap community camping, the sixty dollar a day budget from rental income is doing great, with flights, shipping, etc. all paid for from savings. With this in mind, treat ourselves, for me a small block of cheese, for David a bar of chocolate.

We're back on the Garden Route, on a part tar, part gravel road through the Seven Passes, built in the late eighteen hundreds, cutting through the dense forest and seven fast flowing rivers of the Outeniqua Mountains. The most incredible feat being the bridge over the Kaaimans River, using loaded wagons hauled by teams of thirty or more oxen. Nicknamed Keeromriver, or Turnaround River, as the wagons and travellers had to turn around when faced with it.

It's like stepping back in time, with the main traffic using the alternative motorway route we're completely alone, winding our way down into gorges, over simple stone bridges declared national monuments, laced with intricate moss. A wooden school desk contains a dog-eared ledger, to register in before taking the woodland walk to a giant protected yellowwood tree, simply signed 'Big Tree' at over eight hundred years old.

The days follow each other as mountain passes change to coastal views, we're woken by a stampede of escaped horses, charging towards us. Two weeks into our four week 'exploration' before heading back to Cape Town, sick of dodging showers and the bitter cold nights, book four nights at Cristal Guest House, Jeffrey's Bay, a Mecca for wind surfers. As it's out of season, it's cheaper than camping, a huge tree house, with two bedrooms, bathroom, dining room, kitchen and secure parking with ocean views. Days dissolve around reading, writing, walking and, with my collection of shells, driftwood and bleached rope, I make a wind chime for Jackie and Elaine.

Following the route given us by the South African Dairy farmers, past remote farms planted with miles of dazzling bougainvillea, vibrant against vivid green undulating vineyards, to the Cango Caves. Here, artefacts dating back to the

Stone Age ensure the history lessons I never had are made up for now. I think that David and I have lots in common with the Stone Age man, specifically David with his talons and beard. It's at times like this, that the thing of driving around the world becomes secondary, having the time to really understand and enjoy the country we are in and its people, is quite wonderful.

South Africa is just an incredible country, we're now soaking in hot springs, once again my pinkies become clean. We're having to pay attention now, to make sure we avoid the speckled Cape Tortoise, the world's smallest tortoise, under threat from poaching, loss of habitat and traffic. Stopping to put them back in the bush for safety, realise that tortoise don't just retreat into their shells for protection, they actually bite and spit. We're allowed to drive through a private game reserve, with herds of elephant, giraffe and zebra complete with airstrip to fly guests in for hunting trips.

All too soon our adventure is over, we're back at Stumble Backpackers in our old room, which feels just like arriving home after a holiday, everyone is so pleased to see us. David watches *Top Gear* with the boys, the girls and I drink Tequila. I've never drank Tequila and didn't really fancy it, vaguely remember something about it having worms. Like most things, it's more a marketing gimmick and usually the larvae of the moth, rather than a worm, which to me is equally as bad. I'm not a shot type of person but I'm persuaded to try one, the stuff burns like acid on the way down, even sucking on lime dipped in salt was horrid. For some reason, everyone is convinced that the more shots I do, the more I will like it. I don't, David finds me on all fours gripping the toilet seat vomiting.

We're back at the place who fitted the tent; they assure us, it leaks only because of the necessity for waterproofing! They did this along with giving us a spare litre of the proofing liquid for any spots that might still leak. We feel fobbed off and pretty pissed off, as a brand-new tent would not have been waterproofed, knowing there is nothing we can do, if, or for sure, when it leaks again, as we will be too far away to do anything about it. It was a huge investment for us, the main reason we bought it was because of the old one leaking, consoling ourselves with the fact it's easy to open and close.

We're sat in Lizzybus around the corner from the restaurant to surprise Eileen for her seventieth birthday; Eileen and everyone are seated in the bay window, as we drive up in Lizzybus. What a very special moment this is, Eileen can hardly believe her eyes, everyone in the restaurant comes out to cheer and wave, we feel like royalty. It was an evening full of happy tears, fish pie, burgers, deep fried mars bars and a glass, okay, a bottle or two, of bubbles.

Chapter 17
Our 'Mission' Is Accomplished

Our real mission begins today, heading off in the direction of Johannesburg, saying goodbye to Eileen, Jackie and Elaine is hard. We're given E, a foot-long wood-carved croc, which we zip-wire to the front bull bar. Elaine, being South African, insists Africans are as wary of crocs as they are of snakes and it will make a very good deterrent. It's about pounding out the miles now, along good tarmac roads, in the blistering heat. As a lot of South Africa is fenced, book a campsite for the night. David is chopping wood, when I hear, "Oh fuck." You would imagine holding a piece of wood with one hand and chopping it with the other is something you would not do but for some reason it's something David did. I'm confronted with a flap of skin from his knuckle to the thumb joint, revealing tendons and muscle.

This attracts the attention of a South African man, a community worker living out in the bush, here collecting supplies. A fascinating man, working on different projects, his latest of tree planting. We donate our spare, non-rusting, super strong Sceptre Jerry Can, that can be used for fuel or water, to the community project. Looking at David's hand, it's decided it's nothing more than a bush wound, giving us a little bottle of mercurochrome. I use it to wash out the flap, apply pressure until it seals and the bleeding stops, secure it with six butterfly stitches, then bandage it up. I'm so proud of my efforts, appoint myself once more, Nurse Jayne.

I'm now the full-time driver due to David's self-inflicted wound, bush camping is not always an option, having to pay to use campsites is frustrating. I'm consoled slightly with the fact they all tend to have baths. I'm not normally a bath person but they are just great for warming you up on these bitter cold evenings and to stretch out in after sitting on your arse all day. Old habits die hard, I have a bath first (I like it roasting hot), then David with my help, due to his bandaged hand, uses my bath water, then the hot water is used for washing clothes. A piece of kit that surprisingly has become invaluable to us is our universal bath plug, not having found a single plug in any of the baths.

There is a main motorway route, running from Cape Town to the border of Zimbabwe, at over two thousand kilometres, using this is the quickest but we see nothing of the country. Driving on it now, from Laingsburg to Colesburgh, it's kilometre after kilometre of boring mountains never to be reached, barren flat scrubland but we have a secret weapon, in 'Tracks4Africa.' It gives so many alternative scenic routes and the confidence to use them, it even lists budget guest houses, fuel stations, supermarkets and even better, embassies, not that we need them right now but if we did, quite incredible. This is when David comes into his own, he makes this journey what it is, by always taking the scenic routes, finds the adventure we both crave, hampered before by inconclusive maps, now armed with this, nothing is going to stand in his way.

That is, apart from documentation. Not only does my passport need replacing but the Carnet De Passage (Lizzybus Bond) runs out in twelve days. David had arranged for this to be renewed in England but has been told if the Carnet De Passage runs out, which it will, it has to be renewed in the country you are in. If we want to renew it in England, Lizzybus has to be with us, there is no choice, it has to be sorted here in South Africa.

With this in mind, taking alternative routes is not an option, even with 'Tracks4Africa,' we need to stick to the most direct route. Driving on through scenery of over-grazed grassland, scorched by late summer, with occasional downpours, David is back to driving, I hang my legs out the window, or drape them across him, it alleviates the pains down my legs momentarily.

It's sod's law that now we have to make progress, progress is impossible, the motorway is being re-surfaced, every ten kilometres we have a twenty-minute wait. In a way it's a welcoming break, as I can stand for a bit, have a chat with everyone but as the Carnet De Passage is running out it starts to become irritating. Tomorrow we should make Johannesburg, pull off at the next exit to the riverbank, to sit it out inside Lizzybus hoping the rain will stop. It does; in the majestic weeping willow cascading over us, a flock of tiny birds come to roost, smooth round boulders allow water to tumble and fall, making the most delightful gurgling sounds on its way to somewhere, it's perfect.

Ever since the loss of the coffee pot, David has been reluctant to get up—he loved the little ritual of brewing fresh coffee—so I'm up first. I love this time in the morning, prehistoric-looking birds fly above me, little feathery ones, tails longer than their bodies bob and dance in the water below, a gentle breeze blows the last feathers of cloud away revealing an aqua blue sky.

We arrive at the 'mega city' of Jo'burg which, despite its reputation, is supposedly safer than Cape Town, if you're looking only at murder rates and, as David and I have not resorted to murdering each other just yet, it should remain so. I am terrified, totally freaked out, as above us, below us and beside us, are five lane carriages of speeding traffic. Lizzybus, old and fully laden, is not your fastest vehicle, put me, Miss Daisy, behind the wheel and it compounds this. Still, I hold my ground and my nerve, staying in the centre lane is necessary for any left, right, or straight on last minute instructions from David trying to give directions from a constantly recalculating sat-nav.

We need to get to the Automobile Association (AA) offices, which are in the grounds of the Kyalami Grand Prix Circuit. I've no idea what the Kyalami Circuit is but apparently it means 'my home' in Sesotho and once home to the South African Formula One Grand Prix and Superbike races. David, having watched the races on television, is beside himself to actually be here and tells me I have no soul. It's faced bankruptcy, political unrest during apartheid and fatalities, to be re-built in the late nineteen hundreds. David's euphoria peaks as we drive in Lizzybus on part of the actual track, incorporated into the resident and commercial area, even I begin to feel the significance in this moment.

At the Automobile Association offices, the wonderfully helpful staff explain that although they cannot issue us with a new Carnet, they can extend our original one by three months, which, when ready, will be FedExed to us at a DHL office of our choice, in the next week. This is all arranged on our behalf, even phoning England and emailing the commissionaire of South Africa. Happy to pay the fifty-five dollars, sad we're unable to persuade them to let us do a timed lap of the circuit in Lizzybus, I wanted this for David but at least Lizzybus drove on its hallowed tarmac.

It's time to start thinking about getting ready for our flight home and storing Lizzybus, we go to check out the contact given us for storage. Driving once more with lanes and signs should be a relief but you're still in Africa so this means diddlysquat, honking horns, overtaking and undertaking, cutting in or across is all perfectly acceptable. I'm driving, David is navigating and freaking out as the brakes seem to have an air lock and sometimes they work but sometimes they don't. David has no concept of how terrifying this is for me, only pissed off that

I can't break in time to make the turnings, tempers flare, insults once more are flung, both determined to instil upon the other, how hard it is navigating as opposed to driving, or driving as opposed to navigating and may I just add, driving with intermittent brakes.

When we arrive at the place, we have to let go of our frustrations and revert to the smiling happy David and Jayne, who have just driven alone, down the West coast of Africa, not the David and Jayne, who can't even agree on what is worse, driving or navigating. Lizzybus will not only be in a fenced area topped with razor wire but in a locked and secured hangar-sized unit. They will collect Lizzybus from us on our departure at the airport and return her to us on our return; wow, I thought this only happened to the rich and famous. Now that is all sorted, at a rambling backpackers in the suburb of Johannesburg with secure parking and washing machines book a room and start cleaning. I've suffered with shingles over the years and see once more the familiar patches of pin head puss spreading across my buttocks, to realise it's not just the hours of sitting causing the shooting pains down my legs but another flare up of shingles.

Most houses here are secured behind shards of glass-topped walls, razor wire, or electric fencing, there are lots of gated communities with twenty-four-hour security. We have been warned about scams, specifically by people posing as police, we're to drive with windows closed and doors locked, if pulled over to keep going until you reach a police station.

Driving into Johannesburg to replace the coffee pot, all three lanes on both carriageways have been blocked by the 'police,' I wonder how this advice could be put into practice. They ask where our tax disc is, we explain we don't need one, then ask what we have for them, like a cold drink, it continued like this, until they ask directly for money. We know to be respectful, to be pleasant, to never show irritation but it's hard, when corruption is so blatant, it's a way of life here, not specific to us but in its way, has become specific.

We continue on with our tales of do and daring, giving them nothing, until they just let us through.

The shopping mall is something else, with the tent and roof rack on Lizzybus normally we can't park in underground car parks but here it is higher than normal with specific four-by-four trucks and van parking. It's November, the vast shopping mall spread over several floors is adorned with beautiful, tasteful Christmas decorations, jewellery shops sell huge sparkling diamonds, Rolex watches and Louis Vuitton bags.

I know we don't belong here, it's so alien to our life of digging toilets, or collecting water and totally overwhelming, we replace our coffee pot and leave. Despite all this obvious show of wealth, on the streets people make a living selling barbequed sweetcorn, a box of matches or packet of tissues. Traffic lights once again are places where bodies are draped with everything you didn't know you wanted or needed and beggars. Although advised to drive with windows closed, we don't, as we sense no threat. I'll admit we were a bit concerned, when waiting at a red light, the guy in the car behind us got out and ran up to us. He gave us a box of twenty low energy light bulbs. Why? Because we drive a Land Rover.

It's the first time we see 'whites' and 'blacks' begging. Mark, an unemployed qualified teacher, had a sandwich-board over him, with 'unemployed, hungry with family and medical bills' written on it. On crutches, both his legs having metal pins sticking out seeping puss, he tells us about Broad-Based Black Economic Empowerment. From what I understood, it was a quota system (supposedly voluntary but enforced) where up to seventy percent, or more, of middle-high management and government positions had to be filled with a black workforce.

I could see the vision but it would be years before it was workable, due to the training and education needs but what do I know. I wonder about sharing these bits of my journey but realise it's life as I found and find, it—a slice of the reality of people living here, for them and us.

Mosquitoes are a huge problem in our room, even burning coils, spraying everything in DEET and sleeping in a long-sleeved shirt, the bastards get me. This is our last day before the long journey home, David is miserable, as he has no desire whatsoever to go back but the realisation of what he can bring back with him, for his mistress, cheers him up a little. It's strange when you think, only a few months ago, he had every intention of shipping Lizzybus back from here, to sell her and forget all about this journey, now he wants nothing more in life than to keep going.

Johannesburg, known as the city of gold, sits high on a plateau, originally an arid place inhabited by a few Boer farmers, transformed by the discovery of gold in the late eighteen hundreds, emerged from a gold rush town to a large modern industrial city. We visit the Apartheid Museum, opened by Nelson Mandela; at the entrance, the seven pillars of the constitution, democracy, equality, reconciliation, diversity, responsibility, respect and freedom.

When issued a ticket, you're randomly segregated, black or white, your journey through this part of the museum is based on this. Inside, grey concrete or bronze walls are stark, inset with pictures or small television screens, with news footage and personal accounts of the time. Once outside, the skies darken, we sit watching forked lightning and torrential rain in sombre mood. On returning to the backpackers, find all our now dry washing is folded neatly on the bed, ready for us to leave.

To all who have taken the time to be with me on this journey so far, thank you, I have been lonely many times but never quite alone, reached highs and lows, been amazed and amazed some more. A whole lifetime has happened in just over one short year, any remnant of life as I knew it gone, the focus became water, food, shelter and Lizzybus maintenance. From barren burnt landscape, to all of nature's jewels, the scenery ever-changing, ever the same.

If not for David, I know I would never have made it out of Birmingham with my sense of direction, let alone Africa. David says of all the people, in all the world, there is no one else he would sooner have experienced this journey with. Now that's a revelation and something for me to cling onto. Before we left, I realise now, we were at a crisis point in our relationship. This journey has not solved that but shifted its focus, finding something bigger than us, more consuming, more challenging, something we have both embraced and cannot seem to let go of.

We leave tomorrow back to our life that was, I get to hold my grandson Ben, the mother I love deeply but who no longer recognises me, see the dream home of my daughter, talk endlessly to my sister, who will be buying new pillows for our weary heads (she has a thing about pillows!), renew my passport and the Carnet de Passage. We're almost half the people we were physically but twice the people we were in every other way. Did we enjoy it? Most of the time. Are we glad we did it? Most of the time. Would we do it all again? Absolutely, but will three weeks in England change our minds?

Lizzybus, our home, our life, is waiting for us in Africa. They say you can take the person out of Africa but you can't take the spirit of Africa out of the person: we're beginning to understand this.

Epilogue

When 'Will' Is More Than 'Wont', Your Journey Continues: Book 2.

Three weeks later...

There are seven continents in the world: Europe, Africa, Asia, Australia-Oceania, North America, South America, and Antarctica. We are one and a half continents, twenty-six countries, and one hundred thousand miles into a journey that became our journey, our life. The goal is to drive Lizzybus around the world, top to bottom, crossing lines of longitude latitude, or pole to pole, who knows? That sentence just puts it into some sort of order, giving it purpose. For now, having driven down the west coast of Africa, we will continue east, crossing the continents and the countries within them. Of course, we want to go to every country, or should I say David wants to go to every country, and we will try, but it will depend on their stability, the availability of visas, that Lizzybus keeps going and us not having killed each other.

It's the oddest thing to stand here in the queue at check-in seeing Johannesburg, South Africa, as our destination; a country that has become very significant to us as it's where we left Lizzybus, our past, our present and our future. Looking around, I see the collection of happy holidaymakers and sad farewells. It will take just over a day to return to a place that took over a year to drive to in Lizzybus. I suppose I'm different now as I'm a grandmother and a mother-in-law, but these are life events that happen to us all. What has changed is David and I because everything we thought we knew or valued was taken from us; voluntarily it's true, but nonetheless gone, and replaced by the unknown.

On arriving in Johannesburg, Lizzybus has washed off her African dust and is waiting for us with the guy who stored her. She starts with the first turn of the key, smells of Africa, oil and us. I'm filled with a sense of belonging and purpose. We are back in the same backpackers we left three weeks ago. In our room, the concrete blocks support a homemade wooden bed frame, wire springs protrude from the hair-stuffed mattress and rat droppings which are a reminder to keep all food stuff secure. It takes a while for our eyes to adjust to the single hanging light bulb before we dump the bags, eat a bowl of noodles and sleep away the trauma of another goodbye…

Africa, we are back.

Ingram Content Group UK Ltd.
Milton Keynes UK
UKHW021831010623
422728UK00003B/20